A PATH *to* JEWISH SURVIVAL

Richard B. Stanger

A Path to Jewish Survival
Copyright © 2024 by Richard B. Stanger
All rights reserved.

This book, or any portion of it, may not be reproduced or transmitted electronically, mechanically, or by any other means including but not limited to photocopying, scanning, downloading, etc., without prior written permission of the author. For sales inquiries, contact: apathtojewishsurvival@gmail.com.

Cover and interior design by the Virtual Paintbrush.

ISBN (hardcover) 979-8-218-34814-4
ISBN (paperback) 979-8-218-27725-3
ISBN (ebook) 979-8-218-34815-1

Library of Congress Control Number: 2023923446

First Edition 2024

Published by Bennett Press
bennettpress@gmail.com

apathtojewishsurvival.net

TO MY WIFE JANE

In Memoriam for the millions of Jews
killed over the generations
because of *Sinat Chinam* and *Lashon Hara*.
May their memory be a blessing.
And may we find the wisdom and strength to
change this tragic aspect of our destiny.

ואהבת לרעך כמוך

And You Shall Love Your Fellow Jew as Yourself!
(VAYIKRA 19:18)

Haskama (Endorsement) from Rabbi Herschel Schachter

```
Rabbi Hershel Schachter                                      הרב צבי שכטר
24 Bennett Avenue                                       ראש ישיבה ורב בכולל
New York, New York 10033                             ישיבת רבינו יצחק אלחנן
(212) 795-0630
```

אמנה דברים

אשר נתן ה' חכמה ותבונה ליאמ"ח הרב הגאון ר' אברהם יוסף שליט"א אשר הואיל בטובו לחבר ספר נחמד ונעים, מלא וגדוש בעניני הלכה ומנהג, ועל הכל הוסיף כמה גרגרים נחמדים בעניני דרש ואגדה, וקראו בשם "אוצרות" ובוודאי ימצאו בו הקוראים טעם לשבח, וישמחו לראות חידושי תורה נחמדים ונעימים, וכל הקורא בו ימצא קורת רוח יתירה, ובפרט שהמחבר הוסיף בכל מקום הערות הנוגעות להלכה למעשה, ויהי רצון מלפני אבינו שבשמים שיזכהו להפיץ מעיינותיו חוצה, ולהמשיך בעבודת הקודש ברוב עוז וחדוה, ולהגדיל תורה ולהאדירה,

כעתירת
צבי שכטר
א' מרחשון תשס"ט

English Translation of Rabbi Herschel Schachter's *Haskama* (Endorsement)

Rabbi Hershel Schachter
24 Bennett Avenue
New York, New York 10033
(212) 795-0630

HaRav Tzvi Schachter
Rosh Yeshiva and Rosh Kollel
Rabbi Isaac Elchanan
Theological Seminary

A Letter of Blessing

From the time of the sale of Yosef, Klal Yisrael is suffering hard from *Sinas Chinam*. A very significant portion of the future redemption is that this matter should be repaired as foreseen in the books of the Prophets. And the honorable friend Dov Ber Stanger*, he should live long, has done a beautiful thing by writing the book *Our Brothers*† for the purpose of repairing this trouble. For if we will all try to understand the other person's point of view, we will then be able to relate to the other person as a brother and not as an outsider. And that's why the author has explained all the different points of view. May it be Hashem's will that the author should succeed in his goal and there should be much mutual love in Israel. And rather than failing with *Sinas Chinam*, which has existed among us for so many generations, we should have *Ahavas Chinam* as is fitting for brothers.

Sincerely,
Tzvi Schachter

8 Adar 5783
March 1, 2023

---

*   Dov Ber Stanger is the author's Hebrew name.

†   *Our Brothers* was the working title of this book at the time this endorsement was written.

TABLE OF CONTENTS

Introduction: The Leading Threat to Jewish Survival Today 1

PART ONE: THE DIFFERENT STREAMS OF JUDAISM

Chapter One: A Primer on Orthodox Judaism 15

Chapter Two: Conservative Judaism and Its Duality 52

Chapter Three: Reform Judaism and Its Growing
Connection to Tradition 103

Chapter Four: The Hidden World of Reconstructionist Judaism . . 142

Chapter Five: The Rich Life and Traditions of Sephardic Jews . . . 157

PART TWO: A FRAMEWORK FOR ACHDUT

Chapter Six: Overview 171

Chapter Seven: Strengthening Orthodox Judaism 176

Chapter Eight: Can Conservative Judaism Survive?. 182

Chapter Nine: Where Should Reform Judaism Go Next? 187

Chapter Ten: Can Reconstructionist Judaism Become
the Next Chabad? 193

Chapter Eleven: What We Can All Learn from Sephardic Judaism 195

PART THREE: THINKING DIFFERENTLY

Chapter Twelve: Overview 201

Chapter Thirteen: Can Orthodox Eyes See the Jewish World Differently? 203

Chapter Fourteen: How Conservative Jews Should View Other Jews. 229

Chapter Fifteen: Reforming Reform Jews' Perspective 238

Chapter Sixteen: Reconstructionist Jews Are Few But Mighty – What Do They Think?. 246

Chapter Seventeen: The Magic of the Sephardic Jewish Perspective 254

PART FOUR: TAKING ACTION

Chapter Eighteen: To All Jews: Yes, We Can! 263

Chapter Nineteen: Hear No Evil, Speak No Evil 274

Chapter Twenty: Choose Life!. 297

Endnotes. 305

Bibliography 315

Glossary of Italicized and Frequently Used Terms 319

Introduction

THE LEADING THREAT TO JEWISH SURVIVAL TODAY

OUR SURVIVAL AS a people is at risk today, perhaps more than ever before. This book is about what we can do individually and institutionally to ensure our survival, both in Israel and in the Diaspora. We need to take action now.

If I were to ask Jews "what's the biggest threat to our future?" the list of answers might look like this:

The Threat to Israel's Security from Iran and Its Terrorist Proxies on Israel's Borders

On October 7, 2023, Hamas, a terror proxy of Iran, killed 2,400 people and took 234 hostages in an existential attack against Israel in the towns bordering Gaza. Hamas engaged in levels of atrocities, such as raping Israeli women and torturing and beheading Israelis, not seen since the Holocaust. Since October 7, Israel and Hezbollah have been trading arial assaults on each other across Israel's northern borders with Lebanon and Syria. Israel's northern and southern border communities have been evacuated for security reasons. It is presently not clear whether an all-out war with Hezbollah will develop.

Israel has made substantial progress in its war against Hamas, but it has not yet achieved its stated goals of eliminating Hamas and securing the return of all Israeli hostages who are still alive. Whether these goals can be fully realized remains to be seen given continued pressure from the United States for Israel to negotiate a permanent ceasefire with Hamas in exchange for release of the remaining hostages and, in the meantime, to conduct the war in a way that impairs a quick path to complete victory.

At the same time, Iran continues to enrich uranium to levels approaching those needed to develop nuclear weapons. The Western world, led by the United States, has not been able to deter Iran from its nuclear ambitions. This poses on ongoing existential threat to Israel.

The Dramatic Rise in Antisemitism in the Western World

Antisemitism has been increasing in the Western World for at least the last decade. Since the beginning of the war in Gaza, this trend has taken a dramatic turn for the worse, particularly in the United States, as evidenced by reported hate crimes and media support. It's reached a point where opposition to Israel, referred to as anti-Zionism, has become an acceptable antisemitic political position and a justification for hate crimes against Jews. Of particular concern is the level of antisemitism on American college campuses led by antisemitic professors who are supported by sympathetic university presidents, including at elite institutions. It's reached a point where Jewish students no longer feel safe at many colleges and feel particularly vulnerable if they express their political views publicly.

Israeli Policy Regarding Palestinian Rights

Many liberal Jews view the Israel/Palestinian conflict as a civil rights issue, citing the alleged treatment of the Palestinian people under the Israeli "occupation." This group insists on a two- state solution to the conflict and often supports punishing Israel with boycotts and property divestitures, as well as international sanctions, until the sides come to a suitable solution. In contrast, Jews whose views are more to the right might assert that Israel has the legal right to annex all of Biblical Israel presently under Israeli military control. They also believe that a negotiated settlement with Palestinian leadership is not possible, that the Palestinian leadership doesn't care about the welfare of its people, and that Palestinians would fare better under Israeli sovereignty than under a Palestinian state.

Efforts by Israel's Right-Wing to Impose Orthodox Religious Policy on the Broader Population

Over the years, particularly under Netanyahu's leadership, the Israeli Rabbinate's authority to make decisions that affect citizens' everyday lives has increased. To give a few examples:

- Defining who is a Jew. Under Israeli law, all individuals who claim Jewish status by birth must be able to establish that their mothers were Jewish. For many Jews around the world, this is not difficult. However, for some, it can be challenging. For example, because the former Soviet Union prohibited the practice of Judaism for more than a generation, it is difficult for immigrants from Russia to prove their Jewish backgrounds. A remedy for this problem is to allow them to convert to Judaism in Israel. Current Israeli law, however, considers only Orthodox

conversions valid and to obtain an Orthodox conversion, the individual must keep the *mitzvot* (laws of the Torah). This is something that most of these secular Jewish immigrants are not willing to do.
- Closing municipal services on the Sabbath. Most businesses, large parts of the Israeli government, and public transportation in several cities including Jerusalem are closed on the Sabbath, following the Biblical requirement to observe the Sabbath day as holy and to refrain from all regular, weekday work activities. This limits both individual movement and commercial activity in the country on this day. Many secular Jews feel that Israel should apply more flexible principles rather than strict Sabbath laws to this issue, and some would go so far as to adopt the United States Constitution's rule of complete separation between religion and state, because they feel that these restrictions infringe on their individual rights.
- Separating men and women at the *Kotel* (Western Wall in Jerusalem). The Israeli Rabbinate requires the area in front of the *Kotel* to be set up like an Orthodox synagogue with a *mechitzah* (a substantial partition) that prevents men and women from praying together. This frustrates many liberal Jews who are used to mixed seating in their synagogues.

Secular Jews Who Undermine Our Ability to Attain the Ultimate Redemption

By Orthodox Jewish tradition, for *Moshiach* (the Messiah) to come and bring the ultimate redemption, *Klal Yisrael* (the Jewish people) must repent for their sins and commit to following the laws of the Torah. But how can this happen when a very large portion of *Klal Yisrael* ignores those laws? How will *Moshiach* ever come if so many individuals prevent *Klal Yisrael* as a whole from deserving the final redemption?

Assimilation, Atheism, and Agnosticism

Jews who have assimilated away from Judaism, as well as confirmed atheists and agnostics who ethnically identify as Jews, might technically be Jewish, but they have no interest in Judaism, and their children are almost certain to follow suit. They also tend to be highly cynical about Jewish practices. Not uncommonly, committed Jews consider these deserters of the faith to be akin to uninformed children when it comes to Judaism. And these individuals, in turn, can make things difficult for Jews who want to practice their religion.

The Orthodox Community's Discrimination Against Women

Many liberal Jews and their leaders take exception to what they regard as Orthodox religious practices that discriminate against women. Examples are separate seating in synagogues, prohibiting women from becoming rabbis, prohibiting women from wearing pants, requiring married women to cover their hair in public, not letting women participate as leaders of communal prayers, not counting women as part of a *minyan* (a quorum of ten required for Jewish communal prayer), and not permitting women to initiate Jewish divorce proceedings, thus relegating many civilly-divorced women to the status of *agunot* (women who are not permitted to remarry because their husbands refuse to divorce them under Jewish law).

The Non-Orthodox Community's Inappropriate Mixing of Men's and Women's Roles

More liberal Jews believe that gender equality requires treating women and men the same way in all aspects of life except where biological differences make this impossible. For example, they permit women to wear *tallitot* (Jewish prayer shawls that men traditionally wear in synagogue) and *tefillin* (leather boxes and straps containing Hebrew scriptural phrases that traditionally only men wear during morning prayers), and to say *kiddush* (the prayer over wine sanctifying the Sabbath or a Biblical holiday). They also permit men to light the Sabbath candles along with their wives and to say the appropriate blessing together. In the Orthodox tradition, married men generally do not light the Sabbath candles, relying on their wives to fulfill this important obligation for the family. Orthodox Jews believe that women have equal but different roles in certain areas of life with religious significance.

Chassidic and Yeshivish Jews' Rejection of Modern Society

These so-called Black-Hat Jews isolate themselves from aspects of the modern world in order to avoid exposure to outside influences that might tempt them to deviate from the strict commandments of Jewish law. They devote as much time as possible to the study of Torah. They don't want their men seeing alluring, scantily-dressed modern women, nor do they want such things as sporting events, television, or video games to distract their children. They send their children to Jewish schools that teach their way of life to protect them from influences that don't support this mission. This Black-Hat lifestyle bothers liberal Jews and even some Modern Orthodox Jews, as they view it as a denial of the realities of the 21st century and not helpful to promoting the broad acceptance of Jews.

They also don't want their men serving in the Israel Defense Forces and have successfully obtained service exemptions for them since the country's inception. Their resistance to military service is two-fold:

- They believe that protecting the Land of Israel depends at least as much on Torah study as it does on military strength. Accordingly, they assert that by their full-time study of Torah they are doing their part to protect Israel from its enemies.
- They regard military service as a threat to their ability to continue to isolate their young men from the rest of Israel's more liberal society. They do not want them exposed to Western culture and its temptations that run counter to their way of life.

This issue of continuing to exempt Chassidic and Yeshivish men from military service has become a sore point for Israelis whose children serve in the military, particularly because, unlike at the country's inception, Chassidic and Yeshivish Jews now make up a major and rapidly growing part of the Israeli population. Interestingly, an unprecedented number of these Black-Hat Jews voluntarily have joined the IDF in support of the war in Gaza. Yet, an overwhelming majority of Chassidic and Yeshivish men have not done so.

The Chaos Created in Israel by Proposed Judicial Reform Legislation

The current right-wing Israeli government has proposed changing the rules for selecting judges for Israel's courts, including the Supreme Court. It has also proposed changing the standard by which the Supreme Court can invalidate majority-passed legislation in the *Knesset* (Parliament). The intent of these changes is to increase the power of the *Knesset* versus the Supreme Court and provide a new balance between the legislative and judicial branches of government. The left-leaning opposition to the reform proposal sees it as a threat to democracy and the first step toward imposing more religious laws on the Israeli people. The current Israeli coalition government views the reform proposal as a legitimate approach to paring back of the power of a liberal Supreme Court in order to protect against the current excessive judicial freedom to overrule legislation, thus thwarting the voice of the voters who elected the majority of the *Knesset* members.

This issue was threatening to rip Israeli society apart. Both sides engaged in major public demonstrations and the *Knesset* passed some of the proposed judicial reform legislation before the war in Gaza broke out on October 7, 2023. Since then, the Supreme Court has declared the legislation to be invalid. At present, the entire subject of judicial reform is up-in-the-air because of the much higher priority of the war. In fact, all Israelis have put this and other issues aside to show unity for the war effort. Hopefully, after the war, this issue will be addressed in a much less divisive manner, especially since there is strong evidence that Israel's apparent weakness stemming from this volatile issue emboldened Hamas to start the war.

The list goes on. However, the real problem is not the substance of any of these individual concerns or any combination of them. It's that too often every segment of *Klal Yisrael* blames other Jews for our collective challenges. We are so sure that we are right and that, by implication, others are wrong, that we cast aspersions on each other, expressing our hatred that others are not keeping the faith properly. Our sages call this baseless hatred *Sinat Chinam* and attribute the destruction of the Second Temple in 70 CE to it.

This problem has persisted for a long time, and, as I write these words, more than 1,950 years after that destruction, no real change is in sight. I've heard rabbis and scholars alike give speeches decrying this evil behavior, but as they almost always speak only to a single segment of *Klal Yisrael*, their words don't seem to have a palpable effect on our attitudes and behaviors. For example, about a decade ago, I heard an esteemed Modern Orthodox rabbi assert the importance of *achdut* (unity among the Jewish people). He spoke of the need for dialog and understanding with both further-to-the- right Jews and more liberal Jews, asserting that we shouldn't consider our brethren in either direction as "beyond the pale." He described how over time he'd learned about the rich diversity within Judaism that he hadn't previously understood. He admitted that change wouldn't be easy and that he'd already received skeptical feedback from some congregants. I was not surprised. We're so entrenched in our own perspectives that we lack a framework with which to navigate to a fresh point of view.

One of the most compelling prayers in our liturgy is *Acheinu* (translated as "Our Brothers"), which reads as follows, according to the translation in the ArtScroll Prayer Book:

> *Our brothers, the entire family of Israel, who are delivered into distress and captivity, whether they are on sea or dry land, – may the Omnipresent One have mercy on them and remove them from distress to relief, from darkness to light, from subjugation to redemption, now, speedily, and soon – and let us say Amen.*[1]

In 1990, Abie Rotenberg wrote beautiful music to accompany these words in Hebrew. I love the music and the message so much that we played it at our wedding as I walked down the aisle. It conveys a request to *Hashem* (God) to liberate the needy among us from their oppressors. But think about it. What if we are the oppressors? Are we asking God to liberate us from each other? Even considering this question and its consequences brings pain.

In the summer of 1991, there were terrible riots in Crown Heights, Brooklyn. When discussing the situation, then-New York Mayor David Dinkins, spoke about making progress on both sides of the issue. The Lubavitcher Rebbe, Menachem Mendel Schneerson, responded that, "We are not two sides. We are one side." He did not see a Black side and a Jewish side, as Mayor Dinkins did[2]. This re-framing of perspectives was the first step toward bringing order, understanding, and cooperation to Crown Heights.

Bringing *achdut* will require a similar shift in perspective. There is only one side – *Klal Yisrael* – but we need a fresh framework if we are to break almost two millennia of established thought to the contrary.

The biggest threat to Jewish survival in the 21st century is lack of *achdut* among different segments of the Jewish community. In fact, it's worse than that: There is absolute hatred between certain Jewish groups. Amazing as it is, the destruction of the Second Temple, the Holocaust, and close to 2,000 years of exile have done nothing to change this.

The time has come for Jews of all backgrounds and persuasions to develop a fresh perspective on this issue and to bring long overdue change to the Jewish world. We read history, but do we really believe it? Do we learn from it? By tradition, during Talmudic times, a plague during the spring months between the festivals of Passover and *Shavuot* (the Feast of

Weeks) killed 24,000 of Rabbi Akiva's students. For this reason, Orthodox Jews, some Conservative Jews, and many Sephardic Jews observe certain mourning practices during this period. What did these victims do? We're told that they were guilty of *Sinat Chinam* in their relationships with each other. Really? Devout students of the Torah learning under one of the greatest rabbis in history? Somehow we mourn them, but don't quite believe the story. In a recorded lecture, a prominent Modern Orthodox rabbi posits that these students died in a revolt against the Romans[3]. After all, how could such a plague really have happened? Now, after living through the recent COVID-19 pandemic, the traditional version of the story finally rings true. Can't we grasp a simple message: Even observing all the laws of the Torah other than avoiding *Sinat Chinam* will not bring the Messianic age.

The purpose of this book is to convince Jews of all persuasions to reconsider how they perceive other Jews and inspire them to change their approach. It presents a novel framework for thinking about the different streams of Judaism. It then proposes a way for members of each stream to consider the other ones in positive terms. It speaks directly to all Jews about the urgency of changing their perspectives and explains why there is no excuse for *Sinat Chinam*. Finally, it asks every Jew, including those who are secular and unaffiliated, to eliminate *Sinat Chinam* using the direct actions that I propose.

As a first step, we need to understand each other. I'm always surprised by how little Jews of one stream know about the beliefs and practices of Jews who differ from them. For this reason, Part One of this book describes each major Jewish movement, including its members' beliefs, practices, and culture. As you read Part One, you might be surprised at things that fly in the face of traditional stereotypes. Part One presents the following streams:

- Orthodox Jews
- Conservative Jews
- Reform Jews
- Reconstructionist Jews
- Sephardic Jews

I discuss each one in the order that makes it easiest to present their practices, similarities, and differences. The reader should not infer any judgment on my part from this order. I have written each chapter of Part One from the perspective of people who affiliate with that stream. I do not intend to be judgmental in any way, but rather to convey to the reader what it feels like to experience life as an adherent to that movement.

The non-Orthodox streams of Judaism are firmly established and have significant numbers of adherents, mostly in North America. They play less of a role in other countries, including Israel, where the issues that this book addresses refer to the tension between Orthodox Jews, including religiously-observant Sephardic Jews, on the one hand, and liberal Jews of all persuasions on the other hand. These tensions also appear in the political arena in Israel, where coalitions of right-wing and center-left-wing political parties, respectively, have become institutionalized channels for *Sinat Chinam*. Nevertheless, the concerns that this book presents are universal, and go beyond regional and national distinctions.

Part Two sets forth the novel framework in detail, drawing on the material in Part One and inserting the different Jewish streams into a unified metaphorical picture of *Klal Yisrael* that, stream-by-stream, can work to bring the Messianic age.

In Part Three, I address Jews in each stream of Judaism directly, discussing how its adherents think about Jews in other streams. I then explain why these attitudes need to change and why there is no excuse for continuing *Sinat Chinam*.

Part 4 speaks to all Jews individually. It calls on them to act now, irrespective of any institutional changes that might come in response to the framework for *achdut* that Part Two proposes.

This book does not place fault on or blame any Jew or stream for the present state of affairs. Our attitudes and behaviors are so ingrained that it no longer matters how they developed. What matters is whether we can find the path, the compassion, and the will to change.

As you read, you will see that I have italicized and defined certain Hebrew and Yiddish words. My purpose is to make the text easy for all Jews to read. Some of the italicized words present the Ashkenazi pronunciation, while others use that of Modern Hebrew. I've made no attempt to be consistent, instead using the pronunciation that is most common in each specific context. I have defined the italicized words in the Glossary at the back of the book.

For ease of presentation, I've framed the discussion of eliminating *Sinat Chinam* among Jews as a prescription for helping to bring the Messianic age. There is much more at stake. History has shown that if we don't change, we all will suffer. As long as we continue our current behavior, we are at severe risk of being driven from the Land of Israel and facing increased persecution in the diaspora. We have entered the land of Israel and been expelled from it several times over the course of history. In all cases, major nations have played a key role in whether we were able to stay in Israel and whether we could live safely in the diaspora. In historical order:

- the Assyrians, who, in 720 BCE, destroyed the Northern Kingdom of Israel;
- the Babylonians, who, in 586 BCE, destroyed the First Temple in Jerusalem;

- the Persians, who allowed us to defeat *Haman*[4] and then, in 538 BCE, to return to Israel and establish the Second Temple in Jerusalem;
- the Greeks, who threatened our religious freedom until the Maccabees defeated them in 140 BCE;
- the Romans, who, in 70 CE, destroyed the Second Temple in Jerusalem;
- the Crusaders, who tortured and uprooted European Jews between 1095 and 1291;
- the Spanish Inquisition in 1492, which ended the great Jewish civilization of Spain that had begun during or before Second Temple times;
- the Pogroms and other persecutions in Europe that came in waves between 1821 and 1921;
- World War I, which, over five years from 1914-1918, devastated most of Europe and threatened its Jewish communities;
- on a positive note, the *Balfour Declaration* that, in 1917, recognized the principle that a Jewish State should be established in then Palestine;
- the Russian Revolution in 1917, which destroyed the Jewish way of life for millions of Jews;
- the Holocaust, which began with *Kristallnacht* in November 1938 and lasted until the end of World War II in 1945, during which the Nazis and their supporters killed six million Jews;
- the United Nation's establishment of the State of Israel in 1948;
- the Six Day War in 1967, which returned the Kotel in Jerusalem to Jewish control.

Today, Israel faces an existential threat from Iran both through Iran's continuing nuclear program, and through

Iran's armed terrorist proxies on Israel's borders and within the country. Similarly, diaspora Jewry is facing an existential threat from a dramatic global rise in antisemitism.

Irrespective of your particular Jewish beliefs, the evidence is irrefutable that continued *Sinat Chinam* within *Klal Israel* has put Jewish survival at risk both in our ancestral homeland and in the diaspora.* To address this dire threat, we will need to change. The book is a prescription that will guide *Klal Yisrael* to make the necessary changes. It is a must read for all Jews.†

---

*   All streams of Judaism believe that our role in the world is to make it a better place by observing and modeling our moral standards that the Torah and the Prophets describe. When we visibly fail to accomplish this, as has been the case since the destruction of the Second Temple, we undermine the very purpose of our existence.

†   Throughout the book, I've made every effort to make the language gender neutral. Where this was not possible without making the text cumbersome, I defaulted to the masculine form, intending it to include the female gender as well.

Part One

THE DIFFERENT STREAMS OF JUDAISM

Chapter One

A PRIMER ON ORTHODOX JUDAISM

ORTHODOX JUDAISM HAS several sub-streams. While they have many similarities, there are also important differences. The taxonomy that this book uses to identify each sub-stream follows the general classifications used in the United States, Europe, Australia, and New Zealand. Israelis tend to prefer the term "Religious" rather than Orthodox, and categorize the different sub-streams slightly differently, although actual practices in Israel do not vary from those in the United States as far as the subject matter of this book is concerned.

Orthodox Judaism is based on the traditional Ashkenazi Judaism that existed in Europe until the emergence of the Reform movement in the 1800s. Since then, the term "Orthodox" has been applied to traditional Ashkenazi Judaism in its different forms.[1]

The best starting point for discussing Orthodox Judaism is *The Thirteen Principles of Faith* that *Rambam* (Rabbi Moses Maimonides) wrote in the 12th century. All Orthodox sub-streams subscribe to these principles. *The Thirteen Principles of Faith* read as follows:[2]

1. *I believe with complete faith that the Creator, Blessed is His Name, creates and guides all creatures, and that He alone made, makes, and will make everything.*
2. *I believe with complete faith that the Creator, Blessed is His Name, is unique, and there is no uniqueness like His in any way, and that He alone is our God, Who was, Who is, and Who always will be.*
3. *I believe with complete faith that the Creator, Blessed is His Name, is not physical and is not affected by physical phenomena, and that there is no comparison whatsoever to Him.*
4. *I believe with complete faith that the Creator, Blessed is His Name, is the very first and the very last.*
5. *I believe with complete faith that the Creator, Blessed is His Name, – to Him alone is it proper to pray and it is not proper to pray to any other.*
6. *I believe with complete faith that all the words of the prophets are true.*
7. *I believe with complete faith that the prophecy of Moses our teacher, peace upon him, was true, and that he was the father of the prophets – both those who preceded him and those who followed him.*
8. *I believe with complete faith that the entire* Torah *now in our hands is the same one that was given to Moses, our teacher, peace be upon him.*
9. *I believe with complete faith that this* Torah *will not be exchanged nor will there be another* Torah *from the Creator, Blessed is His Name.*
10. *I believe with complete faith that the Creator, Blessed is His Name, knows all the deeds of human beings and their thoughts, as it is said, 'He fashions their hearts all together, He comprehends all their deeds.'*
11. *I believe with complete faith that the Creator, Blessed*

is His Name, rewards with good those who observe His commandments, and punishes those who violate His commandments.

12. *I believe with complete faith in the coming of the Messiah, and even though he may delay, nevertheless I anticipate every day that he will come.*
13. *I believe with complete faith that there will be a resuscitation of the dead whenever the wish emanates from the Creator, Blessed is His Name and exalted is His mention, forever and for all eternity.*

   For Your salvation I do long, HASHEM,
   I do long, HASHEM, for Your salvation.
   HASHEM, for your salvation I do long.
         [ed.: Italics in original text.]

The following is an excerpt of the Artscroll siddur's explanatory commentary on *The Thirteen Principles of Faith*:

Historically, Judaism never separated belief from performance. In the Torah, the commandment to believe in God is not stated any differently than the commandment to lend money to a fellow Jew in need, or to refrain from eating non-kosher food. As the centuries rolled by, however, philosophical speculation and dogmas became prevalent among other religions and, in time, began to influence a number of Jews. To counteract this trend, medieval Rabbinical authorities felt the need to respond by defining the principles of Judaism. The 'Thirteen Principles of Faith' are based upon the formulation of Rambam [Maimonides] in his Commentary to Mishnah (Sanhedrin, ch. 10) and have achieved nearly universal acceptance. ...

The Thirteen Principles fall into three general categories: (a) the nature of belief in God; (b) the authenticity, validity, and immutability of the Torah; and (c) man's responsibility and ultimate reward.[3]

The meaning of *The Thirteen Principles of Faith* according to the Artscroll Siddur is as follows[*]:

A) The Nature of Belief in God

1. *God's Existence.* There is no partnership in creation. God is the sole Creator and the universe continues to exist only because He wills it so.
2. *God is a complete and total Unity.* He is not a collection of limbs and organs, as are man and animals. Unlike everything in Creation, He cannot be split as can a rock or divided into component elements. This concept appears in the first verse of the Shema. [ed.: The *Shema* is a prayer quoting the Torah that Orthodox men recite four times daily. It opens with: "Hear, O Israel: *Hashem* is our God, *Hashem*, the One and Only."]
3. *God is not physical* nor can the human imagination grasp His essence.
4. *God is eternal and the First Source.* Everything in the created universe has a moment when it came into existence; by definition, no creature can be infinite. God transcends time, however, because time itself is His creation.
5. *We should direct our prayers only to God.* It is tempting to beseech the angels or such mighty forces as the sun or constellations, because God has entrusted

---

[*] Some of the text below is paraphrased for brevity.

them with carrying out His will. However, this is illusory. None of them has any power independent of that which has God assigned them. There are no intermediaries; we pray directly to God.

B) **Authenticity of the *Torah***

6. *God communicates with man.* In order for man to carry out his divinely ordered mission, he must know what it is. Prophecy is the means by which God communicates His wishes to man. It is a gift that man can attain upon reaching heights of self-perfection.
7. *Moses' prophecy is unique.* Moses' prophecy is not only true, but of a quality unapproached by that of any prophet before or since. It is essential that his prophecy be unrivaled so that no later 'prophet' could ever claim that he had received a 'Torah' that was superior to that of Moses.
8. *The entire* Torah *is God-given.* God dictated every word in the Torah to Moses. There is no difference between [the 'trivial' verses] … and [the important verses].… The same applies to the Oral Law that explains the Torah. Moses received all of it from God.
9. *The* Torah *is unchangeable.* Since both the Written and Oral Law come from God, they cannot be improved upon in any manner.

C) **Man's Responsibility and Ultimate Reward**

10. *God knows man's thoughts and deeds.* Man's individual deeds are important to God and so are the hopes and thoughts that drive him. God is aware of everything man thinks and does.

11. *Reward and punishment.* No one acts in a vacuum and no deed goes unrewarded or unpunished. This includes the dictum that one cannot cancel out a bad deed with a good one. God treats each independently.
12. *The Messiah will come.* We are to conduct our lives according to the Torah and retain the belief that the Messiah will come at the time that God deems proper. This faith includes the principle that only the Davidic dynasty will provide the Messianic King.
13. *The dead will live again in the Messianic era* when the world will attain a new spiritual and physical level of perfection. Those who have not been found too unworthy to enter this exalted state will live again to enjoy it. [ed.: Judaism holds that the righteous of other faiths will also enjoy these rewards.][4]

The song *Yigdal*, which appears in virtually all Jewish prayer books, summarizes these principles.[5]

All sub-streams of Orthodox Judaism subscribe to *The Thirteen Principles of Faith*. The best definition of an Orthodox Jew is one who believes in and lives by these principles and observes the laws of the Torah as halachic (Orthodox Jewish legal) authorities later codified it. On a train from Warsaw to the Treblinka concentration camp during the Holocaust, Reb Azriel David Fastag put the 12th of these principles to music.[6] The song spread like wildfire among the Jewish inmates of the Nazi concentration camps and the death camps. A large but unknown number of inmates sang it as they were led to the gas chambers. An escapee from the train introduced the song and the music to a well-known Chassidic composer who later escaped from Poland to the United States. Today, the song, *Ani Ma'amin* ("I Believe"), is familiar throughout the Jewish world and is sung frequently, including on *Yom HaShoah*

(Holocaust Remembrance Day observed on the 27th of the Hebrew month of Nisan) by those Jewish congregations that observe this day. There are now several different tunes for *Ani Ma'amin*. You can find a good sampling of them by searching for "*Ani Ma'amin*" on YouTube.

The hallmarks of Orthodox Judaism are strict observance of the Jewish Sabbath (*Shabbat* or *Shabbos*), Jewish holidays, *Kashrut*, Jewish laws of family purity, as well as daily prayer and consistent time spent studying halacha. All Orthodox Jews take these *mitzvos* seriously. The details of these practices are beyond the scope of this book, but when I refer to them in the text, I will explain them, as necessary.[7]

Orthodox Jews adhere to the Hebrew calendar, which God gave the Jewish people during the Exodus from Egypt. In this calendar, days and weeks coincide with the solar calendar, while the lunar calendar determines the months and years; periodically it adds a full month to the year to keep the seasons consistent with the solar calendar. The first book of the Torah[8] established the seven-day week, based on the six days of creation and the seventh day when God rested.[9] The Hebrew calendar determines the Jewish holidays, meaning that they do not have fixed dates on the solar calendar. For example, Chanukah can begin as early as late November or as late as late December in any given year.

The Torah designates *Shabbos* and several Jewish holidays as days of complete rest from daily activities, particularly work. These holidays include the three Pilgrimage Festivals during which Jews in Israel visited Jerusalem in ancient Temple times: *Pesach*, *Shavuos* in the spring, and *Succos* in the fall. They also include *Rosh Hashana* and *Yom Kippur* in the fall. Every *Shabbos* is a day of great joy for an Orthodox Jewish family, and the Pilgrimage Festivals are times of special celebration. It is an Orthodox tradition that goes back two thousand years for men to give their wives special gifts just before each of the Pilgrimage Festivals. Orthodox Jews also celebrate the lesser Jewish Holidays of Chanukah and Purim, as well as observing several fast days during the year, most of which are linked to the destruction of the ancient Temple in Jerusalem or to events leading up to its destruction. Many Orthodox Jews observe other significant dates on the Hebrew calendar as well.

The Hebrew calendar does not include Mother's Day and Father's Day because the Ten Commandments require one to honor one's parents every day rather than only on specific holidays. Nor does it recognize Halloween, Saint Patrick's Day, and Valentine's Day because of the Christian origin of these holidays. Modern Orthodox Jews in America generally celebrate Thanksgiving Day as a non-religious holiday, but no Orthodox Jews observe Christmas and Easter.

An important characteristic of Orthodox Judaism is how its adherents observe *Shabbos* and Jewish holidays. Non-Orthodox Jews also might observe them, but in far more limited ways. My discussion of the respective streams of Judaism will expand on some of the specifics of these differences, but they include the frequency of attending synagogue services, the observance of the prohibition of work activities on these days, and the performance of specific rituals, including special festive meals, related to these days.

Shabbos is one of the distinctive elements that has preserved Orthodox Judaism over the millennia. It brings families and communities together to refrain from all work and spend 25 hours every week eating, praying, and socializing. This markedly distinguishes Orthodoxy from other streams of Ashkenazi Judaism and might explain the far lower assimilation and intermarriage rates among Orthodox Jews than among Jews of other streams of Ashkenazi Judaism.

Another distinguishing feature of Orthodoxy is the success of marriages among Orthodox couples. This stems from dating practices that focus on exclusively looking for a marriage partner, careful discussion between prospective marriage partners to ensure that their future goals are aligned, and an attitude toward the sanctity of marriage that embraces "giving to your spouse" rather than negotiating for "what I can get." This creates a special bond within Orthodox Jewish couples. They are partners in living a Jewish life and therefore, equals, despite their different roles. It is important to keep this in mind in contrast to the media's frequent portrayal of the diminished, repressed role of women in the Orthodox world.

Most practicing Orthodox Jews read Hebrew fluently, pray exclusively in Hebrew, and have a working knowledge of the major texts of Jewish law. Even though many are not familiar with the details of each text, they at least know of their existence and how to use them. Today, many of these texts have been translated into English, which makes them more accessible. To assure that their children will have the requisite Hebrew literacy and knowledge of Jewish laws and customs to practice Orthodox Judaism properly, Jewish families send their children to Orthodox schools rather than to public schools or secular private schools.

Many Orthodox men participate in *daf yomi*[10] (translated as the "daily page") where they learn a designated page of Talmud each day, often under the leadership of an instructor. There are many choices available for *daf yomi* study, including in-person classes, internet-based instruction, dial-in based instruction, and personal study of the text alone or with a colleague. It takes seven-and-a-half years to complete the study of the Talmud at this pace. No matter where or how one studies, everyone learns the same page each day, so all participants finish the cycle at the same time. To celebrate this significant accomplishment, ceremonies are held in locations around the world in venues ranging in size from *shuls* to sports stadiums.

When a Jew from another stream of Judaism becomes Orthodox, the individual will often need time and instruction to gain the Hebrew literacy needed to pray in Hebrew, participate in Jewish rituals in Hebrew, and navigate Jewish legal texts. The same is true for those who convert to Judaism without prior Jewish literacy.

Chassidic Jews

Chassidic Judaism began in the 18th century under the leadership of Rabbi Israel ben Eliezer, better known as the Baal Shem Tov (literally in Hebrew, "the carrier of a good name") who was born close to the year 1700 in then Poland, now Ukraine. By his early 30s, the Besht, as he came to be called in admiring abbreviation, had become widely known for the many miracles that he performed for the benefit of sick or needy Jews. The study of the Besht's life is beyond the scope of this book, but I highly recommend it to readers who wish to understand 18th century Jewish life in Poland, in both the *shtetel* (village) and rural Jewish communities.

Jewish theology espouses both Love of *Hashem* and Fear of *Hashem*. The Besht brought fresh energy and meaning to the former concept, drawing on the mystical, Kabbalistic teachings of the *Zohar* (leading textual source of Kabballah) and the Arizal (Rabbi Luria Ashkenazi), who lived in Israel from 1534 to 1572 and by tradition, authored the *Zohar*. The Besht's teachings attracted a great following during his life. His style, message, and reputation were electric, and drew the admiration and following of tens of thousands of Jews. The established Jewish leadership, however, was not supportive of the Besht. They feared that he would become another false *Moshiach* like Shabbetai Zevi – a Sephardic Rabbi who in the mid-17th century declared himself to be *Moshiach* and attracted countless followers throughout the Jewish world. In the end, he converted to Islam under pressure from the Ottoman authorities, thus exposing himself as a false messiah.

A lead skeptic of the propriety of Chassidism was the Vilna Gaon – the most prominent Ashkenazi Rabbinic leader and scholar of the time. His opposition was so well known that the legend arose that the great Chassidic Rabbi and Master, Rabbi Levi Yitzchak of Berditchev dreamed about a battle in Heaven after the Vilna Gaon's death over whether to admit his soul to the highest sphere of Heaven in light of his attitude toward Chassidim.[11]

Despite this opposition, Chasidism grew rapidly throughout Ashkenazi Eastern Europe during the 17th and 18th centuries. Finally, in 1913, the Yeshivish Orthodox Jewish establishment and the leaders of the Chassidic world formed the governing body *Agudas Yisrael*, often called "the *Agudah*," ending roughly 170 years of friction between these two Orthodox sub-streams. The Chofetz Chaim[12] and the Chortkover Rebbe[13] were prominent proponents of this effort that brought calm after years of discord.[14]

A main characteristic of Chassidim is that they follow the teachings and leadership of the Rebbe who is the leader of the Chassidic movement to which they belong.* These Rebbes are the successors to Rebbes who succeeded the Besht, and their names generally derive from the towns in Eastern Europe where each Chassidic movement, or dynasty, began. Examples are the Satmar Rebbe from Szatmárnémeti, Hungary, now Satu Mare, Romania; the Belz Rebbe from Belz,

---

* Rebbe is the Chassidic term for rabbi.

Poland, now Ukraine; the Skver Rebbe from Skvyra, Ukraine; and the Gerer Rebbe from Góra Kalwaria, Poland. During the years of the rapid growth of the Chassidic movements in Europe, beginning in the 1700s and lasting until the Holocaust, these Rebbes often resided in royal courts, separate from their followers, who mostly lived in modest or impoverished conditions. Each Rebbe, and the members of his court, wore the garments characteristic of the dynasty, clothing that the average Chassid could not generally afford.

The Rebbes taught the philosophy of *Deveikus*, a Hebrew word meaning to cleave, cling, or connect to *Hashem*. Adherents could achieve this connection through prayer or selected *zmiros* (songs) whose words and *niggunim* (melodies) draw one close to *Hashem*. The Rebbes were masters of praying with *Deveikus*.* Their practice was often to pray in private for many hours a day. They prayed for *Hashem* to act kindly toward their followers and to *Klal Yisrael*. Unlike the average Jew, many of these Rebbes could see the spheres of Heaven and anticipate bad decrees. This enabled them to focus their prayers on the specific outcomes that they hoped to help achieve.

A key tenet of Chassidic doctrine is asceticism. Despite their grand courts, the Rebbes lived very simple, non-materialistic lives, using their opulent surroundings to enhance their followers' experience of a visit to the Rebbe, which was indeed a rare event for the average Chassid, reserved for special occasions when he or she sought the Rebbe's prayers or blessings. Examples are asking for help to cure a severe illness, asking for a blessing to have children, and asking for prayers for financial help. The Rebbes were so devoted to their followers that they often did not eat much or well and slept very little in light of the time they needed for their work.

---

* This type of intense prayer is extraordinarily difficult for the average Jew.

Chassidism as I have just described it has changed in many ways since the Holocaust. The grand Rebbe's courts no longer exist, and Chassidim today mostly live in communities close to their Rebbe, who is quite accessible to his followers. Chassidim emphasize modesty in their appearance (*tznius*) and their actions. Modest dress means avoiding wearing revealing garments, which it makes it easy to identify Chassidim, and thus creates a visible barrier to assimilation into broader society.

Most Chassidic men now wear distinctive clothing that represents their dynasty, and which has become much more affordable with the invention of polyester (often replacing expensive silk), and the development of mass clothing manufacturing. The signature look for all Chassidic men is the long black or dark-colored robe or coat (*bekishe* or *kapota*) worn over a white dress shirt. When praying in *shul*, they tie a black cloth belt (*gartel*) around their coats or robes at the waist, to separate their upper bodies from their less clean lower bodies. Male Chassidim wear black hats, and the style of hat identifies the Chassidic dynasty to which a particular Chassid belongs. On *Shabbos*, Jewish holidays, and special occasions such as weddings, many Chassidic men wear fur hats – either *shtreimels* or *spudiks*. Under their hats, Chassidic men wear black velvet *kippos* so that their heads are always covered out of respect for *Hashem*, even when they do not wear their hats. Chassidic men do not wear wedding rings.

Chassidic women wear dark-colored clothing, not necessarily black, and make sure that their outfits cover their skin, other than their wrists, hands, and faces. For this reason, their dresses or skirts extend to mid-calf and they wear stockings all year round. Chassidic women do not wear pants. They also cover their hair once they are married. Hair coverings range from wigs (*sheitels*), to scarves, to tightly woven fabric nets (*snoods*). These coverings ensure that women do not attract the attention of men other than their husbands. In some Chassidic dynasties, married women also shave off their natural hair. While observing this dress code, many Chassidic women still dress fashionably. In observance of *tznius*, many Chassidic men will avert their eyes when passing women in the street, unless the women are members of their family.

Men and women go separately to those activities where they are not able to wear Chassidic dress, such as at the gym, swimming pool, or beach. Thus, for Chassidim, these facilities have separate hours for men and women, or are restricted exclusively to men or women.

Chassidic men pray three times a day, generally with a *minyan*. Before morning prayers, Chassidic men immerse in a *mikveh* (Jewish ritual bath) so they will be in a state of ritual purity when they pray to *Hashem*. Chassidic women immerse in a *mikveh* to achieve ritual purity before marriage and several days after menstruation. Many Chassidic women pray at least once a day, generally in private. In addition to formal prayer, Chassidic women frequently recite *tehillim* (Psalms composed by King David) asking *Hashem* to protect or help their families, heal those who are sick, and help those looking for a marriage partner.

Chassidic life is extremely warm and joyous. There are few pleasures greater than attending a Chassidic wedding, which is likely to continue into the next morning. Joy, warmth, and spirituality overflow during a long night of dancing, singing, and listening to the blessings and folklore of local Chassidic storytellers (*badchanim*) as individuals and small groups of men are honored to dance in front of the *kallah* (Jewish bride).

The same can be said of spending *Shabbos* in a Chassidic community. On Fridays, vendors line the streets selling fresh cut flowers to men who bring them home to their wives. Imagine getting flowers every Friday! Chassidic women are used to it. Then, as sunset approaches, the men go to *shul* to say their evening prayers, and the women light *Shabbos* candles, having already prepared the evening *Shabbos* meal. A palpable silence descends on the community. Sitting in *shul* at the beginning of evening services, one can feel the calm enveloping the sanctuary. The prayers are especially spiritual, as is the warmth between congregants wishing each other a good *Shabbos*.

The *Shabbos* meal is always special. Be prepared for a holiday-like feast of fresh-baked challah, wine, fish, meats, traditional side dishes, and sweet desserts. Come hungry! There is also singing and storytelling. This aspect of Chassidic life is called *leibedik*. Chassidim are careful to refrain from negative speech, especially on *Shabbos*. The same applies to raised voices and arguments. In a Chassidic home, *Shabbos* is a day of rest from these behaviors.

Chassidim generally have large families, with an average of more than five children. Families with ten or more children are not unusual. This adds greatly to the festivity of Chassidic life.

Those who are not part of Chassidic communities sometimes have a negative view of them, and especially of the treatment of women. The media and the film industry have fostered this view, as have certain Chassidic women who have left the fold and elect to project a negative impression of their prior lives to the broader public that has no real context for understanding the Chassidic way of life. I urge my readers not to prejudge the Chassidic world based on what the media portrays. All of my personal experiences have been contrary to these cinematic portrayals. Chassidic women are some of the most joyful, fulfilled people I have ever met. The inevitable exceptions are not a fair stereotype of the norm. The excerpt below, in which a Chassidic writer blogs about her story of Chassidic dating and marriage is a good example of that norm:

> In the non-Jewish world, ours is what you would call an arranged marriage. I dislike that word though because in my mind, that equals a "forced" marriage. And mine, like most others in my community, was anything but. At any time, you have the option of saying no.
>
> As a girl turns 18, it gives matchmakers a green light to start calling the parents. I belong to a certain Hasidic sect, so the suggestions were all going to be eligible young men from the same sect. As I turned 18, the phones started ringing with suggestions. If a suggestion sounded promising, my parents went ahead and made many inquiries.
>
> As much as the Jewish world is big, it's actually very small. We quickly found some mutual acquaintances who could tell us more about the boy. We wanted to know about his character traits, is he kind-hearted? Is he a messy kind of person? Happy? Helpful? Basically, a good person who would make a good husband. We can only do our best and hope the reports we got were truthful. For the first few months, none of the suggestions panned out. The boy was either not right for me or they decided I wasn't right for them.
>
> When I was almost 19, my neighbor from around the block was suggested to me. He was, for our

circles, considered a bit older at the ripe age of 23. My father knew him well from the daily prayers at the synagogue. He didn't need to hear much as he knew him to be a fine young man who was always willing to help others and was known to have a heart of gold. That's what matters most, doesn't it?

As I was told of the potential match, my first reaction was NO WAY! I knew the family superficially, I was aware the father had passed away young and left behind the widow and 12 children, I knew they were a very close-knit family and you always saw the mom and her daughters together, in their own world. So, I was a bit intimidated.

My parents were very interested and thought this would be the perfect guy for me. They agreed to let me think it over and give them an answer. After giving it some thought, I decided I had no valid reason to say no. So, the first step was taken. A meeting was scheduled between the young man's mother and myself. It was really weird to be meeting someone you know for such an intimate purpose.

My stomach turned as I got ready. But I needn't have worried. As soon as she saw me, she said: "You should know, I'm just as nervous as you". That put me at ease a little bit. As the conversation progressed, I relaxed, and the meeting was actually nice. We talked about all kinds of stuff, most of which I barely remember now.

Everything goes through a matchmaker which meant that we went home and waited to hear what the other side had decided. It didn't take very long for them to let us know that they were interested in continuing and the time has come to set up a date for me to meet the potential groom. Well, date is not really what we had. We call it a *b'show* which means a sit-in date. We had made up to meet in a friend's house, on the other side of town so as not to run into anyone we knew.

Most of the ultra-orthodox Jews have an average of 5 dates, I am Hasidic which means we do things a bit differently. We have one or two sit-ins after which the couple usually gets engaged. It sounds weird but research has shown that there are no more divorces in our circles than in the rest of the world. This is what I knew, this is how I grew up and this is my normal.

A sit-in in our world is quite intimidating as it's the first close contact a boy/girl has with the opposite gender as we are separated throughout our childhood.

To say the first few minutes were awkward is an understatement. But it didn't take long for him to make me feel comfortable and for the conversation to really become enjoyable. We spoke about our families, our time in seminary or yeshivah (an institution that focuses on teaching Talmud to boys and young men) and other things. We do not talk about the deeper stuff since we both come from the same background, so it's usually a given that we will be on the same page. We spent a nice few hours together. After the meeting, we both went home.

My parents gave me the option to meet him again the next day. I was young, barely 19 and I probably (most assuredly) didn't realize what a momentous decision this was. I thought it over, I liked a lot of what I saw (of how much one could see from one meeting). Besides all the good things I heard about him, he was also nice and had a great sense of humor. I knew how dedicated he was to his widow mom and I could tell he would go through fire for anyone he cares about. I didn't think I would find out much more by a second meeting and I didn't want to spend the night not sleeping from nerves. So, my decision was made. I would marry that guy.

Since the parents had already taken care of the other important stuff like discussions about money among others, I happily told my parents to go ahead and let the other side know and after the matchmaker called to tell us he wanted to marry me too, we got officially engaged.

It's true, we do actually get married to a stranger and there usually isn't such a thing as falling in love. We just work harder at making our marriage grow and the love, as a result, is a deep, long lasting one. I'm happy to report that after 22 years, I'm still very happily in love and our marriage isn't any different than any of yours.

My dear husband is everything I thought he was; caring, a heart of gold, great sense of humor and does everything for me and the kids.[15] [ed.: I have edited punctuation and added italics for clarity.]

To perpetuate their heritage, Chassidim speak Yiddish as their first language, and Yiddish is the language of instruction in Chassidic schools. Boys and girls attend separate schools. In the lower grades, Judaic studies focus on teaching Biblical Hebrew, as well as the Torah, the Prophets, and Jewish laws and customs. After a few years, the boys begin to learn Talmud.* By high school, the Judaic studies curriculum for boys focuses on the study of Talmud.

By tradition, girls do not receive Talmud instruction. Instead, in the later elementary grades and high school, they have the opportunity for further study of the Torah, the Prophets, *tehillim*, and Jewish laws and customs. Girls' schools' curricula vary from school to school.

American Chassidim are also fluent in English. I have found them to be articulate speakers of English in personal, religious, and business discussions. The media and certain politicians have condemned Chassidic education as lacking proper exposure to both the humanities and the STEM subjects, and several city governments are assessing whether these schools comply with applicable state requirements. This book does not express an opinion on the subject. The controversy will have to play itself out city by city and school by school, and will, I hope, result in outcomes that are acceptable for each Chassidic community.

---

* The complex Jewish texts and commentaries that codify the extensive Oral Law, complementing the written Torah, which *Hashem* gave to Moses at Mount Sinai following the exodus from Egypt. Boys first learn *Mishna*, the terse summary of the Oral Law, which Rabbi Yehuda HaNasi redacted, and then *Gemara*, the more extensive Talmudic discussions and their commentaries, which amplify and clarify the *Mishna*).

To avoid outside influences on Chassidic youth, the Chassidic world strongly discourages the attending of college immediately after high school. Chassidim prefer to spend their time dedicated to work, Jewish studies, and family, instead. At a minimum, they defer college until later in life.

Chassidic Jews are not political Zionists. They do not consider the modern State of Israel to be the first step in fulfilling the prophesy of bringing *Moshiach* or rebuilding of the Temple in Jerusalem. Accordingly, Chassidic Jews do not observe the new Jewish holidays, such as Israel's Independence Day, which the Israeli government established in 1948. They do, however, care about the *land* of Israel, as opposed to the State or the government of Israel. They strongly believe in the right of Jews to settle anywhere within the Biblical borders of the ancient Kingdom of Israel and do not support relinquishing any land within these borders that is presently in the possession of Jews. In Israel, the Chassidic community favors Orthodox-sponsored laws that affect daily life, including *Shabbos* closing laws and the exemption of yeshiva students from military service.

Unique among the Chassidic movements is the Chabad Lubavitch dynasty. The Chabad dynasty had seven successive Rebbes but is not led by a Rebbe today. Instead, the movement has a committee, with several individuals in key administrative positions. Most notable among this group is Rabbi Chaim Yehuda ("Yudel") *Krinsky*, whom many consider the administrative head of Chabad, but who is not the Rebbe of the movement. The last Chabad Rebbe, Rabbi Menachem Mendel Schneerson, died in 1994. By Chabad tradition, the Rebbe, as he is widely called, will never have a successor. He transformed Chabad from an Eastern European Chassidic movement decimated by the Holocaust, into a global powerhouse. Today, Chabad has a presence in almost every major city in the world and can be relied on as a source of information, kosher food, and hospitality for Jews traveling worldwide.

This reflects the fact that Chabad Chassidim are not as insular as other Chassidim. Their stated mission is to bring *Moshiach* through outreach to *Klal Yisrael*, one mitzvah at a time. You can see them at tables in select locations in urban areas and on college campuses, asking Jews on the street to put on *tefillin*, light *Shabbos* candles, or shake a *lulav* and *estrog* on *Succos*. They are hosts to Jews around the world and advocates for increased Jewish observance, even if only by small increments. Thus, according to the 2020 Pew Study, 26% of Conservative Jews, 27% of Reform Jews and 22% of Unaffiliated Jews often or sometimes participate in events at Chabad, while only 24% of Orthodox Jews do so.[16]

Chabad Chassidim have their own prayer book, and they dress distinctively, wearing wide-brimmed fedoras rather than fur hats. Their coats also tend to be longer than those of most other Chassidim.[17]

Yeshivish Jews

The hallmarks of Yeshivish Judaism are the study and strict observance of Jewish law. The Yeshivish stream developed in Lithuania in the 1700s, under the leadership of the Vilna Gaon. For this reason, the stream is sometimes called *Litvish* (Lithuanian) Judaism. The Yeshivish center of learning is the yeshiva. Yeshivish Jews educate their children in the private yeshiva system from grade school through high school, and there are a few yeshivas at the university level. Yeshivas separate boys from girls either for all grades or, in some smaller communities, from sixth grade at the latest. Where a community does not have a suitable yeshiva high school, parents send their children to out-of-town schools with residential facilities. Young children attend Yeshivish pre-schools or day care programs, which women in the community often run out of their own homes.

Yeshivas provide instruction in both general studies and Judaic studies, resulting in a long, demanding school day. In the lower grades, Judaic studies focus on teaching Biblical Hebrew, as well as the Torah, the Prophets, and Jewish laws and customs. There is also a heavy focus on Jewish rituals to reinforce the practices that the students see at home and in *shul*. For example, students often make decorations for the family *succah*, write their own *Megillah* for *Purim*, make their own Chanukah menorahs, and participate in model *Pesach* seders in preparation for the festival. In the older grades, the boys learn Talmud beginning with *Mishna* and then *Gemara*.[18] By high school, the Judaic studies curriculum for boys focuses heavily on the study of Talmud.

By tradition, girls do not receive Talmud instruction and instead, in the later elementary grades and high school, have the opportunity for further study of the Hebrew language, the Torah, the Prophets, *tehillim*, and Jewish laws and customs. Girls' schools' curricula vary from school to school.*

After high school, boys continue the study of Talmud in yeshivas for several years. In the United States' Yeshivish communities, it has become popular for some of this study to take place in Israel. Similarly, it is common for girls from these communities to attend Yeshivish seminaries in Israel for a year after high school.

Generally, Yeshivish men and women do not attend secular colleges. Alternatives are to attend one of the few available Yeshivish colleges or to earn a college degree online. Many Yeshivish women avail themselves of the online option to

---

* Yeshivish all-girls' schools, beginning with elementary school, are frequently called *Bais Yaakov* schools, and sometimes include *Bais Yaakov* in the school's name.

obtain certifications and degrees that qualify them to work while they begin dating or while their husbands continue studying in yeshiva. These women often gravitate to careers in fields such as teaching, accounting, general office work, physical or occupational therapy, art therapy, speech therapy, and nursing – fields with plentiful employment that enable them to support their families.* In Israel, new vocational colleges focusing on careers in technology for *Haredi* women are being established.

After several years of Talmud study, many Yeshivish men begin working. Some of them become rabbis in synagogues or yeshivas. Others choose positions in commercial businesses or non-profit institutions. Still others obtain college degrees, either at Yeshivish colleges or online, and pursue fields such as accounting or business, or move on to study professional disciplines such as law and medicine.

Yeshivish adult men who hold full-time jobs continue their Jewish learning at the local *kollel*.† Some Yeshivish men attend the *kollel* daily, others less frequently, depending on demands at work and home.

Yeshivish young adults generally begin dating between ages 21 and 23 for boys, and at 18 to 20 for girls. The Yeshivish dating process (*shidduchim*) is different from dating in the secular world. Matchmakers (*shadchanim*) who have met the individuals and who keep their dating profiles on file or friends and family introduce men and women to each other as prospective partners. Yeshivish adults date only for marriage and there is no physical contact during the dating process.

---

* The health-related certifications require hands-on work in hospitals or training facilities that do not exclusively serve the Yeshivish community, making some interaction with men unavoidable.

† A *kollel* is a community learning center where adults can study Talmud with a learning partner, listen to lectures (*shiurim*), and say daily prayers with a *minyan*. Yeshivish men with professional or commercial jobs often spend parts of several evenings a week learning at the *kollel*.

Rather, the man and woman meet in a public place, such as a restaurant, and have meaningful discussions about what they want out of their life and their future marriage. Generally, a Yeshivish man or woman will date only one person at a time. If, after a few dates, the couple has a sense that they may be right for each other, the dates and discussions become more serious. Typically, the couple will become engaged after dating for a period of two to six months, depending on their dating frequency and comfort level. At that point, or perhaps sooner, they will meet each other's families. Once they have decided to marry, the wedding will generally take place within the next few months. Engagements lasting as long as six months are rare.

Yeshivish Jews are overwhelmingly of Ashkenazi descent and follow Ashkenazic practices, but Yeshivish Jews speak the local language of their country of residence – e.g., English in the United States and Hebrew in Israel – as their first language. Yiddish is not the primary language of Yeshivish Jews.

Yeshivish Jews dress in a modest or *tznius* way but, unlike Chassidim, do not wear special garments reflecting their background or affiliation. Yeshivish men generally wear dark solid-colored suits in black, blue, or gray, white shirts, and black velvet *kippos*. Recently, some Yeshivish men have started wearing two-layered solid black *kippos* made of fabric other than velvet. This mostly black-and-white scheme is sometimes metaphorically called the "Penguin" look. Yeshivish men past bar mitzvah age wear black fedora hats that often have wider brims than fedoras made for the secular world. Many Yeshivish men who do not work in rabbinic fields only wear their hats when they go to *shul*. Yeshivish men do not wear wedding rings.

Yeshivish women wear clothing of different colors, generally avoiding red as too flamboyant, and make sure that their outfits cover their skin, other than their arms below the elbow, and their faces. For this reason, their dresses or skirts extend to mid-calf, and they wear stockings all year round. They also cover their hair once they are married. Hair coverings include *sheitels*, scarves, *snoods*, and hats under which they tuck all of their hair. These coverings ensure that women do not attract the attention of men other than their husbands. While observing this dress code, many Yeshivish women dress fashionably. Yeshivish women bathe in the *mikveh* several days after each menstrual cycle to achieve ritual purity.

Many Yeshivish families dress their young boys and girls, respectively, in matching outfits, particularly on Shabbos. By age 12, Yeshivish boys stop wearing these outfits in favor of the "Penguin" look.

Yeshivish men and women do not go together to swimming pools, beaches, or gyms. Instead, they frequent fitness facilities that have separate hours for men and women or are restricted exclusively to men or women. The same applies to health clubs and spas.

Yeshivish men pray three times a day, generally with a *minyan*. Many Yeshivish women pray at least once a day, generally in private. In addition to formal prayer, Yeshivish women frequently recite *tehillim* asking *Hashem* to protect or help their families as well as those who are sick, in need, or looking for a marriage partner.

Shabbos and Jewish holidays in a Yeshivish community have many similarities to *Shabbos* in a Chassidic community, but there are a few differences. Yeshivish men wear special clothes set aside for *Shabbos* and Jewish holidays – perhaps a newer hat, a better suit, or a special necktie and nice cufflinks, but they do not wear Chassidic robes or fur hats. Also, the *leibedik* aspects of *Shabbos* and Jewish holiday observance are considerably toned down in comparison to Chassidic practices. But these distinctions are largely superficial. *Shabbos* and Jewish holidays in a Yeshivish home have the same special feeling as in a Chassidic home. All weekday activities cease. Everybody is dressed in special *Shabbos* clothing. People eat sumptuous meals on Friday evening and *Shabbos* day. The same is true for Jewish holidays. *Shabbos* is said to be a taste of the world to come. This is certainly true in the *shuls* and homes of Yeshivish communities.

Shabbos begins in a Yeshivish home when the woman of the house lights *Shabbos* candles. Two candles are sufficient to satisfy this *mitzvah,* but it is customary for women to light additional candles for family members such as children and the spouses of married children. Once a woman adds candles, she is bound to do so every *Shabbos,* at least in her own home.

Like Chassidic Jews, Yeshivish Jews are not political Zionists. Contrary to popular impression, Yeshivish Jews do not consider the modern State of Israel to be the first step in fulfilling the prophesy to bring *Moshiach* or rebuild the Temple in Jerusalem. Accordingly, Yeshivish Jews do not observe the new Jewish holidays, such as Israel's Independence Day. They do, however, care about the *land* of Israel, in contrast to the State or government of Israel. They therefore strongly believe in the right of Jews to settle anywhere within the Biblical borders of the ancient Kingdom of Israel and do not support relinquishing any land within these borders that is presently in the possession of Jews. In Israel, the Yeshivish community and the Chassidic community support Orthodox-sponsored laws that affect daily life, including *Shabbos* closing laws and the exemption of yeshiva students from military service.

In recent years, the term "Yeshivish-Balabatish" has emerged to describe a slightly more liberal form of Yeshivish practice. Unlike Yeshivish Jews in general, Yeshivish-Balabatish Jews will attend some secular sporting events such as professional baseball games. They also dress a little differently; women wear dresses or skirts that cover the knees, but don't extend to mid-calf. Men wear regular clothing, often of a preppy, business-casual style, other than on *Shabbos* or Jewish holidays. In addition, many Yeshivish-Balabatish Jews do not always wear beards or wispy, uncut sideburns like Yeshivish Jews in general.

Modern Orthodox Jews

Modern Orthodox Judaism is a truly American evolution in the Orthodox Jewish world, although there were some early stirrings of a similar concept in late 19th century Germany. Modern Orthodoxy also exists today in former British Commonwealth countries and in Israel. At the turn of the 20th century, the desire to escape persecution and the opportunity to achieve the American dream for their children, if not for themselves, drove large numbers of Jews to come to America from Eastern Europe. They found themselves in a completely unfamiliar environment with regard to religious leadership. For the first time, rabbinical authorities had no real control over their congregants' lives. In fact, not many rabbis came to America in this wave of Jewish immigration. The newcomers also experienced individual liberties that Jews had rarely obtained in Europe. And they felt the pull of the modern world. Finally, very few Chassidim came to America before World War II, so what had been a major influence in Eastern Europe did not exist in America.

Modern Orthodoxy existed before there were any Modern Orthodox institutions or leaders. It was the product of the large influx of Eastern European Jews who wanted to continue observing Orthodox Jewish law but who also wanted to become Americans. Those who learned English would always speak it with an Eastern European accent, but their children blended into American life with relative ease. These children received excellent, free, public-school education, often through college, in the urban areas where most of them settled. This led them to careers in business, accounting, medicine, and law, where they often distinguished themselves in their chosen fields. Education in Jewish studies took place in the home and, for those who chose, at the *Talmud* Torah (an after-school program that delivered a very high quality of learning).

These new immigrant families were also quick to adopt American styles of dress, which at the time were reasonably *tznius*. To fit in generally, many new immigrants wore their *kippot* only at or close to home and in *shul*, and abandoned the beards and uncut sideburns of their ancestors. They also began to wear knitted or suede *kippot* instead of the traditional black velvet ones. Most of the adults spoke fluent Yiddish. Some children learned Yiddish, others did not. But English quickly became the spoken language of these communities. In fact, those who spoke Yiddish found English words creeping into the older language. A good example is The *Jewish Daily Forward* (later just the *Forward*), the popular Jewish Socialist newspaper of that era, written in Yiddish and containing a lot of English transliteration. The paper's headline announcing Franklin D. Roosevelt's victory over Herbert Hoover in 1932 read "Roosevelt is Elected," spelled in Hebrew letters. If you knew the Hebrew alphabet, you could read and understand this headline with no knowledge of Yiddish.[*]

Another factor that drove the assimilation of these families into the American way of life was mandatory military service during World War II. The military experience contributed heavily to refining the speech and dress of the young Orthodox Jewish

---

[*] Yiddish is written using the Hebrew alphabet, but there are some pronunciation differences between the two languages.

men who served. It also enabled them to mix with Americans of diverse backgrounds, providing exposures that might not otherwise have occurred.

The allure of American sports, particularly in New York, which then had three baseball teams, had a meaningful impact on this generation of American Jewish immigrants. For example, residents of Brooklyn, the Bronx, and Manhattan were fierce fans of their respective teams. In the early 1920s, radios became readily available and affordable, making it easy for families to listen to baseball games and follow sports news about their teams. It also exposed the listeners to commercials pushing a multitude of products. Women often sang these commercials' jingles; men in the Chassidic and Yeshivish communities were, and still are, prohibited from hearing these, but they quickly became acceptable in this emerging American Orthodox culture.

Most significantly, as noted, there were no rabbinic authorities to control these changes in Jewish life. Most rabbis were pulpit rabbis who ran daily and Shabbos services and gave sermons to their congregants on Shabbos. They also answered questions on Jewish law, but only when asked, which few congregants did when it came to issues related to cultural assimilation. This led Modern Orthodox Jews to abandon some traditional practices such as women covering their hair and bathing in the *mikveh*, as well as men regularly wearing *tzitzit* (fringes on a special four-cornered garment worn under the shirt in observance of the Torah mitzvah to wear *tzitzit* "on the corners of your garments").[19] In *shul*, Modern Orthodox men continued to wear *tallitot* (Jewish prayer shawls) with *tzitzit* on the corners.

Initially, the *shuls* that these new immigrants and their children attended, and the rabbis that led them, were mostly Yeshivish institutions that continued Eastern European traditions. But the following series of events led to the

formal establishment of Modern Orthodoxy as a sub-stream of Orthodoxy:
- The establishment of the Rabbinical Council of America in 1935. The RCA was the governing body for the American Orthodox world and has become the governing body of the Modern Orthodox movement.
- The establishment of the *Eitz Chaim* Yeshiva on the Lower East Side of Manhattan in 1886, leading to the founding of Yeshiva University. The school began as an elementary school focused on Jewish studies in the model of Eastern European yeshivas. Unlike these yeshivas, however, the school initially included a secular curriculum, although a limited one. Over time, this grew to a full curriculum of secular studies taught in parallel with the Jewish curriculum. By 1928, the school had grown to include boys' and girls' high schools and a full-fledged university, Yeshiva University, with a men's college in Washington Heights and a women's college on Lower Park Avenue, both in Manhattan. Yeshiva University is known today for delivering excellent Jewish and secular education as well as for ordaining most of the Modern Orthodox rabbis in America. Over time, the University added numerous graduate schools, which developed outstanding reputations. This was a dramatic departure from the Eastern European Yeshivish world. The schools became the model for most Orthodox Hebrew Day Schools in America today, even in the Yeshivish world (although, the current trend in today's Yeshivish communities is to decrease the focus on secular education, particularly beginning in high school).
- The influence of Rabbi Norman Lamm. Rabbi Lamm was graduated from Yeshiva University in 1949. He was a pulpit rabbi in Manhattan, then at the Jewish Center,

a major Manhattan Upper West Side Modern Orthodox Congregation, from 1959 to 1976. In that year, he became the President of Yeshiva University, where he served until his retirement in 2003. During his tenure at both institutions, he was a strong advocate of the philosophy of *Torah U'Mada* (Torah and modern culture), the blending of Orthodox Torah observance with a life that embraces contemporary culture. This, coupled with a strong commitment to Zionism, became the foundation of Modern Orthodoxy.

- The influence of Rabbi Joseph Soloveitchik. Rabbi Soloveitchik grew up in Russia and was educated in Russian, Polish, and German institutions, ultimately receiving a Ph.D. in Philosophy in 1932 from the Friedrich Wilhelm University in Berlin. He emigrated to Boston in 1932 where, in 1937, he was involved in founding the Maimonides School, a prominent Modern Orthodox yeshiva to this day. In 1940, the school added a high school which, for the first time, taught Talmud to boys and girls together. In 1941, Rabbi Soloveitchik moved to New York and became the head of the RIETS Rabbinical school at Yeshiva University, where he taught until 1986. He was considered the top *Rosh Yeshiva*[*] at Yeshiva University until his death in 1993. During his tenure, he ordained more than 2,000 rabbis who spread the Modern Orthodox approach to Judaism across America.
- The establishment of the modern State of Israel in 1948. Most of the Eastern European Jews who emigrated to America were Zionists from the time they arrived. In the aftermath of the Holocaust, they became

---

[*] This means literally Head of the Yeshiva and descriptively refers to the main leader of the rabbinical faculty of Yeshiva University.

fervent Zionists. The idea of a Jewish homeland from which Jews could not be expelled or subject to antisemitism depending on the political whims of the time, became an obvious imperative after the Nazis brutally murdered six million Jews, and the post-war plight of countless displaced Jewish refugees who had lost their property and most of their families. While accepting the Rambam's 12th Principle of Faith that the Messianic Age would have to await the arrival of the *Moshiach*, Modern Orthodox Jews felt that they could no longer tolerate hostile governments' religious persecution. The answer was a Jewish homeland with a democratically elected government. Once this became a reality, Modern Orthodox Jews became big supporters of the fledgling state.

- The migration of American Jews from urban areas to the suburbs. As long as immigrant Jews lived in urban areas, there were few truly Modern Orthodox shuls. But in the 1950s, Jews joined the mass American post-war exodus to the suburbs. There, Orthodox Jews established Modern Orthodox shuls and Jewish day schools, led mostly by graduates of Yeshiva University. Thus, a new generation of leaders and institutions embracing the Yeshivah University philosophy and model filled the void that the absence of Jewish leaders in America had created. The suburban Jews left behind the vestiges of the old world, including the Yiddish language.

The vast majority of Modern Orthodox children attend Jewish Day Schools, many of which are co-ed. Following high school, it is common for them to spend a year or two in Israel, in a boys' yeshiva or a girls' seminary. In contrast to the Yeshivish yeshivas and seminaries, these institutions are geared to the Modern Orthodox community. Nevertheless, they, often successfully, encourage their students to adopt more traditional Jewish practices such as dating only for marriage, and women covering their hair after marriage. Instead of, or following time studying in Israel, Modern Orthodox students almost always attend college. Some go to Yeshiva University. Many go to secular public and private colleges that provide kosher dining facilities and daily Jewish Orthodox prayer opportunities at Hillel Houses or Chabad on campus. Despite these familiar forms of support, many of these secular institutions provide environments that tempt students to explore different ideas and practices (including dating more liberal Jews and inter-faith dating), many of which are not consistent with Orthodox Jewish customs. This has led some previously Modern Orthodox students to move away from this sub-stream of Judaism.

Increasingly, however, Modern Orthodox students who do not attend Yeshiva University choose colleges that have a large Modern Orthodox contingent within their student bodies.* Once on campus, these Modern Orthodox students tend to associate closely with each other and attend kosher dining halls and Orthodox prayer services. They also are likely to date each other rather than to mingle socially with the non-Jewish population on campus.

In the decades since Modern Orthodoxy was formally institutionalized, new generations of young Modern Orthodox Jews have adopted more of the laws and traditions associated with Yeshivish Judaism. This trend picked up steam in the 1980s. Modern Orthodox communities have built *mikvehs* that almost all married Modern Orthodox women under the age of menopause use. Similarly, many married Modern Orthodox

---

* Examples are Brandeis University, Columbia University, New York University, the University of Maryland, the University of Pennsylvania, and UCLA.

women have begun to cover their hair, although this has yet to become the prevalent practice. Increasingly, Modern Orthodox men are wearing *tzitzit*. The driving force for these changes has been the increased tendency of the Modern Orthodox rabbinate and Yeshiva University to espouse and teach these more traditional practices. Many of the rabbis at Yeshiva University have adopted the black-and-white dress of the Yeshivish world and have emphasized stricter Jewish observance to their students. As more recent graduates of Yeshiva University have taken teaching positions as rabbis at Jewish Day schools, they also have stressed more traditional Jewish practices in their teaching.

While Modern Orthodoxy has moved closer to Yeshivish Judaism in many respects, a more liberal form of Modern Orthodoxy, known as Open Orthodoxy, has evolved over the last few decades under the leadership of Rabbi Avi Weiss, the Rabbinic leader of the Hebrew Institute of Riverdale in New York City until 2015.[*] A critical goal of Open Orthodoxy was to create a more expansive role for women in synagogue worship. This included modifying the procession after the Torah reading to include passing the *Sefer* Torah to a woman, who carries it through the women's section before passing it back to a man to return it to the ark on Shabbat morning; allowing women to be spiritual leaders of Open Orthodox congregations; and allowing women to be called to the Torah and to read the Torah, in the women's section of the main sanctuary, on the festival of *Simchat Torah*.[†]

Open Orthodoxy is committed to a philosophy of inclusiveness. Rabbi Weiss led the establishment of two new Open

---

[*] Rabbi Weiss was also a leading player in the fight to free Soviet Jewry in the 1970s and 1980s.

[†] *Simchat* Torah is part of the *Shemini Atzeret* holiday following the last day of *Succot*. In Israel, Jews observe *Shemini Atzeret* and *Simchat* Torah on a single day. In the diaspora, *Shemini Atzeret* is a two-day festival, the second day of which is called *Simchat* Torah. This is the day on which the annual reading of the Torah is completed, and a new annual cycle commences.

Orthodox institutions. The first is Yeshivat Chovevei Torah Rabbinical School, whose website describes it as follows:

> Our Modern Orthodox rabbinical school cultivates a love of Torah, a philosophy of inclusiveness, and a passion for leadership. The future of Orthodoxy depends on expanding outward cooperatively to encompass the needs of the larger Jewish community. Yeshivat Chovevei Torah Rabbinical School is committed to training and placing Modern Orthodox rabbis who are knowledgeable, non-judgmental, empathetic, and eager to transform orthodoxy into a movement that meaningfully and respectfully interacts with all Jews, regardless of affiliation, commitment or background. YCT cultivates a love of Torah, a philosophy of inclusiveness, and a passion for leadership. [ed.: Paragraph breaks deleted.][20]

The second is Yeshivat Maharat, whose mission, according to its website, is "[t]o educate, ordain and invest in passionate and committed Orthodox women who model a dynamic Judaism to inspire and support individuals and communities."

> Maharat ordains women with *semikha* [ed.: rabbinical ordination, italics added.] so they may serve Jewish communities as fully credentialed spiritual and halakhic leaders. Ordination is granted after a rigorous course of study and demonstrated command of Jewish law, Talmud, Torah, Jewish thought, leadership and pastoral counseling. Graduates of Maharat are conferred with "toreh toreh" – a decisor of Jewish law, giving

psak halakha [ed.: Rabbinical guidance of Jewish religious practices, italics added]. We encourage our graduates to use the professional title most appropriate to them, in consultation with the communities they serve.

Our graduates are impacting thousands of Jews through teaching, delivering sermons, answering sensitive halakhic and ethical questions, officiating at lifecycle events, and providing pastoral counseling. Over 50 communities have benefitted from our students and graduates, including shuls, schools, Hillels and communal organizations.

Our students and graduates can be found giving divrei Torah and teaching, officiating at weddings and funerals, counseling couples in times of need, visiting patients and families in hospitals, standing next to women as they say kaddish or supporting a new mother during her son's bris.[21]

Open Orthodoxy has not found wide acceptance among mainstream Orthodox leadership, including *Agudat Yisrael*, the Conference of European Rabbis and the Rabbinical Council of America, particularly when it comes to ordaining women clergy. In reaction to this criticism, the name Open Orthodoxy has been removed from the website of Yeshivat Maharat, although as of this writing, it remains on the website of the Hebrew Institute of Riverdale.[22] A movement similar to Open Orthodoxy is emerging in Israel. It seeks to maximize the participation of women in synagogue roles and practices in a manner consistent with halacha.[23]

Chapter Two

CONSERVATIVE JUDAISM AND ITS DUALITY

CONSERVATIVE JUDAISM BEGAN in response to the second Reform rabbinic conference, held in Frankfurt, Germany, in 1845 (See Chapter Three). One of its participants was Rabbi Zachariah Frankel, a traditionalist, who was then the Chief Rabbi of Dresden. Frankel had not participated in the first conference in 1844, but when he heard that the conference had proposed an almost complete break from Jewish tradition, he attacked it as excessively radical. His Reform colleagues ignored his complaints because by his absence he had presumptively forgone his right to influence the conference's conclusions. Perhaps for this reason, Frankel did attend the 1845 conference, but he walked out when 15 of the 31 conference members approved a resolution not to keep the Hebrew language as the main language of prayer in Reform Judaism; 13 voted against it and three members abstained. The conference chair, Rabbi Abraham Geiger, was passionate about establishing Reform Judaism in the context of religious practice but conclusively rejected the principle of the Jewish people as a nation tied to the Holy Land. In Geiger's view, retaining Hebrew as a major language for prayer would have preserved ties to the past that he could not accept.

Frankel left the conference on May 17, 1845, and returned to Dresden. While he rejected Reform's radical departure from tradition, he did not embrace the alternative of keeping all traditional Jewish religious practices and just adjusting some cultural practices, such as dress, to fit with the modern world – the position that Rabbi Samson Raphael Hirsch, whom many now recognize as the father of Modern Orthodoxy, endorsed. Specifically, Frankel did not want to accept the absolute principle of an unalterable Torah given at Mount Sinai. Instead, he preferred a position that recognized the Divine source of the Torah, while investing the Jewish community of each generation with the ability to interpret it anew, taking into account the world in which that generation lived, as well as the emerging historical evidence about how changes in civilizations and cultures over time had influenced its development.

In 1854, Frankel became the head of a new rabbinical school: The Jewish Theological Seminary of Breslau. In 1859, he published the document, *Darkhei HaMishnah* (The Ways of the Mishnah), in which he spelled out his justification for taking a middle ground between Orthodox and Reform.

> In this work, Frankel amassed considerable scholarly support for the contention that Jewish law had always developed in response to changing historical conditions. He never outlined the theological outlines of his position, but by acknowledging the possibility of change and development in Jewish religion and by locating the authority for that change within the community, Frankel was implying that whatever

God had to do with the Torah, its fate had now been rendered into the hands of a human community, which was subject to changing conditions of history. This community had always determined and would continue to determine the shape of Jewish belief and practice in every generation.

In contrast to the polar positions of Reform and Orthodoxy, Frankel was proposing a program of development that would be carefully disciplined, academically justified, and communally based. He attempted to authenticate his approach through an appeal to history and community. He was saying, in effect, that there was nothing radically new in his approach. Since the community had always sanctioned changes in Jewish beliefs and practices over time, it was in fact he, and not Hirsch, who had captured the dynamic of Judaism over the ages.

At the same time, however, Frankel was trying to delineate the parameters within which this process of development took place. Above all, he insisted, the integrity of both the Jewish past and the Jewish community as a whole had to be preserved. It was this broader concern that Frankel felt had been sacrificed by Reform.

Frankel's position was an extraordinary vote of confidence both in the internal dynamics of Jewish life and in the inherent goodwill of the Jewish religious community. He had faith that the caring core of the community, under the guidance of its Rabbinic and scholarly leadership, would intuitively continue to locate the fine balance between continuity and development, between what to retain and what to change. His leap of faith was that Jews would not let Judaism die.[1]

German immigrants to the United States first brought Reform Judaism there starting in the mid-1800s. The growth of the Reform movement in the United States quickly drew criticism from traditionalists, just as it had in Germany. In January 1886, ten weeks after the Reform movement held its Pittsburgh Conference, which established the flagship "Pittsburgh Platform,"[2] defining the guiding principles of American Reform Judaism, a group of traditionalists met in New York and agreed to establish a rabbinical seminary based on the Conservative Jewish principles that Frankel had espoused in Germany. Later that year, the Jewish Theological Seminary of New York (now the Jewish Theological Seminary of America, sometimes referred to as "the Seminary" or JTS) admitted its first class of rabbinical students.

There were two guiding figures in the early days of the American Conservative movement: Rabbi Alexander Kohut and Rabbi Sabato Morais. Kohut was the ideological father of the movement. Having trained at the Breslau Seminary, he had absorbed Frankel's approach to Judaism's future and his rejection of the radical Reform approach to change. In an article published in June 1885, Kohut was explicit:

> The sphere of Reform must be limited, and nothing must be admitted whose results and conclusions cannot be foreseen, for the law must always be firmly established and irrevocable so far

as concerns the Revealed Law and religion... The true idea of Liberty excludes the idea of License. Development does not mean destruction. Recasting is a very different process from casting aside... [The community,] that which has a hold upon the hearts of men and women, which still retains vitality, should be preserved as sacred; attempting to destroy it is equivalent to Temple sacrilege.[3]

Morais, in contrast, was the institutional father of Conservative Judaism, serving as the first president of the Jewish Theological Seminary of New York from 1886 until his death in 1897. Under his leadership, the Seminary became a scholarly institution for study based on the Conservative Jewish principle of enlightened traditionalism that Frankel and Kohut endorsed. They and the faculty had no immediate interest in expanding this principle into an explicit ideology, in large part because they did not want to risk fragmenting their new movement in the way that Reform had when it lost adherents after the publication of the Pittsburgh Platform. The implicit ideology favored finding a middle ground between Orthodoxy and Reform, and adapting to the modern world by loosening the strictures that flowed from an inflexible adherence to the traditional view of halachah based on the Torah and the Oral Law as given at Mount Sinai, while at the same time, keeping tradition and rooting changes to religious practices in a combination of scholarly historical interpretation and the evolving beliefs and lives of the Jewish People. It would take until 1988 for the movement to publish a platform clearly enunciating its ideological position.

The Conservative movement added its rabbinic organization, the "Alumni Association of the Seminary," later re-named the "Rabbinical Assembly," in 1901, and its congregational arm, the United Synagogue of America, in 1913. Thus, the movement's development from an academic center to a full-fledged set of religious institutions took 16 years. This pace of development reflects the centrality of the Seminary as the main force in institutional Conservative Judaism.*

After Morais's death, the position of Seminary President remained open until Rabbi Solomon Schechter, an ardent member of the Conservative movement and a European scholar, assumed it in 1901. It was under Schechter's leadership that the Seminary aggressively assembled the distinguished faculty that drove the growth of Conservative Judaism as a real movement.

Schechter extended Frankel's concept of how the evolution of Conservative religious practices would evolve by coining the term "Catholic Israel," which is best understood to mean the evolving consensus of that portion of *Klal Yisrael* that identified as Conservative. Despite this formulation, it is clear that Schechter was in no rush to make changes. Neither were his successors, Cyrus Adler and Rabbi Louis Finkelstein. Adler was the well-connected businessman and fundraiser who is credited with putting the Seminary on sound financial footing and overseeing its move to its present campus at 122nd Street and Broadway in Manhattan. Finkelstein was the academic who extended and maintained the institution's scholarly excellence, as it replaced the collapsing European institutions of Jewish learning. Together they led the Seminary after Schechter's death in 1915 until Finkelstein's death in 1972. They were willing to listen to calls for change, but neither of them moved to implement them.

There was, however, a distinguished member of the JTS

---

* On March 4, 2020, the Rabbinical Assembly was effectively merged into the United Synagogue of Conservative Judaism, the successor to the United Synagogue of America.

faculty who did not accept this gradual approach to change. His name was Rabbi Mordechai Kaplan. He developed and refined his principles over 54 years at the Seminary, beginning in 1909 and continuing until his departure in 1963 to help found the Reconstructionist movement. Unlike most Seminary faculty members, Kaplan was also a pulpit rabbi. He used this role to implement his ideas at his synagogue. Chapter 4 will explore Kaplan's time at JTS and his approach to Judaism.

A good example of the organic evolution of Jewish practice within the Conservative movement is the mixed seating of men and women in the sanctuary. For the most part, this change evolved without movement-wide consideration. Individual rabbis instituted the practice for their congregations, and by the mid-1950s, it was close to uniform in United States Conservative congregations. The Seminary, however, did not accept mixed seating in its own synagogue until 1984, when women first entered its rabbinical school.

In the late 1940s, the movement established the Committee on Jewish Law and Standards, often referred to as the "Law Committee." The first chair of the Law Committee, Rabbi Morris Adler, explained its role in the report of the Law Committee's 1949 *Proceedings*.

Here's a summary of his explanation:

> The Committee was to study halacha*h* and its precedents, the historical conditions out of which halacha*h* grew, the spiritual intent and purposes of the law, the needs and demands of modern life and thought, and the method by which Jewish living can best be aided and stimulated, and it was to plan activities that might make Judaism more inspiring and meaningful.[4]

Though the size and procedures of the Committee have varied over the years – at this writing [ed.: 1993] the Committee is made up of 25 voting representatives – certain principles have been consistently adhered to: Members of the Committee are appointed by each of the major wings of the Movement (the Rabbinical Assembly, the Seminary and the United Synagogue); they should be recognized scholars in rabbinic literature…; they should represent the various shades of religious opinion within the Movement; and – very important – the deliberations of the Committee may yield two or even more equally legitimate options, leaving the individual rabbi the right to choose among them. The rabbi remains, to use the traditional talmudic term, *Mara d'Atra*, literally, 'Master of the Place,' or ultimate authority in religious matters for the congregation.[5]

The establishment of the Law Committee was itself a major departure from traditional Jewish practice. According to Orthodox practice, until *Moshiach* arrives, and a new *Sanhedrin* (Jewish legal governing body) is established, halachic precedents may only be overturned in very limited, defined circumstances. For the most part, the Law Committee kept the traditional body of Jewish law intact, but over time made some major modifications that it deemed appropriate for the modern era, such as:

- Permitting driving to synagogue on *Shabbat*. To the Law Committee, this decision seemed appropriate for the suburban communities where the Conservative movement was rapidly growing. Insisting that congregants live within walking distance of the synagogue would severely limit growth and synagogue attendance. Of course, once congregants could drive on *Shabbat* for this limited purpose, it became easy to use the car to go to places other than to synagogue, such as sporting events, shopping, etc. This was not the Law Committee's intention, but it quickly became the norm in practice.

- Permitting use of electricity on *Shabbat*. This issue was closely related to driving, as cars rely on electricity to function. Allowing people to use electricity on *Shabbat* made life easier, but it also undermined the *Shabbat* lifestyle of unplugging from the world for 25 hours each week to focus on family, prayer, and spiritual matters. It also undercut the concept of community. Jews who can't travel by cars, trains, or buses on *Shabbat* live near their synagogues. This facilitates *Shabbat* meals and children's play dates. Allowing driving and other uses of electricity on *Shabbat* weakens this community bond. It also invites distractions from the *Shabbat* experience through the use of devices such as televisions, computers, and cell phones.

- Permitting women to participate as fully as men in all aspects of Jewish observance – e.g., serving as rabbis and cantors, being counted toward a *minyan*, being called to the Torah for *alyiot* (personal honors and blessings), wearing *tallitot* and *tefillin*, etc. For the most part, American Conservative congregations adopted these changes without much controversy.[*]

- Granting full and equal rights to members of the

---

[*] The approach to mixed-gender participation in Canadian Conservative synagogues is somewhat different.

LGBTQ+ community. Achieving this change took a long time; it did not become a reality until the second decade of the 21st century.

Notably, the Law Committee has not permitted Conservative rabbis to perform interfaith wedding ceremonies. Both parties must be Jewish for the rabbi to officiate.

By now, it should be obvious that there are two often conflicting approaches to Conservative Judaism: the practices within the walls of the Seminary, and the practices of Conservative congregations and individual Conservative Jews.* This happened because the Seminary was, from its beginning, a scholarly, academic institution, rather than an organization focused on supervising or assisting congregational Rabbis with the mission of implementing the Law Committee's decisions about Jewish practice. In fact, over the years, the Seminary's rabbinical program emphasized scholarship rather than teaching its students how to be effective congregational leaders and teachers. This ivory tower approach to education had its weaknesses, but at first, the overall success of the movement obscured them.

The Conservative movement grew rapidly during the postwar years. At the congregational level, its combination of traditional liturgy and services coupled with the *de facto*, and in some cases explicit, relaxation of halachic requirements, particularly those related to *Shabbat* and *kashrut*, turned out to be the perfect formula for attracting children of Eastern European Jews who moved to the suburbs and craved the modern melting-pot American lifestyle with the feeling, but not the practices, of traditional Judaism.

In the 1990s, meaningful erosion of participation in the

---

* Thus, to use Rabbi Solomon Schechter's term, "Catholic Israel" *de facto* determined Conservative religious practices, irrespective of whether the Law Committee acted.

movement started to become evident, when for the first time, many Conservative synagogues began to see a meaningful decline in their membership. The Pew Research Center's 2013[6] and 2020[7] Jewish demographic studies confirmed the magnitude of this trend, while highlighting the dichotomy between the practices at the Seminary and those of individuals identifying as Conservative Jews. Here are some pertinent highlights from the studies:

- According to the 2020 Pew Study:

    - The median age for adult Conservative Jews was age 62.
    - Only 33% of Conservative Jews surveyed said that religion is very important to them, and only 32% said that religious faith is highly meaningful/fulfilling to them.
    - Only 53% of Conservative Jews surveyed said that it was essential to Jewish identity to be part of a Jewish community.
    - Only 21% of Conservative Jews surveyed said that it was essential to Jewish identity to observe Jewish law.
    - 63% of Conservative Jews surveyed said that not believing in the God of the Torah is compatible with being Jewish.
    - 49% of Conservative Jews surveyed said they were members of a synagogue.
    - 44% of Conservative Jews surveyed said that most of their friends were Jewish.
    - Only 33% of Conservative Jews surveyed said they attended synagogue at least monthly.
    - Only 29% of Conservative Jews surveyed said they often mark *Shabbat* in a meaningful way.

- Only 24% of Conservative Jews surveyed said they keep kosher at home.
- Only 15% of Conservative Jews surveyed said being Jewish is about religion, while 17% said it's about culture, 13% said it's about ancestry, and 28% said it's about all three.

• According to the 2013 Pew Study:

- The fertility rate for Conservative Jews had dropped to 1.8 children per family compared to the generally accepted rate of 2.1 that is needed to keep a constant population.
- 94% of Conservative Jews surveyed said that working on *Shabbat* is compatible with being Jewish.
- Only 16% of Conservative Jews surveyed could understand most Hebrew words and only 14% of Conservative Jews could speak Hebrew.

Other factors also contributed to the decline in affiliation with the movement. As Chapter 3 shows, during the second half of the 20th century, the Reform movement, in successive platforms, added tradition to its liturgy, services, and suggested practices. This blurring of distinctions between the movements, coupled with the more modern, relaxed style of Reform congregations and the willingness of Reform rabbis to perform interfaith wedding ceremonies and warmly accept interfaith couples as congregants proved very attractive to the next generation of Americans, leading many to switch their affiliation to Reform.*

At the same time, Modern Orthodoxy developed a strong

---

* This generation of liberal Jewish Americans was an additional generation removed from the Jewish immigrants from Eastern Europe to whom tradition was important.

presence in suburban communities, which made its institutions more accessible to Conservative Jews. To some Conservative Jews, Modern Orthodox practices began to feel more authentic than the increasingly liberal practices of Conservative congregations, impelling them to switch their affiliation.

In addition, the number of unaffiliated Jews grew to 32% overall, 41% for those Jews ages 18 to 29, and 36% for those ages 30 to 49.[8] Many of these unaffiliated Jews are children of Conservative Jews.

One of the greatest successes of the Conservative movement has been Camp Ramah, which it founded in 1946. The movement put the camp's programming entirely in the hands of the Seminary's undergraduate program, which exercised total autonomy, acting independently of the Committee on Jewish Law and Standards and frequently in opposition to Seminary practice itself.

At Ramah, mixed seating at compulsory worship services was the practice from the very beginning. Women were soon permitted to lead *Birkat HaMazon* [ed.: Grace After Meals] at Ramah, to recite *Kiddush* [ed.: the ritual prayer over wine on Shabbat] and *Havdalah* [ed.: the prayer marking the end of *Shabbat* made over a multi-wick candle, wine, and spices] to lead the *Kabbalat Shabbat* service [ed.: preliminary Friday night *Shabbat* service]…, and to chant the book of Lamentations [ed.: *Eichah* in Hebrew, a book read each year as the central focus of the evening *Tisha B'Av* service] at Tisha B'Av services. In 1974, women at Ramah were given the right to receive *aliyot* and read from the Torah. These public roles were still in dispute in many Conservative congregations, and of course, none of them was accepted at the Seminary itself until 1984. Yet all of these policies were introduced at Ramah without fanfare.

Finally, there was simply no question that Ramah's formal education program – the classes in Hebrew, Bible, Talmud, theology, history, and literature – was addressed to men and women campers and staff alike, without the slightest hint of discrimination.[9]

The Camp Ramah experience provided a gender egalitarian Jewish environment – a precursor to what the movement would later adopt. It also did something else. It immersed Jewish campers, counselors, and other camp staff in a thoroughly Jewish lifestyle, including *Shabbat* observance, *kashrut*, prayer, and study every day, in addition to their recreational camp activities. This experience proved transformational for many participants. It dramatically increased their knowledge of Jewish practices and the Hebrew language, and fostered in them a love of Judaism that helped shape their future lives.

At the time of this writing there are ten Ramah sleepaway camps in the United States and Canada, five day camps in the United States and Israel, and a variety of Ramah Israel summer programs. There are also nine sleepaway camps and four day camps catering to campers with special needs.

The Conservative movement has also benefited from the establishment of Conservative Jewish day schools and high schools. Since their inception close to 50 years ago, these schools have provided Judaic Studies programs coupled with excellent secular education. Most graduates of the high schools attend college, and many of the colleges they attend have outstanding reputations. At this time, only a minority of Conservative Jews attend these Conservative schools, but those who do attend tend to take Conservative Jewish practices very seriously, including *Shabbat* observance and *kashrut*.

In 1988, the Conservative Movement finally published an official platform: *Emet Ve-Emunah, Statement of Principles of Conservative Judaism*.[10] Here's a summary:

God in the World

God –

Conservative Judaism affirms the critical importance of belief in God, but does not specify all the particulars of that belief. … For many of us, belief in God means that a supreme, supernatural being exists and has the power to command and control the world through His will. … This is the conception of God that emerges from a straightforward reading of the Bible. …

Some view the reality of God differently. For them, the existence of God is not a 'fact' that can be checked against the evidence. Rather, God's presence is the starting point for our entire view of the world and our place in it. … God is, in this view as well, a presence and a power that transcends us, but His nature is not completely independent of our beliefs and experiences. This is a conception of God that is closer to the God of many Jewish philosophers and mystics.[11]

Revelation –

Conservative Judaism affirms its belief in revelation, the uncovering of an external source emanating from God. …

The single greatest event in the history of God's revelation took place at Sinai but was not limited to it. … God's communication continued in the teaching of the Prophets and the biblical sages, and in the activity of the Rabbis of the Mishnah and the Talmud. ... The process of revelation did not end there; it remains alive in the Codes and Responsa to the present day.

Some of us conceive of revelation as the personal encounter between God and human beings.

Among them are those who believe that this personal encounter has propositional content, that God communicated with us in actual words. For them, revelation's content is immediately normative, as defined by rabbinical interpretation. The commandments of the Torah themselves issue directly from God. Others, however, believe that revelation consists of an ineffable human encounter with God. The experience of revelation inspires the verbal formulation of human beings of norms and ideas, thus continuing the historical influence of this revelational encounter.

Others among us conceive of revelation as the continuing discovery, through nature and history, of truths about God and the world. These truths, although always culturally conditioned, are nevertheless seen as God's ultimate purpose for creation. Proponents of this view tend to see revelation as an ongoing process rather than as a specific event.[12]

Halakhah — the Conservative movement views *halakhah* as an essential element of Judaism, one that is both vital and modern. It represents what they understand as God's will. It also plays an important role in developing personal discipline and sharpening the moral conscience.

> Halakhah thus establishes a structure of rules to govern human interactions…
>
> The sanctity and authority of Halakhah attaches to the body of the law, not to each law separately, for throughout Jewish history Halakhah has been subject to change…
>
> We in the Conservative community are committed to carrying on the rabbinic tradition of preserving and advancing Halakhah by making appropriate changes in it through rabbinic decision… These include additions to the received tradition to deal with new circumstances and, in some cases, modifications of the corpus of Halakhah…
>
> For religious guidance, the Conservative movement looks to the scholars of the Jewish Theological Seminary of America and other institutions of higher learning…
>
> Authority for religious practice in each congregation resides in its rabbi… In making decisions, Rabbis may consult the Committee on Jewish Law and Standards… The Committee on Jewish Law and Standards issues rulings shaping the practice of the Conservative community. Parameters set by that Committee and at Rabbinical Assembly conventions govern all of the rabbis of the Rabbinical Assembly, but within those bounds there are variations of practice

recognized as both legitimate and, in many cases, contributory to the richness of Jewish life.[13]

The Problem of Evil – Much of the evil in the world is the product of the poor exercise of the free will that Conservative theology recognizes. However, it does not follow that climatic events such as the Holocaust are the result of the actions of sinners among us or even by the Jewish people. In these tragic situations, whatever their source, we can rely on traditional Jewish mourning practices and rituals to comfort us.

> We maintain our faith in God whose will it is that good triumph over evil, even if that triumph is experienced only fitfully in historic time. Humanity can delay God's plan of a world freely united in love and righteousness with Him, but it cannot prevent its ultimate fulfillment. Even if the "Kingdom of God" remains a vision of a distant future, we can attain kinship with the divine by restraining our hurtful, self-aggrandizing impulses, and by dealing justly and compassionately with one another.[14]

Eschatology: Our Vision of the Future – This Messianic hope has three dimensions: the continued life of the individual as an eternal soul and by the ultimate resurrection of the dead; the ingathering of the Jewish people in Israel at some future time; and the emergence of a peaceful world order acknowledging God's all-encompassing presence. We will achieve these gradually, as the world develops a social order worthy of the redemption that our Scriptures describe. Revolutionary attempts to hasten the *Moshiach's* arrival are not the preferred approach.[15]

The Jewish People

God's Covenant: The Election of Israel – This encompasses the obligations of our covenant with *Hashem* and the burdens of being chosen to bring Torah principles to the world; burdens that some have misconstrued over time as conferring superiority or privilege – an unintended result.

> For the modern traditional Jew, the doctrine of the election and the covenant of Israel offers a purpose for Jewish existence which transcends its narrow self-interest. It suggests that because of our special history and unique heritage we are in a position to demonstrate that a people which takes seriously the idea of being covenanted with God can not only thrive despite oppression and suffering, but be a source of blessing to its children and its neighbors. It obligates us also to build a just and compassionate society throughout the world and especially in the land of Israel where we may teach by both personal and collective example what it means to be a "covenant people, a light of nations."[16]

The State of Israel and the Role of Religion – Israel is both a Jewish state and a democracy. It is proper for Jewish principles and practices to permeate all aspects of government activities. "Hence, we welcome the reality that Shabbat, *Yom Tov* [ed.: Jewish holidays], *kashrut*, and other *mitzvot* are officially upheld by the civilian and military organs of the State, and that the Jewish calendar is in general use." However, governmental coercion imposing religious beliefs and practices is not consistent with the concept of a democracy whose majority staunchly protects the rights of minorities. "In view of the wide disparity of outlook among Jews, we believe that matters of personal status should fall under secular law, which should provide civil options for marriage and divorce for those who so prefer, while empowering each religious community to handle its own ritual requirements."[17]

Israel and the Diaspora – The modern State of Israel is truly a miracle. Its continued secure existence is essential to our future. It has become a center of Jewish practice and Torah learning as well as an inspiration to Jews everywhere. Israel and the Diaspora complement and enrich each other, and both are important to our past and our future. We applaud those who make *aliya*, but we don't force Jews to emigrate to Israel. We believe that Judaism is a portable religion that can thrive both in Israel and in the Diaspora.[18]

Between Jew and Fellow Jew – The Conservative philosophy on *achdut*, the subject of this book, is summarized succinctly as follows:

> In the face of the widening rifts that have developed primarily among the religious groups, a fundamental concern must be the furtherance of Jewish unity. Only when Jews live in harmony and peace with each other, and our people embrace fraternal love and respect will we be worthy of messianic redemption.[19]

Relations with Other Faiths – Our strong preference is to have congenial, respectful relationships with those of other faiths. Historically, where this has happened, we have borrowed from each other in ways that have enhanced all of our communities. Where this is not the case, such as where we are threatened by antisemitism, or worse, murdered or severely persecuted, we have responded in kind with harsh words or actions.

> Theological humility requires us to recognize that although we have but one God, God has more than one nation. Our tradition explicitly recognizes that God entered into a covenant with Adam and Eve, and later with Noah and his family as well as his special covenant with Abraham and the great revelation to Israel at Sinai. It is part of our mission to understand, respect, and live with the other nations of the world, to discern those truths in their cultures from which we can learn, and to share with them the truths that we have come to know.[20]

Social Justice: Building a Better World – Jews have an obligation to concern themselves with both the Jewish community and the outside world. We are committed to fighting racial, ethnic, and similar forms of discrimination, as well as poverty and oppression. We need to be concerned for the welfare of widows, orphans, and similarly disadvantaged people.

> In addressing these issues, there are legitimate differences of opinion and approach. Some are willing to compromise in the interests of peace. Others are uncompromising in their demand for justice. Each approach requires both accommodation and cooperation in order to achieve its goals.

> Above all, we must not succumb to apathy, cynicism or defeatism. By our active commitment to the ideals of justice found in biblical and

rabbinic law and lore, we shall fulfill our obligation to be *shutafo shel ha-Kadosh Barukh Hu be-masse bereshhit*, partners with God in the creation of a more perfect world.[21]

Living a Life of Torah

On Women – Women deserve full rights and participation within the Jewish community and this outcome can be achieved fully within Halakha, including addressing the *agunot* situation, for which the Conservative movement has developed an effective approach from its perspective, except in Israel.[22]

The Jewish Home – The Jewish home is a place of sanctity which should reflect "Jewish values such as love, fidelity, purity, *shalom bayit* (domestic tranquility), *kibbud av ve-em* (honor for father and mother), and *kevod ha-briyot*" (giving honor to all of *Hashem's* living creations). It "should be recognizable through Jewish ritual objects, books and art. A *mezuzah* on the door is not only *a* halakhic imperative but a sign of Jewish identity." These objects "should reflect the Jewish ideal of *hiddur mitzvah*, the esthetic that heightens our sense of the holy."[23]

> *Tefillah (Prayer)* –
> As the Hebrew root of *tefillah* suggests, its emphasis is not on petition, but rather on self-examination as a prelude to self-improvement.
>
> One who sees the world as pervaded by God responds to that with *tefillah* on many occasions throughout each day. The synagogue and special seasons or events can be catalysts for prayer, but

only in the soul of one who is ready to seek God…

While there are minimum, fixed times for prayer each day, a Jew is encouraged to pray at any time he or she is moved to pray, either within or outside the usual rubric of prayer. When one is unable to perform the prescribed ritual, as part of a community (*minyan*), one should recite the prayers in private…

Above all, the goal of prayer is to involve us with a sense of holiness of God, which fills the universe…

The *Siddur* [ed.: Jewish prayer book] itself is a book of theology for the Jewish people as a whole, and Jewish prayer, then, is nothing less than a continual renewal of one's attachment to the heart and mind of Judaism.

[T]he Conservative movement urges contemporary Jews to master the art of traditional Jewish prayer, including its Hebrew words and its music.[24]

Talmud Torah *(Jewish Study)* – "*Talmud* Torah [ed: the study of Torah, including all classical Jewish texts] is an essential value of Judaism… Judaism regards study as a cardinal commandment, the highest form of the worship of God." It is a lifelong commitment of every Jew to engage in both formal and informal Jewish education. In addition to studying the classical texts, "a learned Jew must be familiar with Jewish literature, history, philosophy, and the arts. Study of these subjects enhances our understanding of Jewish history and religion."25

The Ideal Conservative Jew

This section of *Emet Ve-Emunah* is so critical to the goal of this book that I quote it in its entirety:

> Throughout most of its history, Jewish life was an organic unity of home and community, synagogue and law. Since the Emancipation, however, Judaism has been marked by increasing fragmentation. Not only do we find Jewish groups pitted against one another, but the ways in which we apprehend Judaism itself have become separate and distinct. That unified platform upon which a holistic Jewish life was lived has been shattered. Participating in a majority culture whose patterns and rhythms often undermine our own, we are forced to live in two worlds, replacing whole and organic Judaism with fragments: ritual observance or Zionism, philanthropy or group defense; each necessary, none sufficient in itself.
>
> Facing this reality, Conservative Judaism came into being to create a new synthesis in Jewish life. Rather than advocate assimilation or yearn for the isolation of a new ghetto, Conservative Judaism is a creative force through which modernity and tradition inform and reshape each other.
>
> During the last century and a half, we have built a host of institutions to formulate and express and embody our quest. As important as these

are, they in themselves cannot create the new Jewish wholeness that we seek. In spite of the condition of modern life, we must labor zealously to cultivate wholeness in Jewish personalities.

Three characteristics mark the ideal Conservative Jew. First, he or she is a *willing* Jew, whose life echoes the dictum, "Nothing human or Jewish is alien to me." This willingness is not only a commitment to observe the *mitzvot* and to advance Jewish concerns, but to refract all aspects of life through the prism of one's own Jewishness. That person's life pulsates with the rhythms of daily worship and Shabbat and *Yom Tov*. The moral imperatives of our tradition impel that individual to universal concern and deeds of social justice. The content of that person's professional dealings and communal involvements is shaped by the values of our faith and conditioned by the observance of *kashrut*, of Shabbat and the holidays. That person's home is filled with Jewish books, art, music and ritual objects. Particularly in view of the increasing instability of the modern family, the Jewish home must be sustained and guided by the ethical insights of our heritage.

The second mark of the ideal Conservative Jew is that he or she is a *learning* Jew. One who cannot read Hebrew is denied the full exaltation of our Jewish worship and literary heritage. One who is ignorant of our classics cannot be affected by our message. One who is not acquainted with contemporary Jewish thought and events will be blind to the challenges and opportunities which lie before us. Jewish learning is a lifelong quest through which we integrate Jewish and general knowledge for the sake of personal enrichment, group creativity and world transformation.

Finally, the ideal Conservative Jew is a *striving* Jew. No matter the level at which one starts, no matter the heights of piety and knowledge one attains, no one can perform all 613 *mitzvot* or acquire all Jewish knowledge. What is needed is an openness to those observances one has yet to perform and the desire to grapple with those issues and texts one has yet to confront. Complacency is the mother of stagnation and the anthesis of Conservative Judaism.

Given our changing world, finality and certainty are illusory at best, destructive at worst. Rather than claiming to have found a goal at the end of the road, the ideal Conservative Jew is a traveler walking purposefully towards "God's holy mountain."[26]

During the period when the Conservative movement was developing *Emet Ve-Emunah* as its statement of principles, Dr. Ismar Schorsch assumed the position of Chancellor of JTS. In 1995, seven years after *Emet Ve-Emunah* was published, Dr. Schorsch published "The Sacred Cluster" in *Conservative Judaism*, the quarterly journal of JTS and the Rabbinical Assembly. "The Sacred Cluster" explains Conservative Judaism as a cluster of core values, rather than as a set of theological propositions. According to Dr. Schorsch, these core values are the glue that attracts and holds Conservative Jews to the movement. These values are not absolute and, like *Emet Ve-Emunah*, provide space for varied practices among different Conservative congregations and individuals. I have included the entirety of "The Sacred Cluster" below because of its importance.

The Sacred Cluster:
The Core Values of Conservative Judaism

If dogmas or doctrines are the propositional language of a theological system, core values are the felt commitments of lived religion, the refraction of what people practice and profess. To identify them calls for keen observation as well as theoretical analysis. Conservative Judaism is best understood as a sacred cluster of core values. No single propositional statement comes close to identifying its center of gravity. Nor does Conservative Judaism occupy the center of the contemporary religious spectrum because it is an arbitrary and facile composite of what may be found on the left or the right. On the contrary, its location flows from an organic and coherent world view best captured in terms of core values of relatively equal worth.

There are seven such core values, to my mind, that imprint Conservative Judaism with a principled receptivity to modernity balanced by a deep reverence for tradition. Whereas other movements in modern Judaism rest on a single tenet, such as the autonomy of the individual or the inclusiveness of God's revelation at Sinai (Torah *mi-Sinai*), Conservative Judaism manifests a kaleidoscopic cluster of discrete and unprioritized core values. Conceptually they fall into two sets—three national and three religious—which are grounded and joined to each other by the overarching presence of God, who represents the seventh and ultimate core value. The dual nature of Judaism as polity and piety, a world religion that never transcended its national origins, is unified by God. In sum, a total of seven core values corresponding to the most basic number in Judaism's construction of reality.

The Centrality of Modern Israel

The centrality of modern Israel heads our list of core values. For Conservative Jews, as for their ancestors, Israel is not only the birthplace of the Jewish people, but also its final destiny. Sacred texts, historical experience, and liturgical memory have conspired to make it for them, in the words of Ezekiel, "the most desirable of all lands (20:6)." Its welfare is never out of mind. Conservative Jews are the backbone of Federation leadership in North America and the major source of its annual campaign. They visit Israel, send their children over a summer or for a year, and support financially every one of its worthy institutions. Israeli accomplishments on the battlefield and in the laboratory, in literature and politics, fill them with pride. Their life is a dialectic between homeland and exile. No matter how prosperous or assimilated, they betray an existential angst about anti-Semitism that denies them a complete sense of at-homeness anywhere in the diaspora.

And their behavior reflects the dominant thrust of Conservative Judaism not to denationalize Judaism. Even in the era of emancipation, Zion remained the goal, as it was for the Torah, an arena in which to translate monotheism into social justice. A world governed by realpolitik needed a polity of a different order. The liturgy of the Conservative synagogue preserved the full text of the daily amida (the silent devotion) with its frequent pleas for the restoration of Zion. Heinrich Graetz, who taught at the Movement's rabbinical seminary in Breslau and authored the most nationalistic history of the Jews ever written, inspired Moses Hess to pen one of the earliest Zionist tracts in 1862 and would not write of the biblical period until he had personally visited Palestine in early 1872. During the last two decades, well over one hundred Conservative rabbis have made aliyah, often at the cost of professional satisfaction, attesting not only to movement ideology, but personal courage.

This is not to say that Conservative Judaism divests the diaspora of all spiritual value or demands of all Jews to settle in Israel. Ironically, the state of Judaism is far healthier outside the Jewish state, where Judaism is indispensable for a resilient Jewish identity. Most Israelis have sadly been severed from any meaningful contact with Judaism by the absence of religious alternatives and by the erosion of sacred Jewish content in the secular school system where 75% of Israel's Jewish children are educated. And yet, the miracle and mystery of Israel's restoration after two millennia out of the ashes of the Holocaust continues to overwhelm Conservative Jews with radical amazement and deep joy.

Hebrew: The Irreplaceable Language of Jewish Expression

Hebrew as the irreplaceable language of Jewish expression is the second core value of Conservative Judaism. Its existence is coterminous with that of the Jewish people and the many layers of the language mirror the cultures in which Jews perpetuated Judaism. It was never merely a vehicle of communication, but part of the fabric and texture of Judaism. Words vibrate with religious meaning, moral values, and literary associations. Torah and Hebrew are inseparable and Jewish education was always predicated on mastering Hebrew. Hebrew literacy is the key to Judaism, to joining the unending dialectic between sacred texts, between Jews of different ages, between God and Israel. To know Judaism only in translation is, to quote Bialik, akin to kissing the bride through the veil.

These are some of the sentiments which prompted Zacharias Frankel, the founder of Conservative Judaism in central Europe, to break with Reform over the issue of Hebrew at the Frankfurt

Rabbinical Conference in 1845. Despite the leniency of Jewish law, he was not prepared to endorse a resolution which would acknowledge that synagogue services could theoretically dispense with Hebrew. Given the rapid shrinkage of Judaism with the advent of emancipation, the fostering of Hebrew for Frankel became a symbol of historical continuity and national unity. Much of his scholarly oeuvre was intentionally written in Hebrew. And the language has remained at the heart of the Conservative agenda ever since.

Hebrew became the language of instruction of JTS's Teachers Institute not too long after its opening in 1909, as well as the language of daily conversation in the Ramah summer camps which it launched in the late 1940s. The Conservative synagogue never expunged Hebrew from the liturgy, and its supplementary Hebrew school, despite the constraints of a very pared-down curriculum, never gave up the struggle to teach a modicum of Hebrew literacy to the young. If anything, the Solomon Schechter day schools of the movement, an achievement of the past two decades, excel in the teaching of Hebrew language.

The revival of Hebrew in the last century-and-a-half, that is *Hebrew Reborn* as Sholom Spiegel put it in the title of his celebratory book of 1930, is as singular a feat as the creation of the Jewish state. Hebrew has been wholly transformed from an unwieldy classical medium of liturgy and learning into a modern Western language fit for the sciences and sensibilities of secular society. Diaspora Jews can little afford to remain deaf to the sounds of Hebrew as they can ignore the fate of the Jewish state.

In a Jewish world of sundry and proliferating divisions, Hebrew must emerge as the common and unifying language of the Jewish people, and nothing would advance that vision more effectively than to redefine Zionism today solely in terms of the ability to speak Hebrew. To restructure the World Zionist Organization by earmarking all of its budget to the intensive teaching of Hebrew to diaspora Jews would create many more Zionists (that is, Jews who appreciate the centrality of Israel) than all the atavistic politics of the current Zionist establishment. The natural bonds of language and culture bind more firmly than those of abstruse ideological constructs.

I offer as example the young Mordecai Kaplan, then dean of the Teachers Institute, struggling to perfect his command of Hebrew to the point where he could preside over its faculty meetings and public events in Hebrew. In the 1920s he made the following poignant entry in his diary:

> *Here is another failure I have to register against myself. Due to the lack of energy necessary to train myself to speak and write Hebrew with ease, I am afraid to venture on those occasions to give an address in Hebrew.*

Of such failures, the fabric of Jewish unity is sewn!

Devotion to the Ideal of Klal Yisrael

The third core value is an undiminished devotion to the ideal of klal yisrael, the unfractured totality of Jewish existence and the ultimate significance of every single Jew. In the consciousness of Conservative Jews, there yet resonates the affirmation of haverim kol yisrael (all Israel is still joined in fellowship)—despite all the dispersion, dichotomies and politicization that history has visited upon us, Jews remain united in a tenacious pilgrimage of universal import. It is that residue of Jewish solidarity that makes Conservative Jews the least sectarian or parochial members of the community, that renders them the ideal donor of Federation campaigns and brings them to support unstintingly every worthy cause in Jewish life. Often communal needs will prompt them to compromise the needs of the Movement.

Such admirable commitment to the welfare of the whole does not spring from any special measure of ethnicity, as is so often ascribed to Conservative Jews. Rather, I would argue that it is nurtured by the acute historical sense cultivated by their leadership. In opposition to exclusively rational, moral or halakhic criteria for change, Conservative Judaism embraced a historical romanticism that rooted tradition in the normative power of a heroic past. To be sure, history infused an awareness of the richness and diversity of the Jewish experience. But it also presumed to identify a normative Judaism and invest it with the sanctity of antiquity. It is that mixture of critical breadth and romantic reverence that imbued men like Frankel, Graetz, Schechter, Kaplan, and Louis Finkelstein with the love of klal yisrael. And, fortunately, they all commanded the literary gifts to disseminate and popularize their views.

The Defining Role of Torah in the Reshaping of Judaism

The fourth core value is the defining role of Torah in the reshaping of Judaism after the loss of political sovereignty in 63 B.C.E. and the Second Temple in 70 C.E. to the Romans. In their stead, the rabbis fashioned the Torah into a portable homeland, the synagogue into a national theater for religious drama, and study into a form of worship. Conservative Judaism never repudiated any of these remarkable transformations. Chanting the Torah each Shabbat is still the centerpiece of the Conservative service, even if all too often it is lamentably done according to the triennial cycle and then without liturgical aplomb. Though historically defensible, the cycle makes a sham of Simhat Torah, even as it suggests the decline of Torah in our lives.

More substantively, the cycle misses a precious chance to reinvigorate Shabbat. As the rhythm of the Jewish week is to be set by Shabbat, so should the content of individual home study be informed by the weekly Torah portion. Conservative Jews increasingly evince a hunger for access to holy texts. To restore the reading of the entire parasha each Shabbat, to train a cadre of congregants, both young and old, to become proficient Torah readers, and to help congregants in studying the parasha prior to Shabbat would create a *kahal kadosh*, a holy community, joined by a sacred calendar and text. Jews would then come to the synagogue on Shabbat morning prepared and primed to listen to the Torah reading, to recapture a touch of the numinous of the Sinai experience which, at best, it is designed to reenact.

For Conservative Jews, the Torah is no less sacred, if less central, than it was for their pre-modern ancestors. I use the word "sacred" advisedly. The Torah is the foundation text of Judaism, the apex of an inverted pyramid of infinite commentary, not because it is divine, but because it is sacred, that is, adopted by the Jewish people as its spiritual font. The term skirts the divisive and futile question of origins, the fetid swamp of heresy. The sense of individual obligation, of being commanded, does not derive from divine authorship, but communal consent. The Written Torah, no less than the Oral Torah, reverberates with the divine-human encounter, with 'a minimum of revelation and a maximum of interpretation.' It is no longer possible to separate the tinder from the spark. What history can attest is that the community of Israel has always huddled in the warmth of the flame.

The Study of Torah

Accordingly, the study of Torah, in both the narrow and extended sense, is the fifth core value of Conservative Judaism. As a canon without closure, the Hebrew Bible became the unfailing stimulus for midrash, the medium of an I-Thou relationship with the text and with God. Each generation and every community appropriated the Torah afresh through their own interpretive activity, creating a vast exegetical dialogue in which differences of opinion were valid and preserved. The undogmatic preeminence of Torah spawned a textually-based culture that prized individual creativity and legitimate conflict.

What Conservative Judaism brings to this ancient and unfinished dialectic are the tools and perspectives of modern scholarship blended with traditional learning and empathy. The full meaning of sacred texts will always elude those who restrict the range of acceptable questions, fear to read contextually, and who engage in willful ignorance. It is precisely the sacredness of these texts that requires of serious students to employ every piece of scholarly equipment to unpack their contents. Their power is crippled by inflicting upon them readings that no longer carry any intellectual cogency. Modern Jews deserve the right to study Torah in consonance with their mental world and not solely through the eyes of their ancestors. Judaism does not seek to limit our thinking, only our actions.

This is not to say that earlier generations got it all wrong. Nothing could be further from the truth. To witness their deep engagement with Torah and Talmud is to tap into inexhaustible wellsprings of mental acuity and spiritual power. It is to discover the multiple and ingenious ways—critical, midrashic, kabbalistic, and philosophical—in which they explicated these texts. Like them, Conservative scholars take their place in an unbroken chain of exegetes, but with their own arsenal of questions, resources, and methodologies. No matter how differently done, the study of Torah remains at the heart of the Conservative spiritual enterprise.

Moreover, it is pursued with the conviction that critical scholarship will yield new religious meaning for the inner life of contemporary Jews. It is not the tools of the trade that make philology or history or anthropology or feminist studies threatening, but the spirit in which they are applied. Rigorous yet engaged and empathetic research often rises above the pedestrian to bristle with relevance. Witness the tribute paid by Moshe Greenberg, professor of biblical studies at the Hebrew University and a graduate of the Seminary, to Yehezkel Kaufmann, who a generation earlier pioneered a Jewish approach to the critical study of the Hebrew Bible.

Yehezkel Kaufmann embodied a passionate commitment to grand ideas, combining the philosopher's power of analysis and generalization with the attention to detail of the philological exegete. His lifework is a demonstration that the study of ancient texts does not necessitate losing contact with the vital currents of the spirit and the intellect.

The Governance of Jewish Life By *Halakha*

The sixth core value is the governance of Jewish life by halakha, which expresses the fundamental thrust of Judaism to concretize ethics and theology into daily practice. The native language of Judaism has always been the medium of deeds. Conservative Jews are rabbinic and not biblical Jews. They avow the sanctity of the Oral Torah erected by Rabbinic Judaism alongside the Written Torah as complementary and vital to deepen, enrich, and transform it. Even if in their individual lives they may often fall short on observance, they generally do not ask of their rabbinic leadership to dismantle wholesale the entire halakhic system in order to translate personal behavior into public policy. Imbued with devotion to klal yisrael and a pervasive respect for tradition, they are more inclined to sacrifice personal autonomy for a reasonable degree of consensus and uniformity in communal life.

Collectively, the injunctions of Jewish law articulate Judaism's deep-seated sense of covenant, a partnership with the divine to finish the task of creation. Individually, the mitzvot accomplish different ends. Some serve to harness and focus human energy by forging a regimen made up of boundaries, standards, and rituals. To indulge in everything we are able to do, does not necessarily enhance human happiness or well-being. Some mitzvot provide the definitions and norms for the formation of community, while others still generate respites of holiness in which the feeling of God's nearness pervades and overwhelms.

The institution of Shabbat, perhaps the greatest legacy of the Jewish religious imagination, realizes all three. The weekly rest it imposes both humbles and elevates. By desisting from all productive work for an entire day, Jews acknowledge God's sovereignty over the world and the status of human beings as mere tenants and stewards. But the repose also conveys an echo of Eden, for Shabbat is the one fragment left over from the lost perfection of creation. Shabbat seeds the tortuous course of human history with moments of eternity, linking beginning to end while softening the massive suffering in between. Stopping the clock and diminishing the self allow others to reenter our lives. We are transposed to another dimension of reality.

Shabbat is an exquisite work of religious art created out of whole cloth by the meticulous performance of countless mitzvot. We join with family, friends, and community in a symphony of ritual—clothing, candles, table-setting, prayer, food, song, and study—to turn Shabbat into the Jewish equivalent of a country home. To gain renewal, we give up a measure of dominion. The hallowed tranquility that ensues helps us reach beyond ourselves. Like the halakha as a whole, Shabbat at its best invests the ordinary with eternity and life with ultimate meaning. Submission to God sets us free.

Never has this heroic effort to generate pockets of holiness in our personal lives been more important than today. Emancipation has thrust Jews irreversibly into the mainstream of contemporary civilization, with incalculable benefit to both. We are determined to live in two worlds and have won the right to be different, individually and collectively, without impairing our integration. The question is whether our Judaism will survive intact? Our sensibilities as Jews have been transformed and the discrepancies between the two worlds beg for accommodation.

The challenge, however, has not induced Conservative Judaism to assert blithely that the halakha is immutable. Its historical sense is simply too keen. The halakhic system, historically considered, evinces a constant pattern of responsiveness, change, and variety. Conservative Judaism did not read that record as carte blanche for a radical revision or even rejection of the system, but rather as warrant for valid adjustment where absolutely necessary. The result is a body of Conservative law sensitive to human need, halakhic integrity, and the worldwide character of the Jewish community. Due deliberation generally avoided the adoption of positions which turned out to be ill-advised and unacceptable.

Nevertheless, what is critical for the present crisis is the reaffirmation of halakha as a bulwark against syncretism, the overwhelming of Judaism by American society, not by coercion but seduction. Judaism is not a quilt of random patches onto which anything might be sewn. Its extraordinary individuality is marked by integrity and coherence. The supreme function of halakha (and Hebrew, for that matter) is to replace external barriers with internal ones, to create the private space in which Jews can cultivate their separate identities while participating in the open society that engulfs them.

Belief In God

I come, at last, to the seventh and most basic core value of Conservative Judaism: its belief in God. It is this value which plants the religious nationalism and national religion that are inseparable from Judaism in the universal soil of monotheism. Remove God, the object of Israel's millennial quest, and the rest will soon unravel. But this is precisely what Conservative Judaism refused to do, even after the Holocaust. Abraham Joshua Heschel, who came to the United States in March 1940, to emerge after the war as the most significant Jewish theologian of the modern period, placed God squarely at the center of his rich exposition of the totality of the Jewish religious experience.

To speak of God is akin to speaking about the undetected matter of the universe. Beyond the reach of our instruments, it constitutes at least 90 per cent of the mass in the universe. Its existence is inferred solely from its effects: the gravitational force, otherwise unaccounted for, that it exerts on specific galactic shapes and rotational patterns and that it contributes in general to holding the universe together.

Similarly, Heschel was wont to stress the partial and restricted nature of biblical revelation.

> *With amazing consistency the Bible records that the theophanies witnessed by Moses occurred in a cloud. Again and again we hear that the Lord 'called to Moses out of the midst of the cloud' (Exodus 24:16)... We must neither willfully ignore nor abuse by allegorization these important terms. Whatever specific fact it may denote, it unequivocally conveys to the mind the fundamental truth that God was concealed even when He revealed, that even while His voice became manifest, His essence remained hidden.*

For Judaism, then, God is a felt presence rather than a visible form, a voice rather than a vision. Revelation tends to be an auditory and not a visual experience. The grandeur of God is rarely compromised by the hunger to see or by the need to capture God in human language. And yet, God's nearness and compassion are sensually asserted. The austerity of the one and the intimacy of the other are the difference between what we know and what we feel. God is both remote and nearby, transcendent and immanent. To do justice to our head and heart, that is, to the whole person, Judaism has never vitiated the polarity that lies in the midst of its monotheistic faith.

I know of no finer example of this theological view than the berakhah which introduces the psalms (*pesukei de-zimra*) of the morning service. Its function is to praise God before we make our petitions. But, in essence, it is really a meditation on the nature of the deity we are about to address. Before we pray, we take a moment to orient ourselves. My quite literal translation of the text encompasses the first few lines, which are all I wish to comment on.

Praised be the one who spoke and the world sprang into being.
Praised be that one.
Praised be the maker of the beginning.
Praised be the one who spoke and acted.
Praised be the one who ordered and executed.
Praised be the one who has compassion for all the earth.
Praised be the one who has compassion for all of nature's creatures.
Praised be the one who rewards those who fear God.

Praised be the one who lives forever and endures till eternity.
Praised be the one who redeems and rescues.
Praised be God's name.

What I find striking and altogether typical of Judaism in this ancient paean is the crescendo of appellations for God through a preference for circuitous verb forms. Despite a fervent desire to encounter and behold God, there is a palpable reluctance to depict or render God concrete, to traduce the mystery. The author takes refuge in verbs rather than nouns.

The very first appellation alludes to the strategy: "Praised be the one who spoke and the world sprang into being"- an awkward name for God that quickly brings to mind the majestic and imageless description of creation in the opening chapter of Genesis. Not a word is wasted there on what God looks like, on what God's sex might be, on what God did before creation. The Torah simply implies that there is but a single God who is absolutely transcendent and chose at some point to call forth the cosmos. And that creation is effected with effortless elegance through ten verbal commands. No consultations, no warfare, no labor!

It is wholly in the spirit of that supreme expression of biblical monotheism that our rabbinic author works. The act of creation becomes the name by which God is known. Theology compels us to turn verbs into nouns. We know God not through appearance, but effect. Only the experience of divine action falls within our ken. Our author even forms an adverb "bereshit" (in the beginning) into a noun and God rises before us as 'the maker of the beginning.'

But an unchanging, soaring, bodiless deity is also beyond human suffering. To counter that conclusion, the prayer immediately moves from creation to love. The God of Israel remains engaged, a soul mate as much as a prime mover. God's compassion extends to our planet and all its creatures as well as to the chosen people, 'those who fear God.' God is not an ineffable 'It' but a caring 'Thou,' or, as Buber once said of his own faith in God: 'If believing in God means being able to speak of Him in the third person, then I probably do not believe in God; or at least, I do not know if it is permissible for me to say that I believe in God. For I know, when I speak of him in the third person, whenever it happens, and it has to happen again and again, there is no other way, then my tongue cleaves to the roof of my mouth so quickly that one cannot even call it speech.'

As this lilting paean makes so clear, for the rabbinic mind God was conceived in polarities, lofty yet loving, imageless yet intimate, hidden yet revealed. Conservative Judaism is very much part of that ancient Jewish quest for a comprehensive understanding of God.

More broadly still, Jewish tradition continues unbroken in Conservative Judaism, where yearning for God wells up primarily not from reason or revelation but from the blood-soaked, value-laden, and textually rooted historical experience of the Jewish people. It is surely in order to ask in closing whether this unique constellation of core values has ever coalesced into a vivifying ideal. I would submit that in its Ramah summer camps the Seminary created an extension of itself: a controlled environment for the formation of a model religious community. Over the past half-century Ramah has compiled an extraordinary record of touching and transforming young Jews to become the most effective educational setting ever generated by the movement. All the core values of Conservative Judaism are present in spades, defining and pervading the culture.

Let me single them out. The centrality of Israel finds expression in the large contingent of Israeli staff members brought over each summer, who often return to Israel themselves enamored of Conservative Judaism in the wake of experiencing Ramah. Their presence also reinforces the use of Hebrew as the camp's official language, while the value of klal yisrael promotes the priority of community and the inclusive spirit of camp programming.

On the religious side of the ledger, the Torah constitutes the lifeblood of camp life. The parasha is a basic text of study during the week and read in full every Shabbat, giving dozens of youngsters the chance to master the skill. A myriad of daily classes and Shabbat study groups symbolize the devotion to learning (in the Conservative manner), and halakha governs every aspect of life, from daily services to human relationships to relating to the environment. Each week culminates in the magnificent choreography of Shabbat that puts Judaism to music by imbuing everyone with a sense of belonging and intimacy, of uplift and holiness. And finally, the engaged figure of a Seminary scholar-in-residence teaches and personifies the core values that animate the whole noble experiment.

Ramah is not the conscious articulation of an ideological blueprint but rather the natural impulse of a vibrant, authentically Jewish religious culture, proof positive that Conservative Judaism bespeaks an organic, distinctive, and transformational reality. What Solomon Schechter once said of Rabbinic Judaism, when he ventured to crystallize its theological underpinnings, holds true no less for its modern counterpart:

> *A great English writer has remarked that 'the true health of a man is to have a soul without being aware of it....' In a similar way, the old Rabbis seem to have thought that the true health of a religion is to have a theology without being aware of it; and thus they hardly ever made—nor could they make—any attempt towards working their*

> *theology into a formal system, or giving us a full exposition of it.*
>
> Today, Conservative Judaism pulsates with many pockets of intense religious energy. Its congregational life, national conventions, USY pilgrimages and Schechter day schools increasingly manifest models of religious community shaped by its core values. More than ever, the lay leadership of these ventures consists of serious Jews for whom Conservative Judaism is hardly 'a halfway house' (Sklare). The longstanding gap between Seminary and synagogue has also been largely transformed into a common calling to perpetuate rabbinic Judaism in an open society. What Conservative Judaism offers the growing number of Jews hungry for the holy is a sacred cluster where standards are coupled with compassion, scholarship with spirit, piety with intellectual honesty, and parochial passion with universalism—a prescription for *salvation in this world and the one to come*. [ed.: Italics included in original text].[27]

Emet Ve-Emunah and "The Sacred Cluster" are aspirational statements. The data from the Pew studies make it clear that there is a large gap between these statements and the practices of affiliated members of the Conservative community. Anecdotal evidence reinforces this disparity. Nevertheless, these publications are important for two reasons. First, they describe the goals of the movement, providing a roadmap that interested Conservative Jews can follow.

Second, they firmly establish the leadership of the

Conservative movement as highly traditional and halachically-based, yet very inclusive, which is consistent with the philosophy of adapting traditional Judaism to the modern era. This is exactly what Conservative Jews want from their leadership, even though it might not reflect the daily practices of the vast majority of Conservative Jews.

It is very important to Conservative Jews that the movement embody the Jewish traditions of their ancestors. When they attend services, they want the prayers to be based on the traditional liturgy. When they consult their rabbi on important issues, often related to lifecycle events, they want him or her to be a well-educated, practicing Jew, on whose halachic answers they can rely. They want and care about being part of what they consider to be the real thing, even if they don't personally practice that way.

At the same time, they want an inclusive environment that recognizes women, members of the LGBTQ+ community, and others as fully participating Jews, to the extent that they wish to participate. This resonates with the social consciousness of Conservative Jews, who tend to be very modern, academically focused, and socially liberal.

It is therefore not surprising that over the years, the Conservative movement has generally moved to the right on many aspects of observance, while moving to the left on issues of inclusion, producing a cluster of values that is more traditional than in the past and that embraces a more diverse community than in the past, particularly regarding synagogue worship. Several changes that have occurred in many Conservative congregations over the decades reflect this evolution:

- Making *Shabbat* morning, rather than Friday evening, the main prayer service for *Shabbat*
- Holding services on *Shabbat* and on weekday evenings

at times based on the Jewish calendar, rather than at a fixed time that does not change with the seasons
- Lighting *Shabbat* candles and beginning *Shabbat* dinner at the proper halachic times on Friday nights
- Introducing the traditional practice of *korim* (kneeling then bending to the floor) during Rosh Hashana and Yom Kippur *Musaf* (ed: Additional) services
- Giving *hazzanim* (cantors) *shtenders* (podiums) facing the *Aron Kodesh* (the Holy Ark in which the Torah Scrolls are kept in the sanctuary) from which to lead prayers, rather than having them face the congregation while leading services
- Reintroducing *seudah shlishit* (the third *Shabbat* meal)
- Wearing large woolen *tallitot* rather than narrow silk prayer shawls at services
- Putting up *sukkot* and purchasing *lulavim* and *etrogim* for the festival of *Sukkot*
- Including women in all aspects of synagogue services
- Editing the prayer book liturgy to make it more gender neutral
- Fully accepting LGBTQ+ community members into the movement, including allowing them to assume clerical positions in synagogues, schools, and summer camps

These changes have made the Conservative movement more attractive to many of its members. The fact that individual Conservative Jews might choose not to follow many traditional practices does not mean that they don't care about the authenticity of these practices. For example, although many Conservative Jews do not have *Shabbat* dinner every Friday night, when they do have it, they want it to be traditional with songs, blessing the children, *kiddush, motzi,* and *birkat hamazon*. They also serve traditional *Shabbat* foods like gefilte fish, chicken soup, and chicken or brisket. They cover the table with a white tablecloth and use their best dishes, glassware, and silverware. These actions create an atmosphere that feels different from the work week.

Similarly, while many Conservative Jews do not strictly observe *kashrut*, the aspects of *kashrut* that they often do keep – e.g., often not eating pork products or shellfish, occasionally eating at kosher restaurants, and keeping a higher level of *kashrut* on *Pesach* – are very important to them.

Conservative Jews revel in feeling that they are a part of Jewish history and tradition based on how they live. Even where they don't observe certain practices regularly, they like to hear about them by listening to their rabbi speak and by reading synagogue publications. Parents rejoice when their children embrace Judaism based on things they are taught in Conservative religious schools and summer camps.

Chapter Three

REFORM JUDAISM AND ITS GROWING CONNECTION TO TRADITION

When Napoleon reigned in Western Europe, from the turn of the 19th century until 1815, he gave Jews broad political freedoms, as well as the right to work in business and professional fields from which they had previously been barred. This freed them from social isolation and exposed them to broader European, and particularly German, society, where they discovered the culture and philosophies that were emerging in the early 1800s. In response, these Central European Jews developed the *Haskalah*, which quickly spread to Eastern Europe, where Jews were not yet politically liberated but aspired to be.

A form of Jewish Enlightenment, the *Haskala* led Jews to adopt secular European practices, reasoning that a form of Judaism that fit enlightened society was more appropriate to their situation than traditional Orthodoxy. They believed that Jews who blended in with their non-Jewish neighbors by dressing secularly, refraining from eating exclusively kosher food, giving up the restrictions of *Shabbat*, and speaking and praying in the local language would not be subject to antisemitism. In time, this movement became Reform Judaism.

Rabbi Abraham Geiger of the Breslau Jewish community was the intellectual leader of this new movement. He organized the first Reform Rabbinical conference in Brunswick in 1844, with successive gatherings in Frankfurt in 1845, and Breslau in 1846. At the conferences, representatives of the Jewish community developed Reform beliefs and practices. This was a dramatic departure from the traditional Jewish approach. Rabbi Geiger would have gone so far as to abolish ritual circumcision, but the community rabbis elected to preserve this, as well as some other practices. They did, however, reject continued adherence to *The Thirteen Principles of Faith* and the observance of strict Torah Law and Oral Law, most notably observance of *Shabbat* and *kashrut*. They also supported the abolition of distinctive dress for Jews, adopting instead the secular dress styles of the time.

The large numbers of Central European Jews who came to the United States between 1820 and 1860 brought Reform Judaism with them. In 1820, there were approximately 2,000 Jews in the United States. By 1860, the United States Jewish population had grown to approximately 150,000. Over time, these new immigrants adopted Reform Jewish practices that felt compatible with their new lives in America. They founded Temple Emanu-El founded in New York City in 1845. It remains the most prominent and best-known American Reform Temple.[1,*]

At first, Reform communities developed across the country with little consistency of practice or theology. This began to change in 1854, when Rabbi Isaac Mayer Wise, an

---

* Reform synagogues are almost universally referred to as Temples, as are many Conservative synagogues. Orthodox synagogues do not use the title "Temple" out of respect for the memory of the Temples in Jerusalem that the Babylonians and the Romans, respectively, destroyed.

immigrant from Bohemia (today part of the Czech Republic), took the pulpit of Congregation B'nai Jeshurun in Cincinnati. He used it as a base from which to build American Reform Judaism. He established a newspaper, *The Israelite* (later *The American Israelite*) and edited a Reform Jewish Prayer book. Over time, he inspired lay leadership to establish the Union of American Hebrew Congregations (now the Union for Reform Judaism), the umbrella organization for Reform Temples. Rabbi Wise established Hebrew Union College, for ordaining Reform rabbis, and the Central Conference of American Rabbis, the central body for defining Reform Jewish practices.

In 1885, at a conference in Pittsburgh that Rabbi Wise chaired, the leadership of the Reform movement adopted a *Declaration of Principles*, which became known as the "Pittsburgh Platform." This defined what became known as Classical Reform Judaism, and stressed beliefs and ethics over religious practices.

Convening at the call of Kaufmann Kohler of New York, Reform rabbis from around the United States met from November 16 through November 19, 1885, with Isaac Mayer Wise presiding. The meeting was declared the continuation of the Philadelphia Conference of 1869, which was the continuation of the German Conference of 1841 to 1846. The rabbis adopted the following seminal text:

1. We recognize in every religion an attempt to grasp the Infinite, and in every mode, source or book of revelation held sacred in any religious system the consciousness of the indwelling of God in man. We hold that Judaism presents the highest conception of the God-idea as taught in our Holy Scriptures and developed and spiritualized by the Jewish teachers, in accordance with

the moral and philosophical progress of their respective ages. We maintain that Judaism preserved and defended midst continual struggles and trials and under enforced isolation, this God-idea as the central religious truth for the human race.

2. We recognize in the Bible the record of the consecration of the Jewish people to its mission as the priest of the one God, and value it as the most potent instrument of religious and moral instruction. We hold that the modern discoveries of scientific research in the domain of nature and history are not antagonistic to the doctrines of Judaism, the Bible reflecting the primitive ideas of its own age, and at times clothing its conception of divine Providence and Justice dealing with men in miraculous narratives.

3. We recognize in the Mosaic legislation [ed.: The Torah and the Oral Law given at Mount Sinai] a system of training the Jewish people for its mission during its national life in Palestine, and today we *accept as binding only its moral laws, and maintain only such ceremonies as elevate and sanctify our lives, but reject all such as are not adapted to the views and habits of modern civilization.* [ed.: Italics added]

4. We hold that all such Mosaic and rabbinical laws [ed.: The Torah and the Oral Law as interpreted by rabbinic authorities] as regulate diet, priestly purity, and dress originated in ages and under the influence of ideas entirely foreign to our present mental and spiritual state. They fail to impress the modern Jew with a spirit of priestly holiness; their observance in our days is apt rather to obstruct than to further modern spiritual elevation.

5. We recognize, in the modern era of universal culture of heart and intellect, the approaching of the realization

of Israel's great Messianic hope for the establishment of the kingdom of truth, justice, and peace among all men. *We consider ourselves no longer a nation, but a religious community, and therefore expect neither a return to Palestine, nor a sacrificial worship under the sons of Aaron, nor the restoration of any of the laws concerning the Jewish state.* [ed. Italics added]

6. We recognize in Judaism a progressive religion, ever striving to be in accord with the postulates of reason. We are convinced of the utmost necessity of preserving the historical identity with our great past. Christianity and Islam, being daughter religions of Judaism, we appreciate their providential mission, to aid in the spreading of monotheistic and moral truth. We acknowledge that the spirit of broad humanity of our age is our ally in the fulfillment of our mission, and therefore we extend the hand of fellowship to all who cooperate with us in the establishment of the reign of truth and righteousness among men.

7. We reassert the doctrine of Judaism that the soul is immortal, grounding the belief on the divine nature of human spirit, which forever finds bliss in righteousness and misery in wickedness. *We reject as ideas not rooted in Judaism, the beliefs both in bodily resurrection and in Gehenna and Eden (Hell and Paradise) as abodes for everlasting punishment and reward.* [ed.: Italics added]

8. In full accordance with the spirit of the Mosaic legislation, which strives to regulate the relations between rich and poor, we deem it our duty to participate in the great task of modern times, to solve, on the basis of justice and righteousness, the problems presented by the contrasts and evils of the present organization of society.[2]

The authors of the Pittsburgh Platform sought to embrace the moral laws of both the Torah and the Oral Law, while firmly rejecting religious practices that they didn't believe would elevate or sanctify the lives of Jews and resonate with modern civilization. They also rejected Zionism and the desire to return to the Biblical land of Israel, opting instead for redemption through assimilation into modern, enlightened society. Finally, they rejected the theological principles of revival of the dead, and reward and punishment, including the afterlife in Heaven as the ultimate reward. Under the Pittsburgh Platform, there was no Messiah whom *Hashem* would send to reward *Klal Yisrael* for adhering to strict religious practices and good works, and who would lead a re-established Jewish monarchy in the Holy Land. Through the eight principles of the Pittsburgh Platform, the Conference soundly rejected *The Thirteen Principles of Faith* as inappropriate for modern Jews who were both emancipated and enlightened.

The worldview and the demographic composition of American Jewry that led to the adoption of the Pittsburgh Platform in 1885 changed very quickly over the next 50 years:

> From 1881 until 1920, the Reform movement grew slowly relative to the increase in the American Jewish population, with 99 congregations consisting of 9,800 members in 1900 and 200 congregations with 23,000 members in 1920 while the American Jewish population increased 14-fold as a result of the mass immigration of Eastern European Jews. The Reform movement went from being the single most important voice of the Jewish American community to being a small minority. Despite the fact that the elite roles of many Reform Jews in American society

allowed them to retain a high profile, they were swamped by the Eastern European organizations and ideologies.

The Eastern European mass immigrations increased the American Jewish population from 250,000 in 1880 to 1 million by 1900 and 3.5 million by 1920. The bulk of the immigrants came from Russia, Ukraine, Lithuania, Poland, Romania and other regions where there had not been full emancipation. Since most of the native populations in their home countries had viewed these Jews as separate from the broader society, they came to America from an insular Jewish background. As a consequence, few joined the Reform movement. The immigrants did not like the Reform service, which they found lacking in traditional Jewish elements. Many Reform Jews maintained a haughty attitude toward the newcomers, preferring not to remember that their own parents or grandparents had arrived in the United States one or two generations earlier under similar circumstances. Indeed, a mythology developed that had the 'German' Jews descended from aristocrats. Historically inaccurate, it reflected a widely held perception.

Nevertheless, over the course of time increasing numbers of Eastern Europeans joined Reform congregations. Under their influence, the Reform movement inched back toward a more traditional approach to Jewish thought and practice, hastened by world events. By the 1920s and especially the 1930s, with the worldwide rise of antisemitism, this direction became clear. Even though the 1885 Declaration of Principles had argued that Jews should remain together solely as a religious group to fulfill their mission of bringing ethical monotheism to the world, the rise in antisemitism threatened Jewish physical survival, a concern that far outweighed theology or ideology.³

These changes led to the adoption of the "Columbus Platform" in 1937, which enunciated three pillars of Judaism: Judaism and its Foundations, Ethics, and Religious Practice:

> In view of the changes that have taken place in the modern world and the consequent need of stating anew the teachings of Reform Judaism, the Central Conference of American Rabbis makes the following declaration of principles. It presents them not as a fixed creed but as a guide for the progressive elements of Jewry.
>
> **Judaism and its Foundations**
>
> 1. Nature of Judaism. Judaism is the historical religious experience of the Jewish people. Though growing out of Jewish life, its message is universal, aiming at the union and perfection of mankind under the sovereignty of God. Reform Judaism recognizes the principle of progressive development in religion and consciously applies this principle to spiritual as well as to cultural and social life.

Judaism welcomes all truth, whether written in the pages of scripture or deciphered from the records of nature. The new discoveries of science, while replacing the older scientific views underlying our sacred literature, do not conflict with the essential spirit of religion as manifested in the consecration of man's will, heart and mind to the service of God and of humanity.

2. God. The heart of Judaism and its chief contribution to religion is the doctrine of the One, living God, who rules the world through law and love. In Him all existence has its creative source and mankind its ideal of conduct. Though transcending time and space, He is the indwelling Presence of the world. We worship Him as the Lord of the universe and as our merciful Father.

3. Man. Judaism affirms that man is created in the Divine image. His spirit is immortal. He is an active coworker with God. As a child of God, he is endowed with moral freedom and is charged with the responsibility of overcoming evil and striving after ideal ends.

4. Torah. God reveals Himself not only in the majesty, beauty and orderliness of nature, but also in the vision and moral striving of the human spirit. Revelation is a continuous process, confined to no one group and to no one age. Yet the people of Israel, through its prophets and sages, achieved unique insight in the realm of religious truth. The Torah, both written and oral, enshrines Israel's

evergrowing consciousness of God and of the moral law. It preserves the historical precedents, sanctions and norms of Jewish life, and seeks to mold it in the patterns of goodness and of holiness. Being products of historical processes, certain of its laws have lost their binding force with the passing of the conditions that called them forth. But as a depository of permanent spiritual ideals, the Torah remains the dynamic source of the life of Israel. Each age has the obligation to adapt the teachings of the Torah to its basic needs in consonance with the genius of Judaism.

5. Israel. Judaism is the soul of which Israel is the body. Living in all parts of the world, Israel has been held together by the ties of a common history, and above all, by the heritage of faith. Though we recognize in the group loyalty of Jews who have become estranged from our religious tradition, a bond which still unites them with us, we maintain that it is by its religion and for its religion that the Jewish people has lived. The nonJew who accepts our faith is welcomed as a full member of the Jewish community. In all lands where our people live, they assume and seek to share loyally the full duties and responsibilities of citizenship and to create seats of Jewish knowledge and religion. In the rehabilitation of Palestine, the land hallowed by memories and hopes, we behold the promise of renewed life for many of our brethren. We affirm the obligation of all Jewry to aid in its

upbuilding as a Jewish homeland by endeavoring to make it not only a haven of refuge for the oppressed but also a center of Jewish culture and spiritual life. Throughout the ages it has been Israel's mission to witness to the Divine in the face of every form of paganism and materialism. We regard it as our historic task to cooperate with all men in the establishment of the kingdom of God, of universal brotherhood, Justice, truth and peace on earth. This is our Messianic goal.

Ethics

1. Ethics and Religion. In Judaism religion and morality blend into an indissoluble unity. Seeking God means to strive after holiness, righteousness and goodness. The love of God is incomplete without the love of one's fellowmen. Judaism emphasizes the kinship of the human race, the sanctity and worth of human life and personality and the right of the individual to freedom and to the pursuit of his chosen vocation. Justice to all, irrespective of race, sect or class, is the inalienable right and the inescapable obligation of all. The state and organized government exist in order to further these ends.
2. Social justice. Judaism seeks the attainment of a just society by the application of its teachings to the economic order, to industry and commerce, and to national and international affairs. It aims at the elimination of manmade

misery and suffering, of poverty and degradation, of tyranny and slavery, of social inequality and prejudice, of ill-will and strife. It advocates the promotion of harmonious relations between warring classes on the basis of equity and justice, and the creation of conditions under which human personality may flourish. It pleads for the safeguarding of childhood against exploitation. It champions the cause of all who work and of their right to an adequate standard of living, as prior to the rights of property. Judaism emphasizes the duty of charity, and strives for a social order which will protect men against the material disabilities of old age, sickness and unemployment.

3. Peace. Judaism, from the days of the prophets, has proclaimed to mankind the ideal of universal peace. The spiritual and physical disarmament of all nations has been one of its essential teachings. It abhors all violence and relies upon moral education, love and sympathy to secure human progress. It regards justice as the foundation of the wellbeing of nations and the condition of enduring peace. It urges organized international action for disarmament, collective security and world peace.

Religious Practice

1. The Religious Life. Jewish life is marked by consecration to these ideals of Judaism. It calls for faithful participation in the life

of the Jewish community as it finds expression in home, synagogue and school and in all other agencies that enrich Jewish life and promote its welfare. The Home has been and must continue to be a stronghold of Jewish life, hallowed by the spirit of love and reverence, by moral discipline and religious observance and worship. The Synagogue is the oldest and most democratic institution in Jewish life. It is the prime communal agency by which Judaism is fostered and preserved. It links the Jews of each community and unites them with all Israel. The perpetuation of Judaism as a living force depends upon religious knowledge and upon the Education of each new generation in our rich cultural and spiritual heritage.

Prayer is the voice of religion, the language of faith and aspiration. It directs man's heart and mind Godward, voices the needs and hopes of the community and reaches out after goals which invest life with supreme value. To deepen the spiritual life of our people, we must cultivate the traditional habit of communion with God through prayer in both home and synagogue.

Judaism as a way of life requires in addition to its moral and spiritual demands, the preservation of the Sabbath, festivals and Holy Days, the retention and development of such customs, symbols and ceremonies as

> possess inspirational value, the cultivation of distinctive forms of religious art and music and the use of Hebrew, together with the vernacular, in our worship and instruction.
>
> These timeless aims and ideals of our faith we present anew to a confused and troubled world. We call upon our fellow Jews to rededicate themselves to them, and, in harmony with all men, hopefully and courageously to continue Israel's eternal quest after God and His kingdom.[4]

The principles of the Columbus Platform represent a significant retreat from the idealistic view of the harmonious unity of Jewish life and a religion based exclusively on moral and ethical Jewish principles. Given the changes in Europe after 1885, it is no wonder that this perspective changed. When the conference adopted the Pittsburgh Platform, German society still stood as the model state that allowed Jews full participation, providing a uniquely Jewish redemption *in situ* after close to 2,000 years of social isolation and economic deprivation. The spread of antisemitism and the rise of the Nazi party turned this utopian philosophy on its head. The theme of civil rights is also notable in the Columbus Platform. Jews became prominent advocates for civil rights in the aftermath of the Civil War, and the text reflected this.

The Columbus Platform provides an unequivocal affirmation of the existence of God who rules everywhere in our world through law and love. It presents God as merciful and as the creative force for all existence. It describes man as created in God's image and possessing an immortal spirit. This is notably different from the references to the God-idea in the Pittsburgh Platform. The Columbus Platform also recognizes both the Torah and the Oral Law as the dynamic sources of life for the Jewish people. It does not subscribe to Divine authorship of the Torah or consider the events at Mount Sinai to have been the Divine revelation of the Torah to the Jewish people, instead describing revelation as a continuing process. It states that "certain of its laws have lost their binding force with the passing of the conditions that called them forth." The Columbus Platform refers to these now-obsolete laws as the products of historical processes that no longer have relevance. This is because Reform Judaism sees both the written Torah and the Oral Law as the result of human endeavor over time rather than being Divine. Thus, as times change, so too does the relevance of particular parts the Torah and Oral Law.

In contrast to the secular approach of the Pittsburgh Platform, the last paragraph of the "Religious Practice" section of the Columbus Platform recognized the preservation of *Shabbat* and the Jewish holidays, elevating the religious aspects of the Reform Jewish experience and giving Reform Jews an ideal to which to aspire that is grounded in religious ritual. The same is true for the Columbus Platform's strong statement about the importance of prayer in synagogue and at home.

Perhaps the biggest departure from the Pittsburgh Platform is the Columbus Platform's endorsement of Zionism and the importance of Israel, including "the obligation of all Jewry to aid in its upbuilding as a Jewish homeland by endeavoring to make it not only a haven of refuge for the oppressed but also a center of Jewish culture and spiritual life." By 1937, with the rise of Nazism and other forms of antisemitism, Reform Jewish leadership had lost confidence that Jews would be safe in foreign lands.

In 1976, in commemoration of the 100th anniversary of

the founding of the Union of American Hebrew Congregations and the Hebrew Union College-Jewish Institute of Religion, the leaders of the Reform movement, meeting in San Francisco, issued a new set of guiding principles known as "A Centenary Perspective," as follows:

Reform Judaism: A Centenary Perspective

Adopted in San Francisco – 1976

The Central Conference of American Rabbis has on special occasions described the spiritual state of Reform Judaism. The centenaries of the founding of the Union of American Hebrew Congregations and the Hebrew Union College-Jewish Institute of Religion seem an appropriate time for another such effort. We therefore record our sense of the unity of our movement today.

One Hundred Years: What We Have Taught

We celebrate the role of Reform Judaism in North America, the growth of our movement on this free ground, the great contributions of our membership to the dreams and achievements of this society. We also feel great satisfaction at how much of our pioneering conception of Judaism has been accepted by the Household of Israel. It now seems self-evident to most Jews: that our tradition should interact with modern culture; that its forms ought to reflect a contemporary esthetic; that its scholarship needs to be conducted by modern, critical methods; and that change has been and must continue to be a fundamental reality in Jewish life. Moreover, though some still disagree, substantial numbers have also accepted our teachings: that the ethics of universalism implicit in traditional Judaism must be an explicit part of our Jewish duty; that women have full rights to practice Judaism; and that Jewish obligation begins with the informed will of every individual. Most modern Jews, within their various religious movements, are embracing Reform Jewish perspectives. We see this past century as having confirmed the essential wisdom of our movement.

One Hundred Years: What We Have Learned

Obviously, much else has changed in the past century. We continue to probe the extraordinary events of the past generation, seeking to understand their meaning and to incorporate their significance in our lives. The Holocaust shattered our easy optimism about humanity and its inevitable progress. The State of Israel, through its many accomplishments, raised our sense of the Jews as a people to new heights of aspiration and devotion. *The widespread threats to freedom, the problems inherent in the explosion of new knowledge and of ever more powerful technologies, and the spiritual emptiness of much of Western culture have taught us to be less dependent on the values of our society and to reassert what remains perennially valid in Judaism's teaching.* We have learned that the survival of the Jewish people is of highest priority and that in carrying out our Jewish responsibilities we help move humanity toward its messianic fulfillment.

Diversity Within Unity, the Hallmark of Reform

Reform Jews respond to change in various ways according to the Reform principle of the autonomy of the individual. However, Reform Judaism does more than tolerate diversity; it engenders it. In our uncertain historical situation we must expect to have far greater diversity than previous generations knew. How we shall live with diversity without stifling dissent and without paralyzing our ability to take positive action will test our character and our principles. We stand open to any position thoughtfully and conscientiously advocated in the spirit of Reform Jewish belief. While we may differ in our interpretation and application of the ideas enunciated here, we accept such differences as precious and see in them Judaism's best hope for confronting whatever the future holds for us. Yet in all our diversity we perceive a certain unity and we shall not allow our differences in some particulars to obscure what binds us together.

1. *God* — The affirmation of God has always been essential to our people's will to survive.

In our struggle through the centuries to preserve our faith we have experienced and conceived of God in many ways. The trials of our own time and the challenges of modern culture have made steady belief and clear understanding difficult for some. Nevertheless, we ground our lives, personally and communally, on God's reality and remain open to new experiences and conceptions of the Divine. Amid the mystery we call life, *we affirm that human beings, created in God's image, share in God's eternality* despite the mystery we call death.

2. *The People Israel* — The Jewish people and Judaism defy precise definition because both are in the process of becoming. Jews, by birth or conversion, constitute an uncommon union of faith and peoplehood. Born as Hebrews in the ancient Near East, we are bound together like all ethnic groups by language, land, history, culture, and institutions. *But the people of Israel is unique because of its involvement with God and its resulting perception of the human condition. Throughout our long history our people has been inseparable from its religion with its messianic hope that humanity will be redeemed.*

3. Torah — Torah results from the relationship between God and the Jewish people. The records of our earliest confrontations are uniquely important to us. *Lawgivers and prophets, historians and poets gave us a heritage whose study is a religious imperative and whose practice is our chief means to holiness.* Rabbis

and teachers, philosophers and mystics, gifted Jews in every age amplified the Torah tradition. For millennia, the creation of Torah has not ceased and Jewish creativity in our time is adding to the chain of tradition.

4. *Our Religious Obligations:* Religious Practice — Judaism emphasizes action rather than creed as the primary expression of a religious life, the means by which we strive to achieve universal justice and peace. Reform Judaism shares this emphasis on duty and obligation. Our founders stressed that the Jew's ethical responsibilities, personal and social, are enjoined by God. The past century has taught us that the claims made upon us may begin with our ethical obligations but they extend to many other aspects of Jewish living, including: creating a Jewish home centered on family devotion: lifelong study; private prayer and public worship; daily religious observance; keeping the Sabbath and the holy days: celebrating the major events of life; involvement with the synagogues and community; and other activities which promote the survival of the Jewish people and enhance its existence. *Within each area of Jewish observance Reform Jews are called upon to confront the claims of Jewish tradition, however differently perceived, and to exercise their individual autonomy, choosing and creating on the basis of commitment and knowledge.*

5. *Our Obligations:* The State of Israel and the Diaspora — We are privileged to live in an

extraordinary time, one in which a third Jewish commonwealth has been established in our people's ancient homeland. We are bound to that land and to the newly reborn State of Israel by innumerable religious and ethnic ties. We have been enriched by its culture and ennobled by its indomitable spirit. We see it providing unique opportunities for Jewish self-expression. *We have both a stake and a responsibility in building the State of Israel, assuring its security, and defining its Jewish character. We encourage aliyah for those who wish to find maximum personal fulfillment in the cause of Zion. We demand that Reform Judaism be unconditionally legitimized in the State of Israel.*

At the same time that we consider the State of Israel vital to the welfare of Judaism everywhere, we reaffirm the mandate of our tradition to create strong Jewish communities wherever we live. A genuine Jewish life is possible in any land, each community developing its own particular character and determining its Jewish responsibilities. The foundation of Jewish community life is the synagogue. It leads us beyond itself to cooperate with other Jews, to share their concerns, and to assume leadership in communal affairs. We are therefore committed to the full democratization of the Jewish community and to its hallowing in terms of Jewish values.

The State of Israel and the Diaspora, in fruitful

dialogue, can show how a people transcends nationalism even as it affirms it, thereby setting an example for humanity which remains largely concerned with dangerously parochial goals.

6. *Our Obligations:* Survival and Service — Early Reform Jews, newly admitted to general society and seeing in this the evidence of a growing universalism, regularly spoke of Jewish purpose in terms of Jewry's service to humanity. In recent years we have become freshly conscious of the virtues of pluralism and the values of particularism. The Jewish people in its unique way of life validates its own worth while working toward the fulfillment of its messianic expectations.

Until the recent past our obligations to the Jewish people and to all humanity seemed congruent. At times now these two imperatives appear to conflict. We know of no simple way to resolve such tensions. We must, however, confront them without abandoning either of our commitments. A universal concern for humanity unaccompanied by a devotion to our particular people is self-destructive; a passion for our people without involvement in humankind contradicts what the prophets have meant to us. Judaism calls us simultaneously to universal and particular obligations.

Hope: Our Jewish Obligation

Previous generations of Reform Jews had unbound confidence in humanity's potential for good. We have lived through terrible tragedy and been compelled to reappropriate our tradition's realism about the human capacity for evil. Yet our people has always refused to despair. The survivors of the Holocaust, being granted life, seized it, nurtured it, and, rising above catastrophe, showed humankind that the human spirit is indomitable. The State of Israel, established and maintained by the Jewish will to live, demonstrates what a united people can accomplish in history. The existence of the Jew is an argument against despair; Jewish survival is warrant for human hope.

We remain God's witness that history is not meaningless. We affirm that with God's help people are not powerless to affect their destiny. We dedicate ourselves, as did the generations of Jews who went before us, to work and wait for that day when "They shall not hurt or destroy in all My holy mountain for the earth shall be full of the knowledge of the Lord as the waters cover the sea."[5] [ed.: Isaiah 11:9] [ed.: italics added]

The Centenary Guiding Principles added a few tenets to guide Reform Judaism as it evolved. First, they acknowledge that "the people of Israel is unique because of its involvement with God…" This statement comes very close to the traditional view that Jews are the chosen people because they chose to accept the Torah. If the Jewish people are unique because of their involvement with God, it must be because they chose to be involved with God. This statement would have been unthinkable at the time of the 1885 Pittsburgh Platform.

Second, the Centenary Guiding Principles state that "[t]hroughout our long history our people has been inseparable from its religion with its Messianic hope that humanity will be redeemed." This statement ties the Jewish people to the hope for a Messianic age through redemption, a notable departure from the Pittsburgh and Columbus principles, although it falls short of endorsing praying for the Messiah to come as *Hashem's* representative to rule in the Messianic age.

Third, the Centenary Guiding Principle referring to the Torah states that "[l]awgivers and prophets, historians and poets gave us a heritage whose study is a religious imperative and whose practice is our chief means to holiness." Making study of Jewish texts an essential act was not a part of prior Reform doctrine. Under the Centenary Guiding Principles, the concept of Torah includes works from varied sources beyond the written Torah, the Oral Law, and the commentaries and Codes of Jewish Law that followed over the centuries. Note that the obligation in the Centenary Guiding Principles is a general communal obligation, rather than the individual obligation of every Jew, as in traditional Judaism.

Fourth, the Columbus Platform recognized the importance of Jewish ritual observance but fell short of defining how this translates to individual practice. The Centenary Guiding Principles, in contrast, stated that "[w]ithin each area of Jewish observance Reform Jews are called upon to confront the claims of Jewish tradition, however differently perceived, and to exercise their individual autonomy, choosing and creating on the basis of commitment and knowledge." The language "called upon" is a big step toward bringing traditional ritual back to adherents of the Reform movement. And making this a commitment for "each area of Jewish observance" raises the bar still more.

Fifth, the Centenary Guiding Principles state unequivocally that the State of Israel is critical to the Jewish future. They also encourage *aliyah* (emigration to Israel) for individuals who believe that doing so would enhance their lives. Further, they "demand that Reform Judaism be unconditionally legitimized in the State of Israel." Today, in many instances, the Orthodox movement controls the Jewish lifecycle in Israel, much to the frustration of Reform Jewish leadership, which has worked hard over several decades to build religious institutions there, and to gain authority for Reform rabbis to act as recognized, ordained rabbis for all aspects of the Jewish lives of their followers.

In May 1999, the Central Conference of American Rabbis again issued a set of principles to guide the Reform community and its leaders. This latest set of principles has become known as the "New Pittsburgh Platform." It reads as follows:

Central Conference of American Rabbis

May 1999 Sivan 5759

Preamble

On three occasions during the last century and a half, the Reform rabbinate has adopted comprehensive statements to help guide the thought and practice of our movement. In 1885, fifteen rabbis issued the Pittsburgh Platform, a set of guidelines that defined Reform Judaism for the next fifty years. A revised statement of principles, the Columbus Platform, was adopted by the Central Conference of American Rabbis in 1937. A third set of rabbinic guidelines, the Centenary Perspective appeared in 1976 on the occasion of the centenary of the Union of American Hebrew Congregations and the Hebrew Union College Jewish Institute of Religion. Today, when so many individuals are striving for religious meaning, moral purpose and a sense of community, we believe it is our obligation as rabbis once again to state a set of principles that define Reform Judaism in our own time.

This "Statement of Principles" affirms the central tenets of Judaism–God, Torah and Israel–even as it acknowledges the diversity of Reform Jewish beliefs and practices. It also invites all Reform Jews to engage in a dialogue with the sources of our tradition, responding out of our knowledge, our experience and our faith. Thus we hope to transform our lives through *kedushah*, holiness.

God

We affirm the reality and oneness of God, even as we may differ in our understanding of the Divine presence.

We affirm that the Jewish people is bound to God by an eternal *b'rit*, covenant, as reflected in our varied understandings of Creation, Revelation and Redemption.

We affirm that every human being is created *btzelem Elohim,* in the image of God, and therefore every human life is sacred.

We regard with reverence all of God's creation and recognize our human responsibility for its preservation and protection.

We encounter God's presence in moments of awe and wonder, in acts of justice and compassion, in loving relationships and in the experiences of everyday life.

We strive for a faith that fortifies us through the vicissitudes of our lives–illness and healing, transgression and repentance, bereavement and consolation, despair and hope.

We continue to have faith that, in spite of the unspeakable evils committed against our people and the sufferings endured by others, the partnership of God and humanity will ultimately prevail.

We trust in our tradition's promise that, although God created us as finite beings, the spirit within us is eternal.

In all these ways and more, God gives meaning and purpose to our lives.

Torah

We affirm that Torah is the foundation of Jewish life.

We cherish the truths revealed in Torah, God's ongoing revelation to our people and the record of our people's ongoing relationship with God.

We affirm that Torah is a manifestation of *ahavat olam*, Gods eternal love for the Jewish people and for all humanity.

We affirm the importance of studying Hebrew, the language of Torah and Jewish liturgy, that we may draw closer to our people's sacred texts.

We are called by Torah to lifelong study in the home, in the synagogue and in every place where Jews gather to learn and teach. Through Torah study we are called to *mitzvot* [commandments], the means by which we make our lives holy.

We are committed to the ongoing study of the whole array of *mitzvot* and to the fulfillment of those that address us as individuals and as a community. Some of these *mitzvot*, sacred obligations, have long been observed by Reform Jews; others, both ancient and modem, demand renewed attention as the result of the unique context of our own times.

We bring Torah into the world when we seek to

sanctify the times and places of our lives through regular home and congregational observance. Shabbat calls us to bring the highest moral values to our daily labor and to culminate the workweek with *kedushah*, holiness, *menuchah*, rest and *oneg*, joy. The High Holy Days call us to account for our deeds. The Festivals enable us to celebrate with joy our people's religious journey in the context of the changing seasons. The days of remembrance remind us of the tragedies and the triumphs that have shaped our people's historical experience both in ancient and modern times. And we mark the milestones of our personal journeys with traditional and creative rites that reveal the holiness in each stage of life.

We bring Torah into the world when we strive to fulfill the highest ethical mandates in our relationships with others and with all of God's creation. Partners with God in *tikkun olam*, repairing the world, we are called to help bring nearer the messianic age. We seek dialogue and joint action with people of other faiths in the hope that together we can bring peace, freedom and justice to our world. We are obligated to pursue *tzedek*, justice and righteousness, and to narrow the gap between the affluent and the poor, to act against discrimination and oppression, to pursue peace, to welcome the stranger, to protect the earth's biodiversity and natural resources, and to redeem those in physical, economic and spiritual bondage. In so doing, we reaffirm social action and social justice as a central prophetic focus of traditional Reform Jewish belief and practice. We affirm the *mitzvah* of *tzedaka*, setting aside portions *of* our earnings and our time to provide for those in need. These acts bring us closer to fulfilling the prophetic call to translate the words of Torah into the works of our hands.

In all these ways and more, Torah gives meaning and purpose to our lives.

Israel

We are Israel, a people aspiring to holiness, singled out through our ancient covenant and our unique history among the nations to be witnesses to God's presence. We are linked by that covenant and that history to all Jews in every age and place.

We are committed to the *mitzvah* of *ahavat Yisrael*, love for the Jewish people, and to *k'lal Yisrael*, the entirety of the community of Israel. Recognizing that *kol Yisrael arevim zeh bazeh*, all Jews are responsible for one another, we reach out to all Jews across ideological and geographical boundaries.

We embrace religious and cultural pluralism as an expression of the vitality of Jewish communal life in Israel and the Diaspora.

We pledge to fulfill Reform Judaism's historic commitment to the complete equality of women and men in Jewish life.

We are an inclusive community, opening doors to Jewish life to people of all ages, to varied kinds of families, to all regardless of their sexual orientation, to *gerim*, those who have converted to Judaism, and to all individuals and families, including the intermarried, who strive to create a Jewish home.

We believe that we must not only open doors for those ready to enter our faith, but also to actively encourage those who are seeking a spiritual home to find it in Judaism.

We are committed to strengthening the people Israel by supporting individuals and families in the creation of homes rich in Jewish learning and observance.

We are committed to strengthening the people Israel by making the synagogue central to Jewish communal life, so that it may elevate the spiritual, intellectual and cultural quality of our lives.

We are committed to *Medinat Yisrael*, the State of Israel, and rejoice in its accomplishments. We affirm the unique qualities of living in *Eretz Yisrael*, the land of Israel, and encourage *aliyah*, immigration to Israel.

We are committed to promoting and strengthening Progressive Judaism in Israel, which will enrich the spiritual life of the Jewish state and its people.

> We affirm that both Israeli and Diaspora Jewry should remain vibrant and interdependent communities. As we urge Jews who reside outside Israel to learn Hebrew as a living language and to make periodic visits to Israel in order to study and to deepen their relationship to the Land and its people, so do we affirm that Israeli Jews have much to learn from the religious life of Diaspora Jewish communities.
>
> We are committed to furthering Progressive Judaism throughout the world as a meaningful religious way of life for the Jewish people.
>
> In all these ways and more, Israel gives meaning and purpose to our lives.[6]

The New Pittsburgh Platform adds several principles, reiterates others, and does not mention a few that appeared in the Centenary Guiding Principles. The additions are a strengthened commitment to the lifelong study of Torah; specific mention of the value of observing the *Shabbat* and the Jewish Holy Days and Festivals; and the importance of learning Hebrew, of gender equality in all aspects of Jewish life, of setting aside a portion of one's earnings for *tzedakah*, of affirmatively accepting inter-faith couples and converts into Reform homes and institutions, of actively seeking new participants in Reform Judaism, and of reaching across ideological and geographical boundaries to all Jews in *Klal Yisrael*.

The statement about gender equality was the culmination of decades of debate on this subject. The Reform movement ordained its first woman rabbi in 1972, but some congregations took far longer to give women full equality and to accept women as clergy. Since 1999, the Reform movement has published prayer books with gender-neutral language, including their references to God. The 1999 statement did not include LGBTQ+ equality, but this too was achieved when:

> [t]he Union for Reform Judaism approved a broad resolution in support of transgender rights in November 2015, setting a positive example for religious organizations all over the world. The resolution, approved at the biannual meeting of the URJ in Orlando, Florida, calls for Reform institutions to use gender-neutral language and also for Reform camps and buildings to have gender-neutral restrooms. Sponsors of the resolution suggested members of the URJ participate in activism on behalf of the transgender community and recommended that Reform religious school staff undergo training on gender issues. Suggestions included in a 9-page pamphlet to help members understand the resolution, vary from dividing children by birth month instead of gender during activities, to avoiding titles of "Mr." and "Mrs." on nametags.[7]

Another significant development occurred under the leadership of Alexander Schindler, who became the President of the Union of American Hebrew Congregations in 1973. The UAHC adopted the "Patrilineal Descent Resolution," which, for the first time, established the presumption that a child of a Jewish male parent would be considered Jewish provided the child was raised as a Jew.[8] This approach created tension among different streams of Judaism regarding the Jewish status of individuals with Jewish fathers but non-Jewish mothers. And that is not the only "who-is-a-Jew" issue. A similar issue exists with respect to conversions to Judaism under the auspices of non-Orthodox rabbis.

In contrast to Orthodox and Conservative rabbis, most Reform rabbis are willing to officiate at marriages between a Jew and non-Jew. This has helped intermarried couples remain within the Reform Jewish community, making it more accessible for non-Jewish spouses who later choose to convert to Judaism.

As the history of the adoption of Reform principles and platforms shows, Reform Judaism evolves in response to historical events and changes in society. Over time, there has been a sharp pivot toward Zionism[9] and a trend toward adding more tradition into Reform Judaism's formal platforms.

Yet, Reform Jewish practices do not always follow the formal platforms. Thus, according to the 2020 and the 2013 Pew Studies:[10,11]

- 14% of American Reform Jews believe that being Jewish is mainly a matter of ancestry, 27% of American Reform Jews believe that being Jewish is mainly a matter of culture, only 10% of American Reform Jews believe that being Jewish is mainly a matter of religion, and only 21% of American Reform Jews believe that being Jewish is mainly a matter of all three.[12]
- When responding to the question of what is essential to Jewish identity, 79% of American Reform Jews said remembering the Holocaust, 49% said caring about Israel, 31% said being part of a Jewish community, and only 5% said observing Jewish law.[13]
- In terms of Hebrew literacy, only 4% of American Reform Jews said they can understand all or most Hebrew words, and only 2% said they can have a conversation in Hebrew.[14,15]

It is important to realize that the multiple principles and platforms are not mutually exclusive. Their authors did not intend subsequent platforms to repeal earlier principles, except in cases where there is a clear contradiction between the two, such as Reform Judaism's perspective on Zionism. Rather, new platforms focus on principles of emerging importance without comprehensively restating every principle that governs the beliefs and practices of Reform Judaism.

From a big picture perspective, we can expect that Reform Judaism's principles will continue to change over time. The Reform Jewish concept of Continued Revelation (as opposed to a single Revelation event at Mount Sinai) requires evolution, rather than adherence to fixed principles, as times change and as Reform clergy and academics seek to determine what beliefs and practices best suit each generation of Reform Jews in light of past experience, what has the most meaning at a given moment, the broader values of society, and the need to support Jewish continuity.

Describing Reform Judaism in terms of its published principles does not accurately describe life in a Reform congregation or the breadth of the Reform movement's accomplishments for its more than 1.5 million members across nearly 850 Reform congregations. Every Reform Temple has a core of devoted Jewish families who actively participate in *Shabbat* services on Friday nights and Saturday mornings. They also are deeply involved in the range of Jewish learning opportunities that their Temple offers. Where possible, their children attend one of the Reform movement's 15 overnight camps and the movement's 12 Jewish Day Schools in the United States and Canada. These camps and schools provide Reform youth with the opportunity for recreation and learning, coupled with extensive exposure to Reform's progressive, inclusive Jewish values. Members of this core family group are dedicated Reform Jews who take living a Jewish life extremely seriously.

Members of the broader congregation also participate in Temple-sponsored activities, even when their attendance at *Shabbat* services is more sporadic, and, in many instances, focused on *Rosh Hashana* and *Yom Kippur* as well as lifecycle events such as *Bar* and *Bat Mitzvot*. These activities include visiting the sick, providing meals through soup kitchens and shelters, participating in the movement's Campaign for Climate Justice, and helping to support campaigns for greater democracy in Israel. This is only a sampling of the types of activities that the Reform movement and its Temples sponsor.

Reform youth are very active in the movement's youth groups. The national umbrella youth group organization is NFTY (National Federation of Temple Youth), which has branches throughout North America. These branches provide local youth programming, offering Reform high school students a Jewish, social, communal, social action, and recreational experience that integrates Reform values with their daily lives.

Almost all children of families belonging to Reform Temples participate in the congregations' religious schools. They learn Hebrew, the weekly Torah portion, Jewish songs, and the meaning of both *Shabbat* and the Jewish Holidays, and absorb Reform Judaism's progressive values, which shape their beliefs and actions over their lives.

As Reform youth approach the age of 13, their congregation's clergy prepares them for their upcoming *B'nei Mitzvot*. In this *Shabbat* morning ceremony, they will play an important role by chanting from the Torah with proper Hebrew pronunciation and traditional Jewish cantillation notes.

Reform rabbis, cantors, assistants, and their support staffs are the glue that holds Reform congregations together. Those who have not closely observed Reform congregations in person probably have no idea just how capable the Reform clergy is at addressing individual and congregational needs. They are both talented and charismatic. The breadth of their training in interpersonal and pastoral skills in unequalled within *Klal Yisrael*. It is this aspect of Reform Judaism, more than any other, that attracts so many Jews to the Reform movement.

Another highly spiritual aspect of Reform Judaism is its use of music in Temple services. From the start, Reform Temples used organs in their sanctuaries in pursuit of their goal of fitting in with the broader, particularly Christian, society. This was true in Germany as well. But that changed dramatically in the 1970s when an American folk singer, Debbie Friedman, began composing liturgical music, drawing on texts from the Torah, *tehillim*, and the prayer book. Her songs were perfect for the Reform movement. They were highly spiritual; they combined snippets of Hebrew with English, which made learning them easy for an audience that for the most part was not literate in Hebrew; they conveyed deep meaning; and they were not too long. Debbie's beautiful voice enhanced these inspiring songs. However, her music was not well suited for the somewhat church-like sound of the organ. As a result, many Reform Temples switched from organs to guitars, pianos, and small ensembles of musicians playing string and reed instruments.

Debbie Friedman's best-known songs are *Misheberach* and *Havdalah*. *Misheberach* in its classic form is a *Shabbat* prayer recited toward the end of the Torah reading, asking *Hashem* to heal the sick. Congregants recite the prayer with particular people in mind. Debbie took its opening words and the words *refuah shleima* (a complete healing or recovery), both in Hebrew, and composed a two-verse song, mostly in English. She used egalitarian language, including the Biblical

Matriarchs as well as the Patriarchs, which matched the principles of Reform liturgy. Her version of *Misheberach* is beautiful in every respect. Listening to it as part of a Reform service is a moving experience. The entire congregation stands and sings *Misheberach* together, often to musical accompaniment. Many in the congregation tear up as they think about the sick friends and relatives for whom they are praying. Most congregants know the song without the need to look at their prayer books. Reform Temples throughout the movement use this song in their liturgy and many Conservative congregations have adopted it as well.

The *Havdalah* prayer marks the conclusion of *Shabbat*. It includes blessings over wine, spices (to dampen the shock of the loss of the peace of *Shabbat*), a flame from a multi-wick candle, and the separation of the holiness of *Shabbat* from the profane nature of the rest of the week. Debbie's composition uses the Hebrew text of *Havdalah* with no English additions. The beauty of the song brought the *Havdalah* ritual back to the Reform community, both in the synagogue and in the home. It too spread quickly beyond the Reform world to the Conservative movement and, selectively, to Orthodox congregations and families.

Debbie was prolific, recording 22 albums before her untimely death in 2011 at the age of 59, from a chronic neurologic condition. She gave countless performances to packed concert halls and synagogues, as well as in Jewish meeting venues all over America. She delighted in teaching her songs to even 60 children at a time, while sitting on a low chair and playing her acoustic guitar.

Her influence spawned a generation of Jewish folk singers who sang her songs and composed their own. Reform and Conservative cantors, more and more of whom were women, used Debbie's music heavily in their public worship during weekly *Shabbat* services. It can truly be said that Debbie Friedman transformed the communal prayer experience of the Reform movement and heavily influenced the music of the Conservative movement.

This thoroughly American use of music has had a profound influence on the Reform observance not just of *Shabbat*, but also of its High Holy Day services, particularly the afternoon service on *Yom Kippur*. The Reform version replaces the traditional Jewish liturgy with a text in Hebrew, English, and Yiddish that chronicles the Jewish journey through history. It is set to beautiful music performed on a variety of instruments allowing for a transition of styles from traditional to operatic to folk and rock music.

Chapter Four

THE HIDDEN WORLD OF RECONSTRUCTIONIST JUDAISM

RECONSTRUCTIONIST JUDAISM IS the brainchild of Rabbi Mordechai Kaplan, a JTS-ordained Rabbi who, following his ordination in 1902, began his career as Assistant Rabbi at a Modern Orthodox synagogue in New York City. Over the next several years, his belief in Orthodoxy weakened. In 1909, he left the pulpit and joined the Seminary faculty, where he would remain for 54 years. There he developed a new version of Judaism, defining it first and foremost as a civilization. According to Kaplan, the Jews as a civilization created many things: the Hebrew language; their history and its mythological origins, which they borrowed heavily from other cultures; their beliefs and practices; their institutions; their art; and their ties to the Land of Israel. They also created the Torah, "not one internally coherent text but, rather, a composite of separate documents with multiple internal contradictions, overlappings, and borrowings from the sacred literature of other peoples edited some seven centuries after

Moses…"¹ According to Kaplan, not only was the Torah not given to the Jewish people at Mount Sinai, it was not even Divinely inspired, and certainly not by the God traditionally portrayed by Judaism and described in Jewish liturgy. Kaplan's definition of God

> is not a being, not a personal being, certainly not supernatural, and not "beyond" nature, for there is no beyond to nature; nature is simply all there is. Rather God is a power, a process, a force, an impulse that pervades all things, and impels us to evolve and to implement visions of an ever-more-perfect social order. God is "the power that makes for salvation."
>
> Does this God reveal? Certainly, says Kaplan, but not from a mountaintop, not in words and letters, not only from the outside in but also from the inside out, from within ourselves, through the workings of the human conscience and human creativity. God reveals through our urge to acquire knowledge in order to tame the forces of chaos in ourselves, in nature, and in history, thus bringing about the vision of the world as perfected.²

Kaplan believed that nature is supreme and that our thoughts, yearnings, and creations are all part of nature. He also believed that over time, nature "impels us to… implement visions of an ever-more-perfect social order" and that this aspect of nature is what represents God.

"In 1945, Kaplan published his Reconstructionist Prayerbook, which adapted the traditional liturgy to his new theology, eliminating references to traditional doctrines, such as that of the chosen people, the resurrection of the dead, and the personal Messiah."[3] It was Kaplan's hope that he could bring the Conservative movement in line with his thinking, and this is what probably kept him at the Seminary for so long. But that didn't happen.

"His heyday was in the years prior to World War II, when generations of rabbinical students, most of them dropouts from Orthodoxy, came to the Seminary precisely because he was teaching there. But from the 1950s on, American Jews turned more traditionalist, and the mood of the students swung against Kaplan and he felt more and more isolated."[4]

Kaplan left the Seminary at age 82 in 1963. The Reconstructionist Rabbinical College (RRC) was created in 1968.

> The decision to open the school was made by the lay-led organization of the movement, the Federation of Reconstructionist Congregations and Havurot (today the Jewish Reconstructionist Federation) meeting in Montreal in June 1967. Kaplan previously had resisted establishing a seminary that would mark Reconstructionism as a denomination rather than a school of thought. He maintained a life-long allegiance to the Jewish Theological Seminary where he taught for decades. However Reconstructionist congregations, insufficiently served by Reform and Conservative rabbis, pushed Rabbi Ira Eisenstein [ed.: a distinguished Reconstructionist leader and Kaplan's son-in-law] and lay leaders to make this decision.
>
> Eisenstein became the RRC's first president. The college included two unique features. Reflecting

Kaplan's vision of living in two civilizations [ed.: Jewish and American], students were to pursue doctoral studies in religion simultaneously at a secular university. (However this dual-studies program would later be dropped.) Second, the curriculum would be based on Kaplan's concept of Judaism as an evolving Jewish civilization, studying each period sequentially and integrating history and literature from each time period. The five-year rabbinic curriculum devotes a year each to the biblical, rabbinic, medieval, modern, and contemporary periods. Open to both men and women, from the beginning RRC included faculty from diverse Jewish backgrounds.

The college opened in September 1968 in Philadelphia near Temple University, as the college was to collaborate with the Temple religion department and provide access to other graduate programs. Given the existence of only a handful of Reconstructionist congregations, for many students their first exposure to the movement in practice came as students. In 1974, the second graduating class included Sandy Eisenberg Sasso, the second woman rabbi in the United States.

In 1984 the college moved from its inner-city location to its current home in a former mansion in suburban Wyncote. Around that time, the college leadership wanted to enrich the curriculum and increase the Hebrew level of students. The number of RRC courses increased, including courses by visiting non-Jewish scholars. In 1983 RRC became the first rabbinical seminary to officially admit openly gay students. A mekhinah (preparatory) year for some students was also added. The college continued to expand in the late 1980s as faculty and student enrollment significantly increased... The college received full academic accreditation in 1990.

In the 1990s and early 2000s the college strengthened its financial base and expanded its programs, publications, and facilities. Cantorial studies and a master's program in Jewish studies were added. Three academic centers were established to support research, publications, and education in the wider community: Jewish ethics; Kolot, a center on Jewish women's and gender studies; and Hiddur, a center on aging.

By 2005, RRC had graduated 283 rabbis and two cantors. Of these, 153 were male and 132 were female. Enrollment in 2005 was 76 rabbinical students, two cantorial students, and two masters' candidates. RRC publishes the *Reconstructionist* journal (1935 -).[5]

There are Reconstructionist congregations in 27 states in the United States, as well as in Brazil, Canada, Curacao, Germany, Italy, the Netherlands, and Russia.

In determining Reconstructionist customs and religious practices, the main guiding principle has been Kaplan's oft-repeated motto: "The past has a vote, not a veto."[6] Kaplan understood that if Judaism is a civilization, then its past is important in guiding its future. He also believed that as a civilization changes, so to do its practices. To Kaplan, 20th century democratic America, where Jews had full rights as citizens, was so profoundly different from both Biblical times and previous diaspora times that Jewish civilization needed to change to survive and remain vital. This reconstructed civilization would need both its history and its new practices to be relevant. There was no place in Kaplan's theology for the concept of Divinely given law that was immune from change over time.

Let's look at the application of this principle to the practice of keeping kosher. Suppose a group of Reconstructionist Jews, either a full congregation or a sub-group such as a study group within a congregation, wants to establish a position on *kashrut* because some members of the group have doubts about the continued relevance of traditional *kashrut* observance.

> Since the intuitions of the members of the group are in conflict with traditional observances, a process of revaluation is in order. That revaluation, in the case of a ritual practice, has two components – one intellectual and the other experiential. First, the group would want to seek out new meanings for the observance of *kashrut*. A list might include making our homes more Jewish, allowing anyone to eat in our homes, getting in touch with Jewish tradition, making eating something we do with more attention, becoming aware of *tza'ar ba'alei hayyim* (the traditional concern with the pain of living creatures), and supporting the kosher food industry so that Jews who choose to keep kosher can do so. They would want to experiment

with keeping kosher, perhaps cooking kosher meals together or eating out in a restaurant and ordering only 'kosher' items,* or learning how to make their dishes and utensils kosher, or buying a kosher cookbook and making special meals.

Members of the group might find that they differ over which meanings enhance their personal practice, depending on individual perspectives, circumstances and background. The *experience* of keeping kosher itself is likely to affect each member's views of the practice in unanticipated ways. The meaning and significance of a ritual observance cannot always be reduced to a clearly articulated value. Rituals have subliminal power that condition one's outlook, so that sometimes the original reason for taking on a particular practice proves not to be the most important one. This is part of what we mean when we say that Judaism is a *civilization*, and that Jews who immerse themselves in that civilization are transformed by it.

Eventually, some members of the group might choose to keep some portions of the traditions of *kashrut*, as opposed to attempting to take on all of them. They might, for example, become vegetarians or observe an eco-*kashrut*, in which they eat foods based upon their impact on the

---

* This approach is often called 'kosher style,' where food items are not established as kosher in the traditional sense because they lack proper preparation – such as ritual slaughtering in the case of meats – rabbinical supervision, or a *kashrut hekhsher* (kosher certification). Rather, they are items that could be potentially kosher if properly prepared and supervised. Food like pork products and shellfish, which can never be kosher according to the halacha, can't be kosher style either.

environment; both of these are completely compatible with traditional *kashrut*. They might eat only special foods but not have special dishes, keep kosher only in the home, choose specific foods from which to refrain, or buy only kosher meat. Their initial choices will not be irrevocable; their *kashrut* practice is likely to continue to change as part of the dynamic processes of their lives. For some, *kashrut* may become a central component of their Jewish identities, sanctifying their tables and leading to a greater appreciation of their blessings. Others may find that, for a variety of reasons, *kashrut* never resonates with any power. Still others may decide to adopt a form of "*kashrut*" that is unrelated to traditional observance. For all of them, engaging in this experiment with the experience of traditional *kashrut* will have enriched their appreciation of the Jewish heritage.

In addition, the group might decide that, apart from variations in personal observance of *kashrut*, the synagogue ought to serve as a repository for more traditional practice, and that *kashrut* should be observed in the communal kitchen. In point of fact, all Reconstructionist groups that own their own kitchens have decided to keep them kosher. They take the category of *kashrut* seriously and formulate a communal *kashrut* policy.[7]

In the Reconstructionist observance of *kashrut*, we care not only about *what* we eat but *how* we eat. We seek to cultivate an awareness of our blessings, utilizing *berakhot* (traditional blessings) that sanctify the meal and slow us down to appreciate our bounty and notice its tastes and textures. We recite the *Birkat Hamazon* after the meal to express our thanks, and there are many different forms of these blessings that Reconstructionists have created to do so. Eating is a religious act, and it is also a political act, especially in today's consumer economy. We seek to take responsibility to distinguish between our wants and needs, to care about what is healthful for us as individuals and for the world as a whole.

As we do so, *kashrut* links us with our ancestors' transformation of the table into a sacred altar. Their blessings infuse our consciousness. As we adopt their customs, we are linked to them, reminded of their values. And to their concerns, we add our own.[8]

When last surveyed, 35% of Reconstructionists asserted that they observe *kashrut*, and that they are more ritually observant than their parents were. According to the Reconstructionist program, this is information to applaud. The fact that a significant percentage of Reconstructionists are choosing to keep kosher is evidence that a democratic, non-coercive process is effective. We seek to create communities in which members come to lead ever more intensive and meaningful Jewish lives – lives that are enriched by study, ethical practice and ritual observance. We do not, however, expect each Jew to find the identical path to this goal. The goal is engagement, involvement, and enrichment. It is not uniform belief or practice.⁹

A large percentage of Reconstructionists observe *Shabbat* in some meaningful way. The acknowledged goal is 25 hours of prayer, study, feasting, and rest each *Shabbat*, but few start there. Most begin with a special Friday night *Shabbat* meal with *kiddush*, *motzi* (blessing over the challah), and traditional Jewish foods. Over time many add *Shabbat* songs (*zmirot*), both traditional and contemporary, to the meal, along with *birkat hamazon*.

Shabbat morning is a busy time in Reconstructionist synagogues. The sanctuary is almost always packed. The *Shabbat* service is traditional, but without references to the traditional tenets that Reconstructionists don't accept, such as Jews as the chosen people and the Torah as a the Divinely scribed document that they received at Mount Sinai. Thus, for example, when individuals make the blessing upon being called to the Torah, they generally omit the phrase *asher bachar banu mekol ha-amim* (who has chosen us from among all the nations). Some traditionalists within the congregation still prefer to include this, and that is acceptable. Often, the Torah reader does not read directly from the Torah scroll. Instead, he or she reads the words of the Torah from a *chumash* (book version of the text of the Torah) that includes the vowels for the words as well as their cantillation notes, neither of which appears in the Torah scroll. The person called to the Torah follows the reading in the Torah scroll, running a *yad* (traditional silver pointer) along the lines of text.

On *Shabbat*, Reconstructionist congregations omit the *Musaf* (additional) prayer service that follows the Torah reading in more traditional synagogues. There are two reasons for this omission. First, Reconstructionists do not yearn for the day when animal sacrifices will again be brought to the altar of the Temple in Jerusalem, which is the main content of *Musaf*. Second, and related, is that without these references, the service comes close to repeating the morning prayer service (*Shacharit*) that comes before the Torah reading.

A Reconstructionist *Shabbat* morning service often has the feel of a town hall meeting. Should the rabbi, or a designated lay member of the congregation, make a point about the service, members feel free to stand and comment. Often, a real discussion takes place. The same is true during the announcements at the conclusion of the service (which cover subjects like births, deaths, and upcoming programming). In many congregations, instead of one person presenting them from the front of the sanctuary, the individuals to whom they are relevant stand and make them known. From start to finish, the *Shabbat* morning service feels like a democratic event.

Following services, the congregation enjoys *kiddush*, which some congregants use as *Shabbat* lunch. Following *kiddush*, congregants might get together in groups or with immediate family for *Shabbat* lunch. Others visit with friends, and still others do various activities, such as visiting a park or museum. The point in all cases is to make the day feel distinct from a regular workday. In the evening, some families make *Havdalah* to mark the end of *Shabbat*.

Reconstructionist congregations often have excellent religious schools. These provide instruction several evenings a week and on Sundays, and teach a broad range of Judaic studies, although not the *Talmud*. Their Hebrew curriculum is particularly strong. As a result, children attending these schools are very well educated in Judaic studies and are quite literate in Hebrew.

Years ago, I heard a story that brings out how

Reconstructionists think carefully before imposing a decision on a minority. By a one-vote majority, a Reconstructionist congregation decided to require boys to wear *kippot* in the congregation's religious school. As a result of the close vote, the group agreed to engage in further discussion before implementing the change.

Ethical behavior is a main tenet of Reconstructionist Judaism, but,

> [not] through pious pronouncements from the pulpit about ethical obligations, demanding that members be honest in their work lives or faithful in their relationships. These have no compelling power in North America, where no Jew is *forced* to join a synagogue and so no rabbinic exhortation has commanding authority. Rather, the Reconstructionist approach is based on the belief that values are acquired through acculturation – when individuals are members of communities that play central roles in their lives, that embody the values that are to be conveyed, and that encourage members to study Jewish texts together as they explore what is right and wrong in specific circumstances.

> Thus, the Reconstructionist Rabbinical College's Center for Jewish Ethics publishes materials for people interested in studying classical Jewish texts on the Ethics of Speech or Biomedical Ethics …, for example, in order to learn what Jews in the past have taught. Studying the voices of the past allows us to deepen and refine our questions, to benefit from the wisdom and insights of our

ancestors, and to confront together the ways in which we do and don't share our ancestors' values. Above all, such study gives Jews access to sources from which they are otherwise cut off. Group discussions promote a climate in communities in which people become aware of the possibilities for guidance when they confront difficult and painful choices. What do I owe the business associate who is acting unscrupulously? How do I confront the community member who is acting hurtfully to me? … When is it acceptable to direct the hospital staff not to resuscitate my parent? Jewish sources have much to say on all these matters.

Reconstructionists believe that the very future of Jewish communities depends on our members' belief that our traditions can offer serious guidance for our ethical dilemmas. If the Jewish community is *only* an institution where I can belong, celebrate, and worship, but is *not* the place to which I turn when I have excruciating choices to make, then it is really a leisure-time social club that I choose to attend when it is convenient. Jewish civilization will flourish if and only if Jewish people find it an essential and invaluable source of wisdom and direction.

But if Reconstructionists don't view texts and traditions as authoritative, how can we be guided by them? Through the working of the community. Reconstructionist communities seek to counter the cultural bias in North America that places a supreme value on individualism, personal autonomy, and privacy. It is not the case that a person's ethical behavior is nobody else's business. If Judaism is a civilization, then how you conduct your business, how you treat or mistreat other people, and how much you contribute your time and money to community building and social action *matter as much* as how much you pray.[10]

Reconstructionist communities work hard to be inclusive. Here are some examples:

- Giving women full and equal rights in all synagogue rituals and activities.
- Accepting as Jews individuals whose only Jewish parent is the father, provided the individual was raised as a Jew.
- Welcoming interfaith couples into the community. While conversion of the non-Jewish partner is preferable, it is not mandatory. The hope is that in time, it will happen. Some Reconstructionist rabbis will officiate at inter-faith marriage ceremonies, most will not. But all are supportive of the couple and their community participation.
- Fully including Jews with disabilities in the community.
- Fully supporting LGBTQ+ individuals and same sex couples as members in the community.

Because the Reconstructionist movement is relatively small compared to the other streams of Judaism, there is not much information available about its members. For example, the 2013 and 2020 Pew Studies do not provide data on Reconstructionists' beliefs, priorities, or practices. Nevertheless, it is evident that the movement follows a clear and consistent philosophy and in so doing, is able to attract dedicated members who belong to thriving congregations that are cohesive communities.

The Reconstructionist movement views hastening the Messianic age as a behavioral goal of Jewish civilization rather than as a reward from God for the performance of Torah commandments. In their view, because man is the only known being with the ability to alter its conduct, it is up to man to behave in a way that improves the world so that evil behaviors and their consequences cease. And it is up to Jews to take the lead in bringing this result. Under Reconstructionist theology, attaining this state will bring the Messianic age, without any supernatural intervention.

Chapter Five

THE RICH LIFE AND TRADITIONS OF SEPHARDIC JEWS

W\HEN WE REFER to Sephardic Jewry today, we include non-Ashkenazi Jews of many origins, in addition to the Jews who migrated from the Holy Land to the Iberian Peninsula, as described below. This broader Sephardic world includes Jews from the former Ottoman Empire, Persia, Greece, and Western Europe, who speak a variety of languages such as Farsi, Judeo-Greek, Judeo Arabic, and Judeo-Turkish.

For example, many think of the members of the Persian Jewish community as part of the Sephardic Jewish movement, although they did not emigrate from Spain to their present countries of residence. Jews came to Persia after the destruction of the First Temple in Jerusalem in the sixth century B.C.E. When, in 538 B.C.E., King Cyrus of Persia issued an edict permitting the Jews to return to Judea, many chose to stay in Persia. Most of their descendants remained there until the establishment of the modern State of Israel in 1948. At that point, most Persian Jews immigrated to North

America and Israel, as living conditions in Persia, now Iran, became more difficult. Unlike the Sephardic Jews who speak Judeo-Spanish languages such as Ladino, many Persian Jews have Farsi, the traditional language of Persia, as their mother tongue.

What Sephardic and Persian Jews have in common is the fact that their communities maintained many of the traditions that they brought from the ancient land of Israel, influenced not by the evolving traditions of the Ashkenazi Jewish world, but instead by the cultures around them. This has affected their customs, outlooks, and religious practices.

The classic Sephardic Jewish community originated from a series of Jewish migrations to the Iberian Peninsula, now Spain. The precise history of the earliest Jewish migration to the area is not known, but Sephardic tradition contains stories that date early migrations to the traveling Phoenician merchants in the 10th century B.C.E. – the time of King Solomon's reign – as well as stories of migrations after the destruction of the First Temple in Jerusalem in the sixth century B.C.E. According to most historians, Jews first came to Spain with the conquering Roman legions. But the largest migration of Jews to Spain happened after the Romans destroyed the Second Temple in Jerusalem in 70 C.E. Historians believe that soon after this destruction, the majority of all Jews lived in Spain; by the 11th century, the Jews of Spain made up 90% of the world's Jewish population. This percentage declined rapidly thereafter, both because of the rapid growth of Ashkenazi Jewry and as a result of the Spanish Inquisition.

The life and history of these Sephardic Jews was significantly different from the experiences of the Jews who settled in other parts of Europe and came to make up the Ashkenazi Jewish communities. Sephardic Jews rose to prominence in, among other fields, commerce, medicine, politics, and science.

They tended to settle in mercantile areas such as port cities, although there were Jewish peasants living in smaller villages. Sephardic Jews wore the dress of their Spanish neighbors, which helped them to fit in with the general population.

During the period of the Roman Empire, the Spanish rulers treated the Sephardic Jews very well, which probably led many diaspora Jews of that era to settle there. This period ended when the Visigoths invaded Spain in 409 C.E. These Germanic Christians were intolerant of non-Christians. In 638 C.E., the monarch declared that non-Catholics no longer had the right to live in Spain but did not enforce this rule strictly. Still, Jews and other minorities suffered, and many were killed in mass murders throughout the country.

The end of this dark period came in 711 C.E., when the Moors – Moslems from Morocco – invaded Spain. This led to an extended era of greater tolerance and prosperity for Sephardic Jews. The years from roughly 900 to 1100 C.E. are known as the "Sephardic Golden Age." This period included several civilization-enhancing developments. The Jews both contributed to this progress and benefited from it. Here are some examples:

- The first manufacture of paper, greatly facilitating the publication of books and the growth of voluminous public libraries.
- The introduction of Arabic numerals, facilitating financial and mathematical calculations that had been cumbersome to do using Roman numerals.
- The development of the principles underlying both algebra and trigonometry.
- The translation of Greek philosophy into Hebrew, Arabic, and Latin, paving the way for the European Renaissance.

- The creation of a system of printed vowels for the Hebrew language, making it easier to learn and read Hebrew.
- The proliferation of poetry, the arts, and scholarship.
- The rapid growth of global travel and trade under the leadership of Jewish businesses.

The region produced its leading Jewish scholars between 1086 and 1248. Chief among these were:

- Sholmo ibn Gabirol (1021-1058). Gabirol was a renowned poet and philosopher. His poetry took two main forms: poems in praise of God and love poems. A popular anthology of love poetry includes the English translations of one of his best-known love poems, *For a Marriage*, as well as one of his spiritual poems, *The Love of God*.[1] Scholars also credit him with having written the 37th Lamentation, *O Zion*, which is a part of the mournful readings on the morning of *Tisha B'Av*. Gabirol's main philosophical publication was *Fons Vitae* (Fountain of Life), a secular work on which later philosophers, including Thomas Aquinas, drew heavily, although it did not gain acceptance in the religious Jewish community.

- Yehudah HaLevi (1075-1141). HaLevi was a prominent scholar during a difficult period for Sephardic Jews. He lived most of his life dodging the persecution of both the indigenous Christians who were rebelling against Moslem rule, and the invading Crusaders. His major work was *The Kuzari*, a religious philosophical book, written in Arabic, that explained the struggles of Jewish life in his time through a story about the

Khazars at the end of the eighth century who experienced similar religious struggles.

The Khazar king decided to interview three scholars, one Christian, one Moslem, and one Jew, to determine which of the three monotheistic religions was most authentic. After carefully undertaking this exercise, the king proclaimed Judaism as the true religion and adopted it for himself and his entire kingdom. In the process of questioning the Jewish scholar, the king expressed his displeasure with the disconnect between the Jewish love for The Holy Land that Jewish prayers express and the reality that individual Jews opt for the financial benefits and creature comforts of living in exile over moving there. The king was so persuasive on this point that the Jewish scholar decided to uproot himself from his home in exile and move to the Holy Land.[2]

HaLevi also authored the 36th Lamentation, *Oh Zion, Will You Not Inquire*, reflecting his own "life-long yearning to flee from the exile and to walk on the sacred soil of the Holy Land." Ultimately, he left Spain to move there, though it is uncertain whether he arrived. Historians believe that he only got as far as Egypt, while tradition holds that he reached Jerusalem, where an Arab horseman trampled and killed him, as he was kissing the ground near the Temple Mount.[3]

- Moses ibn Ezra (c. 1055-1155). Moses ibn Ezra was one of the great poets of his era, writing mostly liturgical, penitential poetry, although his early poetry was a celebration of life, especially love, wine, and nature. He was also a master of poetic form and style, whose technique set the stage for much Medieval Jewish liturgical poetry. His *Selichot* (penitential poems that many congregations, both Ashkenazi and Sephardi recite from the days before *Rosh Hashana* through *Yom Kippur*, and on other specified days throughout the year) are among his best works. He lived a troubled life, wandering around Christian Spain, which he abhorred.

- Abraham ibn Ezra (from approximately 1090 to the mid-1160s). By any measure, Abraham ibn Ezra was a genius. He had deep knowledge of science and mathematics, and he authored incisive commentaries on the *Tanach* (a Hebrew acronym for the Torah, Prophets, and other Holy writings), as well as several works on science, Jewish mysticism, and philosophy. He spent over three decades traveling around Europe and the Middle East, although many Jewish communities would have been thrilled to have him stay as their rabbinic leader.

- Moses Maimonides (1135-1204). Maimonides, also known as the *Rambam* (an acronym for his Hebrew name, Rav Moshe ben Maimon), was born in Spain but lived most of his life in Egypt, serving as the Sultan's physician and writing prolifically on Jewish subjects. Some believe that if *Rashi* (Rav Shlomo Yitzchaki, 1040 - 1105, who lived in France) was the greatest Medieval Jewish scholar, contributing to the understanding of Biblical and Talmudic texts, *Rambam* was the greatest mind of that era, based on his works on Jewish philosophy and theology as well as his authorship of the first Code of Jewish Law, the *Mishneh Torah* (often called *Yad Chazakah*, literally a "strong hand"). He wrote this work in order to preserve the rules of Jewish religious practices that he feared would be lost in the difficult times through which he was living, and to make them accessible to a wide audience that did not have access to the Talmud or the expertise to interpret it. His best-known philosophical work is *The Guide for the Perplexed*, which advocated for a rational approach to Judaism as completely compatible with belief in God. He also authored *The Thirteen Principles of Faith*, which express the theological tenets of Orthodox Judaism.[*,4]

Historians generally mark the end of the Golden Age at about 1100 C.E., when the Christians began the reconquest of Spain. It took them some 800 years. As they gained control, the Christians made life increasingly difficult for Sephardic Jews. As the 15th century approached, antisemitism exploded throughout Spain. Roving mobs burned synagogues and killed thousands of Jews. The ensuing years saw hundreds of thousands of Jews forced to convert to Christianity or murdered. Those who survived did so by going into hiding and practicing Judaism in secret. It was a horrific time for Jews throughout all of Western Europe, but especially for the Jews of Spain. In 1480, the Spanish rulers, Ferdinand and Isabella, ordered all Jews to live in ghettos, where they would have no contact with Christians. In 1478, they established the Spanish Inquisition, which led to the Alhambra decree on March 31, 1492, ordering all Jews to leave the country by July 31 of that year.

Many of those who fled settled in the lands of the Ottoman Empire, which treated them rather well, permitting

---

[*] See Chapter One, which discusses *The Thirteen Principles of Faith* at length.

them to practice Judaism. There, they were largely absorbed into the local Ottoman Jewish communities. Many of the Sephardic customs and traditions that exist today evolved in these Mediterranean Sephardic communities. Other Spanish Jews moved to the Netherlands, Germany, and the Americas. It was during this period that Eastern Europe began to emerge as the epicenter of Jewish life.

The Mediterranean Sephardic Jews continued to live in port cities, where they became merchants, bankers, and professionals, unlike the peasants who settled in the small villages of Eastern Europe. Sephardic Jews adopted the dress styles of their host countries, as well as the local cuisine. Instead of the *Yiddish* of Ashkenazi Jews, they spoke Judeo-Spanish languages, of which Ladino is best known, as well as Judeo-Arabic languages. Their music was also different, focusing on romantic stories, in contrast to the klezmer dance music of Eastern Europe.

Greater differences would emerge in the late 1700s, as the Emancipation swept through Western and Central Europe, and the Enlightenment began to affect all of Europe, ultimately leading to the establishment of the Reform and Conservative movements in the Ashkenazi Jewish world. The Sephardic communities were mostly insulated from these changes. As a result, differences in Sephardic religious practices among communities, families, or individuals have not given rise to separate Jewish movements.[5]

Today, there are large Sephardic Jewish communities in both North America and Israel. In Israel, Sephardic Jews make up the majority of the Jewish population. Sephardic Jews closely identify with each other based on their post-Spain communities (e.g., Algerian, Egyptian, Iraqi, Moroccan, Syrian, Tunisian, and Yemenite). Many people from these communities still live close together and maintain their familiar synagogues, cultures, customs, and cuisines.

The two greatest Halachic authorities on Jewish religious law and practice for Sephardic Jews were the *Rambam* and Rav Yosef Karo (1488-1575), a Spanish Jew who immigrated to the town of Safed in Ottoman Galilee, now Israel, in about 1535. He is best known as the author of the *Shulchan Aruch* (Code of Jewish Law, literally translated as the "Arranged Table") published in 1565. Karo intended the *Shulchan Aruch* to be the definitive Code of Jewish Law, resolving conflicts among the previous post-Biblical halachic sources. For the Sephardic Jewish community, the *Shulchan Aruch*, along with Karo's *Beit Yosef* (the longer codification of Jewish law on which the *Shulchan Aruch* is based), continues to be the definitive authority on Jewish religious law and practice, often to the exclusion of later Ashkenazi authorities such as the Vilna Gaon, and the Chofetz Chaim.*,6

Rabbi Ovadia Yosef (1920-2013) was an Iraqi Jew whose family moved to Jerusalem in 1924. He became the Chief Sephardic Rabbi of Tel Aviv in 1968 and the Chief Sephardic Rabbi of Israel in 1973.† He believed that because Yosef Karo was the leading post-Talmudic rabbinic authority of the Holy Land, Karo's *Shulchan Aruch* should be the highest authority on Jewish Law and religious practice, to the exclusion of the works of Ashkenazi *poskim* (rabbinic legal authorities). Using this position as a springboard, Yosef unified religious practices and traditions across much of Israel. His called his efforts in this regard "restoring the crown to its former glory." By this he meant that he was returning Sephardic Jewry to its religious past when the broader Sephardic population accepted the *Shuchan Aruch* and the *Beit Yosef* over other halachic works and followed their prescribed practices. His efforts bore significant fruit.

Rabbi Ovadia Yosef later became the official leader of

---

* Chapter One discusses these distinguished Ashkenazi authorities.
† To this day, there are separate Sephardic and Ashkenazi Chief Rabbis in Israel.

the Shas political party in Israel, representing the religious Sephardic community – a position he accepted in order to increase the number of Torah-observant Jews in Israel and to create institutions that would support the observance of Torah and *mitzvot* in Israel, including founding or improving Jewish educational opportunities for Sephardic youth. In the process, he dramatically elevated the status of Sephardic Jews in Israel, as well as their level of religious observance, although this still varies by individual and community.[7]

Sephardic Jews in America also have a range of halachic observance. Most Sephardic Jews are very traditional, with lifestyles that typically include daily individual prayer and observing the laws of family purity. There is no recent published data on their overall level of *Shabbat* observance. Anecdotal data indicate that its extent varies considerably among families and individuals. While American Sephardic Jews overwhelmingly enjoy a traditional *Shabbat* dinner on Friday nights, they are less likely to observe the rest of *Shabbat*. A considerable number of Sephardic Jews attend *Shabbat* morning synagogue services and eat *Shabbat* lunch. Far fewer strictly observe the technical laws of *Shabbat* such as not conducting business affairs and avoiding recreational activities like golf, swimming, or tennis.

With respect to *kashrut*, American Sephardic Jews' individual practices also vary considerably. Anecdotal data indicate that most American Sephardic Jews keep kosher homes but with differences in their level of strictness. Outside of their homes, some Sephardic Jews will only eat in kosher restaurants, while others will eat dairy but not meat in non-kosher restaurants. Others will eat all food, except pork products and shellfish, in non-kosher restaurants, and still others will eat all foods in non-kosher restaurants.

Sephardic Jews in America and Israel begin *Shabbat* with a

festive Friday night dinner in which the extended family participates. This is a special time for Sephardic Jews, when the spirit of *Shabbat* permeates their lives in a tangible and memorable way. Guests at a Sephardic *Shabbat* table can sense the distinctiveness of the evening, with its connection to tradition and to *Hashem*'s cessation of creation.

Sephardic communities have some famous *Shabbat* culinary traditions. After *kiddush*, the meal begins with traditional dips and salads served with *challah* and pita. In some Sephardic traditions, this course includes a fish in sauce. Many of the appetizers have a Middle Eastern origin that reflects Israeli cuisine today. Next come meat appetizers of ground beef or lamb wrapped in phyllo dough and seasoned with Middle Eastern or North African spices. Sometimes, the meats are served on top of dough as in the case of *lachmagine*, where the meat covers a small, circular crust, much like the topping on a pizza.

A Middle Eastern- or North African-style soup often follows the first course. Then comes the main course, which often includes several chicken or meat dishes, and rice or other traditional grains such couscous or tabouleh. Dessert, usually a variety of baked goods reflecting Sephardic tradition, ends the meal.[8]

Unlike Ashkenazi Jews, American Sephardic Jews do not label each other by their level of observance as Orthodox, Conservative, etc. In fact, they are extremely respectful of each other's choices in this area. They therefore serve as a model for accepting each other's religious differences rather than using these disparities as a reason for *Sinat Chinam*, as too often occurs among Ashkenazi Jews.

In Israel, the political tension between the religious right and the secular Jewish population, including secular Sephardic Jews, has reached a crisis level. This development has created *Sinat Chinam* between religious Jews and secular Jews, including secular Sephardic Jews.

Part Two

A FRAMEWORK FOR *ACHDUT*

Chapter Six

OVERVIEW

LET'S BRIEFLY LOOK at the origins of the barriers to achieving *achdut* across the different movements of *Klal Yisrael*. Following the revelation at Mount Sinai until the fall of the First Temple in the sixth century B.C.E., there was only one stream of Judaism, requiring all of *Klal Yisrael* to keep the laws of the Torah. Fixed prayer as we know it today did not exist, and the focus of community observance was on the *Avodah* (rituals, including animal and grain sacrifices, lighting the Menorah, and baking and displaying the shew bread) in the Temple. Jews were to contribute agricultural tithes to Priests and Levites who performed the Temple rituals. They were also to visit the Temple on each of the three pilgrimage festivals of *Pesach, Shavuot* and *Sukkot*. Many also chose to come to the Temple to observe the dramatic *Avodah* of Yom Kippur.*

After the First Temple fell to the Babylonians, the observance of this pure form of Torah Judaism was no longer possible. What replaced it was what we now call "Rabbinical

---

* In all, there are 613 *mitzvot* in the Torah. A good number of these *mitzvot* cannot be performed today because they are tied to the existence of the Temple in Jerusalem.

Judaism," which consisted of daily communal and individual prayer services that took the place of ritual sacrifices. As Jews began to migrate to different parts of the world, differences in prayer liturgy emerged, but the basic format – the order of the prayers and the number of blessings recited – changed very little. Despite its varying regional forms, all of *Klal Yisrael* were what we today call "Orthodox Jews," whether or not particular individuals actually fulfilled most of the required *mitzvot*, although the term "Orthodox" did not yet exist.

At different times in the history of Rabbinic Judaism, there were groups of Jews who insisted that the only valid *mitzvot* were those commanded according to the words of the written Torah and that, therefore, the Oral Law, including rabbinical interpretations and decrees, could not be considered valid halacha. The most prominent examples of these groups were the *Sadducees* who lived from the second century B.C.E. until the destruction of the Second Temple in 70 C.E.; the *Essenes* (often referred to as the "Dead Sea sect") who lived from the second century B.C.E. to the first century C.E.; and the Karaites, who were most prominent in the Moslem world from about 900 to about 1100 C.E. Nevertheless, Rabbinical Judaism remained reasonably consistent until the 1770s, when the *Haskalah* led to the development of Reform and Conservative Judaism in the Ashkenazi world.

Before the *Haskalah*, Ashkenazi rabbinic authorities generally had civil authority over their Jewish communities. This let them enforce halacha. That changed with the *Haskalah*, a product of the Emancipation that allowed Central European Jews to participate as citizens or quasi-citizens of their countries of residency, and who were therefore subject to secular civil law. This, for the first time, enabled the establishment of non-Orthodox movements, which asserted that their evolving theologies represented valid progressions within Rabbinic

Judaism, consistent with modern times. Although the Emancipation did not extend to Eastern Europe, the expectation that it would in the near future enabled the *Haskalah* to have a strong influence even in that region.

Jews who, under the influence of the *Haskalah*, abandoned their adherence to traditional Jewish beliefs and practices became known as *Maskilim*. Traditional Ashkenazi rabbinic leadership, both Yeshivish* and Chassidic, fiercely opposed the *Haskalah* and the *Maskilim*. The effort to prevent this new movement from expanding dominated the agenda of the Ashkenazi rabbinic leadership from the beginning of the *Haskalah* until the Holocaust. The leaders of the *Haskalah*, in turn, were determined to reform Judaism so as to make it relevant to the modern world as they perceived it. They had a vision of the Emancipation and the Enlightenment extending throughout all of Europe, and saw a bright future for Jews as successful, prosperous citizens of modern European society. In their eyes, the traditional rabbinic leadership was stuck in the Middle Ages. Ironically, neither group was, particularly Zionist. The traditional rabbinate believed that the return of *Klal Yisrael* to Israel would have to await the coming of *Moshiach*, while the *Maskilim* believed that the Jewish future was in Europe and America.

In time, the *Haskalah* led to multiple streams within Ashkenazi Jewry, including the Reform movement; the Conservative movement, established in reaction to Reform's dramatic break with tradition; and the Modern Orthodox sub-stream, which developed as a way to allow Jews to embrace halacha fully, while also accepting the modern world. It also gave rise to the term "Orthodox" – the label that early Reform leaders used to describe what they considered an outmoded approach

---

* The term "Yeshivish" was not in use at the onset of the *Haskalah*. It is not clear when this term entered the Jewish lexicon. Originally, the term for non-Chassidic Orthodox Jews was "*Misnagdim*."

to Rabbinical Judaism, in contrast to their modern approach.

Our barriers to *achdut* today stem from these divisions. The reactions of the different Jewish movements, both at a leadership level and among individuals, to each other's religious practices are strained at best, despite occasional positive public pronouncements to the contrary. To the casual observer, it might seem that all Ashkenazi Jews accept diverse religious practices, but make no mistake, there are deep-seated, longstanding resentments among these groups.

Liberal Jews look at Orthodox Jews as adhering to an antiquated, overly restrictive set of beliefs and practices that has no place in the modern world. Orthodox Jews see more liberal Jews as victims of a secular culture that is bereft of core Jewish values, and as belonging to religious movements that lack authenticity. Each believes that the others are delaying the arrival of the Messianic age, however one defines it.

This is precisely the problem that this book addresses. It would be unrealistic to think that different Jewish movements can be persuaded to accept each other's theologies. What they should be able to recognize, however, is that each movement, according to its aspirational principles, has objectives that, if achieved, would encourage its adherents to engage in greater observance of *mitzvot* and *middot*. Achieving this change in perspective would lead to greater respect among the different movements, which, in turn, would break the barrier of *Sinat Chinam* that has delayed the Messianic age for almost 2,000 years.

The novel framework that this book is proposing uses this principle. Imagine that each movement's objectives were paths on a gameboard. As the movement's adherents achieve specific objectives, they move along the path from left to right.* When adherents abandon objectives, they move backwards from right to left. On the far-right side of the board is the Messianic age. When enough individuals get to that part of the board, we will achieve the Messianic age – i.e., win the game. This is different from a typical board game in several respects:

- While the concept of a gameboard is helpful for understanding the framework, there is no tangible gameboard. Like God, these paths on the gameboard cannot be measured in either space or time.
- There are no dice and there is no spinner. Each Jew advances along a chosen path based on how that Jew lives.
- There is no competition among Jews. We are all playing together to achieve a single objective. Even the players are not fixed. New players will be born, and players will die between now and the Messianic age.

To visualize how this can work and to understand each movement's path, we need to look at the respective movements one by one and describe their objectives, so that each reader can decide whether achieving them would help to bring the Messianic age. The next several chapters provide this perspective.

---

* Using movement across the imaginary gameboard from *left to right* as the favorable direction is not intended to be an analogy for movement across the political spectrum from *left to right*. Rather, it mimics the format of charts in English, which read from left to right. If I had written this book in Hebrew, my analogy would have used *right to left* – the direction in which the Hebrew language is written and read.

Chapter Seven

STRENGTHENING ORTHODOX JUDAISM

AT FIRST BLUSH, outsiders might think that Orthodox Jews generally perceive themselves as far along their path, having mostly done their part to help bring the Messianic age, but this is not the case. In fact, most Orthodox Jews are quite concerned that they are not strict enough in certain areas of observance, and engage in serious self-reflection, penitence, and repentance (*teshuvah*) each year from the first day of the Hebrew month of *Elul*, which precedes *Rosh Hashana*, through *Yom Kippur*.

The Torah enumerates 613 *mitzvos* that Jews are to observe. This includes 248 positive *mitzvos* – specific commandments that the Torah requires them to do, like building a *succah* for *Succos* and eating *matzah* on *Pesach*. There are also 365 negative *mitzvos* – specific commandments not to do certain actions, such as cooking on *Shabbos* or eating leavened products on *Pesach*. Several *mitzvos* apply only in Israel, for example, not planting crops during the *shemitah* year (every seventh year). Many *mitzvos*, such as bringing *korbanos* (animal and grain offerings), can only be performed in the

Temple in Jerusalem, and hence Jews do not currently observe them. There are also numerous rabbinical *mitzvos*, designed to protect against the transgression of the Torah *mitzvos*. An example of these is the prohibition against carrying things in quasi-public places on *Shabbos*, unless these areas are specifically made permissible for carrying under a rabbinic procedure known as establishing an *eruv*.*

There are also *middos* (ethical commandments), in both the Torah and the Oral Law, such as not placing a stumbling block in front of a blind person.[1] The 613 *mitzvos* include or allude to many, but not all of these. These *middos* are extremely important, and observing ritual practices without also observing the *middos* is not acceptable. The fact that the second five of the Ten Commandments relate to prohibitions *ben adam l'chavero* (between fellow Jews) rather than between Jews and *Hashem* serves to emphasize this point. Since *the middos* are interpersonal, Orthodox Jews cannot atone for violating them through prayer. Instead, it is necessary first to seek forgiveness directly from the person whom one offended. Thus, it is common for Orthodox Jews to ask many of their acquaintances for forgiveness (*mechilah*) before *Yom Kippur*, in case they somehow offended them. For atonement for these transgressions to be effective, one must also have both a sincere intention to refrain from similar transgressions in the future and a plan for accomplishing this correction in the coming year.

Many *middos* have their source in *Vayikra* (Leviticus) Chapter 19, which begins: "HASHEM spoke to Moses, saying: Speak to the entire assembly of the Children of Israel and say to them: You shall be holy, for holy am I, HASHEM your God."[2]

---

* An *eruv* is a fence or wire that marks the perimeter of the community and has been properly designated as such under Jewish law. The requirements for permissible *eruvim* (plural for *eruv*) are not relevant to the topic of this book.

Rambam maintains that the concept of holiness is not limited to the observance of any particular category of commandments. Rather, it is an admonition that one's approach to all aspects of life be governed by moderation, particularly in the area of what is permitted. In Rambam's memorable phrase, someone who observes only the letter of the law can easily become… *a degenerate with the permissions of the* Torah, for such a person can observe technical requirements of the commandments while surrendering to self-indulgence, gluttony, and licentiousness. But God demands more of a Jew than obedience to the letter of the law. The commandment to be holy tells us, as the Sages put it… *Sanctify yourself in what is permitted to you* (*Yevamos* 20a),[3] by not refraining only from what is expressly forbidden, but from too much of what is permitted.[4] [ed.: Italics in original text.]

Here is a list of some of the other *middos* that are prominent in *Vayikra* Chapter 19:

- Not to steal
- Not to deny falsely
- Not to lie
- Not to swear falsely in God's name
- Not to cheat
- Not to rob
- Not to delay even a day before paying a worker his wage
- Not to curse the deaf
- Not to place a stumbling block in front of a blind person
- As a judge, not to commit a perversion of justice

- As a judge, not to favor the poor
- As a judge, not to honor the great
- To judge your fellow righteously
- Not to gossip
- Not to stand idly by while another's blood is shed
- Not to hate your brother in your heart
- To take care not to embarrass your fellow when reproving him
- Not to take revenge
- Not to bear grudges
- To love your fellow as you love yourself
- To use fair measures of length, weight, and volume[5]

It takes tremendous self-control to observe these *middos* because they run contrary to aspects of human nature. According to Jewish theology, we have within us a good inclination (*yetzer hatov*) and an evil inclination (*yetzer hara*). God gave us the important mission of repairing the world (*tikkun olam*) by overcoming our evil inclination, so that it is our good inclination that governs our words and deeds. This is not an easy task. One of the *middos* is not to gossip and to avoid negative speech about others (*lashon hara*) because of the damage it can inflict on them. One must work hard to accomplish this, because gossiping is intrinsic to our nature.

As I write this book, I am reminded of the portion from the Prophets, Isaiah 1:1-27, that we read publicly in our synagogues on the *Shabbos* before *Tisha B'Av* rebuking the Israelites for their poor *middos*, despite their meticulous performance of important *mitzvos* in the Temple. Here is a particularly poignant part of that passage:

> *Hear the word of HASHEM, O chiefs of Sodom;*
> *give ear to the* Torah *of our God, O people of*

> *Gomorrah. Why do I need your numerous sacrifices? – says HASHEM – I am satiated with elevation-offerings of rams and the choicest of fattened animals; and the blood of bulls and sheep and he-goats that I do not desire. When you come to appear before Me – who sought this from your hand, to trample My courtyards? You shall not continue to bring me a worthless meal-offering – incense of abomination is it unto Me; [New] Moon and Sabbath, calling of convocation, I cannot abide mendacity with assemblage. Your [New] Moons and your appointed festivals, My soul hates; they have become a burden upon Me [that] I am weary of bearing. And when you spread your hands [in prayer], I will hide MY eyes from you; even if you were to increase prayer, I do not hear; your hands are full of blood.* **Wash yourselves, purify yourselves, remove the evil of your doings from before My eyes; desist from doing evil. Learn to do good, seek justice, strengthen the victim, do justice for the orphan, take up the cause of the widow.**[6] [ed.: Italics in original text; bold added for emphasis.]

Properly observing all of the *mitzvos* and the *middos* is a tall order, in fact, perfection is not within reach. Even Moses, the most righteous of all Jews, fell short of that standard. Because of this, God denied him the privilege of leading the Israelites into the Land of Israel. Despite the difficulty, Orthodox Jews can, and must, work hard and hope to do much better than presently. This is what it will take to bring the Messianic age.

Let's return to our board game analogy. As we improve, we move across the board toward the Messianic age. Along the way, we never know our score, the value of our individual *mitzvot* or *middos*, or how much we lose when we fail to perform them properly. This doesn't matter because in our hearts we know whether we are progressing. Nor will our individual scores bring *Moshiach*. In order for *Moshiach* to arrive, all of *Klal Yisrael* needs to move across the board as a group by racking up a score only known to *Hashem*. Orthodox Jews can't get there alone, and they certainly won't get there by exhibiting poor *middos* toward the rest of *Klal Yisrael*, or to each other.

So, how will Orthodox Jews know whether they are making progress? The answer is: it will be obvious. When a community changes its ways, the changes are readily apparent. When it becomes visibly just and fair, and lives rigorously by Jewish values and *middos*, things will feel very different from the present situation. Imagine an end to gossip, *lashon harah*, lying, cheating, and jealousy.

Please don't ask what you might be thinking: *How can we ever get there if our counterparts in other movements are so far off the mark? Lashon hara* about Jews who adhere to other movements will only delay *Moshiach*. In fact, don't even think it! The next few chapters will discuss the path for each other movement.

The imperative that this book presents is for each Jew to move from criticism of Jews who adhere to other movements to understanding the different paths and recognizing that as they make progress across the imaginary board, *Klal Yisrael* moves closer to the arrival of *Moshiach*.

Chapter Eight

CAN CONSERVATIVE JUDAISM SURVIVE?

*E*MET *VE-EMUNAH*[1] SETS forth the Conservative movement's statement of guiding principles. "The Sacred Cluster"[2] embellishes *Emet Ve-Emunah* by discussing the movement's values. Chapter Two: Conservative Judaism presented both of these publications in detail. I indicated that these documents are aspirational statements describing how a Conservative Jew should live. I presented data from the 2013 and 2020 Pew Studies showing a significant gap between the standards of these publications and the practices of most Conservative Jews. I also noted that the practices of the JTS faculty are very much in line with the movement's aspirations. The same is true of the movement's pulpit rabbinate.

The final section of *Emet Ve-Emunah* presents a clear description of the Conservative Jew who attains the aspirations that these documents prescribe.[3] I quoted this section in full in Chapter Two, and summarize it here, in outline form, for ease of discussion:

- Being "a *willing* Jew" includes
    o a "commitment to observe the *mitzvot*"
    o a "commitment… to advance Jewish concerns"

- a life pulsating "with the rhythms of daily worship"
- a life imbued "with the rhythms of… *Shabbat*"
- a life filled "with the rhythms of… *Yom Tov*"
- "Universal concern and deeds of social justice"
- "The content of… professional dealings… is shaped by the values of our faith and conditioned by observance of *kashrut*, of *Shabbat* and the holidays"
- "The content of communal involvements is shaped by the values of our faith and conditioned by observance of *kashrut*, of *Shabbat* and the holidays"
- "the home is filled with Jewish books, art, music and ritual objects"
- "the home is sustained and guided by the ethical insights of our heritage"

- Being a "*learning* Jew" involves
  - being able to read Hebrew, participate in worship, and benefit from our literary heritage
  - having knowledge of classic Jewish texts and being "affected by their message"
  - being acquainted "with contemporary Jewish thought and events"
  - Engaging in lifelong Jewish learning "for the sake of personal enrichment, group creativity and world transformation"

- Being a *striving* Jew means
  - being open "to those observances" not already part of your life
  - Desiring "to grapple with those issues and texts" not yet explored
  - Being a "traveler walking purposefully towards 'God's holy mountain.'"

Unquestionably, these are lofty goals. They reflect the practices of the Seminary and the Conservative rabbinate, but not those of most Conservative Jews. The degree of effort that pulpit rabbis have made to close the gap between the practices of their congregants and these aspirational standards varies. While there has been some progress toward this objective, the 2013 and 2020 Pew Studies clearly show that the gap is not closing.

The Conservative movement is at a crossroads. For decades, it has prospered because of its traditional appeal coupled with a tacit acceptance of the fact that its adherents overwhelmingly fall well short of the movement's official aspirations. From a membership growth perspective, this tactic was successful. Now, however, as membership is declining (see Chapter Two), it is clear that this approach, which had its limitations from a theological practice perspective, can no longer sustain the movement's vitality, and perhaps even its continuity.

Probably the movement's best way forward would be for it to encourage its adherents to embrace the concept of *The Ideal Conservative Jew* – a concept about which, as I understand from my discussions with Conservative pulpit rabbis, most adherents barely know. This approach would be consistent with Conservative theology and with the practices of the Seminary and the Conservative rabbinate. It would reflect the values of the movement's founders, who felt strongly about making tradition and halacha Conservative cornerstones, while taking into account modern academic approaches toward interpreting historical texts to derive practices that resonate with our world without arbitrarily rejecting millennia of Jewish tradition and scholarship. However, asking Conservative Jews who do not presently reflect the standards of *Emet Ve-Emunah* in their practices to move in this direction could be difficult; many might resent strong efforts to change their longstanding approach to religious life.

This alternative would require the Conservative movement to invest considerably in *kiruv* efforts, working closely with its members and potential members to bring their practices more in line with the principles of *Emet Ve-Emunah*. This could be complicated, however, as it involves asking prospective members to follow practices to which many members of the congregation do not adhere.

Perhaps the best approach with respect to existing congregants would be to direct a substantial portion of programming to gentle *kiruv* education and participation. This would be most effective if it included the participation of those existing members of the congregation whose practices already align with the movement's principles. Opening their homes to others in a community-building way could generate a positive response. Nothing brings Jews together more than sharing practices like *Shabbat* in a home environment. But this needs to be lived, not just preached, and it needs to be sustained.

Another key *kiruv* element could be increasing attendance at Conservative Jewish day schools and enhancing the schools' *curricula* in the direction of *kiruv* by adding *Emet Ve-Emunah* and the study of Conservative principles. This, combined with encouraging school and synagogue families to host in-home *Shabbat* events, could have a notable impact on the youth of Conservative families. It will not be cheap. It is expensive to build new schools, or even to add new attendees to existing schools, but the results could be dramatic.

Camp Ramah has always been a major asset of the Conservative movement. Now, more than ever, the movement needs to expand its appeal and accessibility to a larger number of families, and to extend the camp experience beyond the summer months with programming throughout the year that will reinforce the powerful exposures to Jewish practice that Camp Ramah provides. This too will cost money, but the results would be well worth the price. Perhaps a good model is the Taglit Birthright approach, which provides free trips to Israel to first-time visitors and to select others. A highly subsidized initial summer at Camp Ramah would go a long way toward developing a new generation of Conservative Jews.

To support these initiatives, the Conservative movement would need to give its pulpit rabbis new resources to help orchestrate change and increase community participation. The United Synagogue of Conservative Judaism would have to lead this effort both financially and through strong advocacy.

At the same time, the Rabbinical School at the Seminary would need to emphasize the new roadmap to its students, which would require it to modify the type of preparation that it offers. This would be a big departure from the historically scholarly approach that the Seminary has taken toward training future pulpit rabbis.

All of these initiatives would require the Conservative movement to re-brand itself in a way that compellingly synthesizes past, present, and future. And it would need the movement to recognize this as a 20-year program of change whose full achievement could take at least two generations.

I have just presented a possible direction that the Conservative movement could take to counter its decline in membership and define its path toward helping to bring the Messianic age. But it is the movement's leadership that needs to determine this direction. If it decides to undertake a serious effort to guide its adherents toward its stated aspirational principles, it will have chosen an ambitious path for its adherents to follow across our imaginary game board. If it opts for a different way forward, I hope that the goals of that approach will be similarly ambitious, leading to a path that other movements can appreciate and respect as helping *Klal Yisrael* bring the Messianic age.

Chapter Nine

WHERE SHOULD REFORM JUDAISM GO NEXT?

THE BEST STARTING point for describing the Reform path is to examine the principles that the movement's most recent statement of principles sets forth. These appear in the New Pittsburgh Platform, which Chapter Three presents in its entirety, and which I have excerpted below:[1]

God

"We affirm the reality and oneness of God..." to whom "the Jewish people is bound"... "by an eternal *b'rit*, covenant..."

"We affirm that every human being is created... in the image of God, and therefore every human life is sacred."

"We trust in our tradition's promise that, although God created us as finite beings, the spirit within us is eternal."

Torah

"We affirm that Torah is the foundation of Jewish life."

"We affirm the importance of studying Hebrew, the language of the Torah and Jewish liturgy, that we may draw closer to our people's sacred texts."

"We are called by the Torah to lifelong study in the home, in the synagogue and in every place where Jews gather to learn and teach."

"We are committed to the ongoing study of the whole array of *mitzvot* and to the fulfillment of those that address us as individuals and as a community. Some of these *mitzvot*, sacred obligations, have long been observed by Reform Jews; others, both ancient and modern, demand renewed attention as the result of the unique context of our own times."

The importance of Shabbat is "to culminate the workweek with *kedushah*, holiness, *menuchah*, rest and *oneg*, joy."

"The High Holy Days call us to account for our deeds. The Festivals enable us to celebrate" our seasonal joy. "The days of remembrance remind us of our tragedies and triumphs…"

"And we mark the milestones of our personal journeys with traditional and creative rites that reveal the holiness in each stage of life."

"We bring Torah into the world when we strive to fulfill the highest ethical mandates in our relationships with others and with all of God's creation. Partners with God in…

repairing the world… to help bring nearer the Messianic age…" "[W]e reaffirm social action and social justice as" a traditional belief and practice. "We affirm the *mitzvah* of *tzedaka*… for those in need."

Israel

"We are committed to the *mitzvah* of *ahavat Yisrael*, love for the Jewish people, and to *k'lal Yisrael*, the entire community of Israel. Recognizing that *kol Yisrael arevim zeh ba-zeh*, all Jews are responsible for one another, we reach out to all Jews across ideological and geographical boundaries."

"We are committed to strengthening the people of Israel by supporting individuals and families in the creation of homes rich in Jewish learning and observance."

The New Pittsburgh Platform sets forth an ambitious agenda for the Reform Movement. At the same time, the 2013 and 2020 Pew Studies make it clear that the Movement's adherents are not paying meaningful attention to many aspects of it. The average Reform Jew has little, if any, awareness of the Movement's published principles, and the Reform pulpit clergy have not focused on closing this gap. The Reform Movement has been successful in promoting active participation in social justice and *tzedaka* initiatives. It has also become the most open movement by including all genders, recognizing patrilineal descent in determining who is a Jew, and fully accepting interfaith couples, including allowing clergy to officiate at interfaith wedding ceremonies. If the leaders of the Movement are serious about all of their principles, they need to focus on the elements of the New Pittsburgh Platform that relate to ritual participation and acts of *chesed* – fulfilling "the highest ethical mandates in our relationships with others…"

To understand this landscape better, I spoke with several Reform pulpit rabbis. They uniformly acknowledged the gap between principles and practices in the areas of ritual and *chesed*. As we discussed the subject in detail, a clear pattern emerged. A key tenet of Reform Judaism is particularism, which allows each individual to look at the broad menu of practices available and choose those that he or she finds most meaningful. In theory, this would result in most individuals picking a representative mix of the practices that the New Pittsburgh Platform delineates, but for two fundamental reasons, this hasn't happened. First, the typical Reform Jew does not know about these principles. Second, the typical Reform Jew does not have the knowledge with which to make informed choices. The way to address this issue is different for ritual practices than it is for *chesed*.

From a ritual practices standpoint, a good way to start would be to pick one practice at a time and introduce it across the Movement. One Reform pulpit rabbi suggested encouraging all Reform Jews to light *Shabbat* candles. This is an easy *mitzvah* to observe. If, in a particular year, every Reform pulpit rabbi spoke about this *mitzvah* during the High Holy Days and every Temple distributed candlesticks, candles, lighting instructions, and the simple prayer, in Hebrew, transliterated Hebrew, and English, it is likely that a large number of families would adopt the practice. This could have far-reaching impact, as it would both bring *Shabbat* into the homes of Reform Jews, and pave the way for introducing other practices, one at a time.

Another suggestion was putting *mezuzot* on the entry doorposts of all rooms rather than just by the front door. The rabbi who suggested this felt that the presence of a *mezuzah* on each door would spiritually transform the home. He suggested a similar approach for introducing this *mitzvah* – emphasizing it as an initiative at High Holy Day services, coupled with distribution of the *mezuzot* to congregants along with instructions and the appropriate blessing in Hebrew, transliterated Hebrew, and English. This too is an easy *mitzvah* on which to act.

Either of these *mitzvot*, or many others, would be a good beginning. Using this approach, it might take a decade or more to make a meaningful difference in Reform ritual practices. But after waiting almost 2,000 years for the Messianic age to arrive, this does not seem like an unreasonable time horizon.

With respect to *chesed*, the consensus among the rabbis whom I approached was to re-design the Reform religious school curriculum so as to emphasize *chesed* in different ways. One rabbi suggested focusing on the parts of the Torah and the Prophets that teach *chesed* and finding ways to relate these teachings to our daily interpersonal interactions. Others proposed telling young children age-appropriate stories that contain *chesed* teachings. The Movement could publish books of these stories especially for reading on *Shabbat*. Older students could confront more complex daily issues from a *chesed* perspective, under the guidance of trained teachers. In addition, religious schools could add specific *chesed* projects to the curriculum. With a little imagination, these projects could provide children with a rich *chesed* experience that would influence their interpersonal behavior and social consciences for a lifetime.

This too will take years to penetrate the movement in a meaningful way, but again, we've waited close to 2,000 years for the Messianic age. Another decade or so is certainly not too long.

With the New Pittsburgh Platform, the Reform Movement laid out its path on our imaginary game board. But the Movement cannot meaningfully progress along this path until it puts more of its principles into action. In some areas, such as social justice and inclusion, this has already happened. In others, most notably ritual practices and *chesed*, it has not. With consistent focus and a pivot from unguided particularism to informed, nurtured particularism, the Reform Movement has the opportunity to help hasten the Messianic age.

Chapter Ten

CAN RECONSTRUCTIONIST JUDAISM BECOME THE NEXT CHABAD?

THE RECONSTRUCTIONIST MOVEMENT is unique among the streams of Judaism in that it explicitly rejects the basic tenets of Biblical Judaism, especially the revelation at Mount Sinai and the concept of Jews as a people chosen to bring about a better world. It also rejects the existence of God as supernatural, accepting the view of Rabbi Mordechai Kaplan that nothing, not even *Hashem*, can be beyond nature. At the same time, the Reconstructionist movement accepts Jewish tradition as an important guide to current practice, one that Reconstructionist groups and congregations should take into account when determining which practices to adopt in order to give meaning to Jewish life in a particular time and place.

As Chapter 4 demonstrated, Reconstructionist congregations and their members take Judaism very seriously and, once they have adopted a practice, they follow it consistently. Reconstructionist Jews care deeply about *chesed*, individual rights, and respectful behavior. They attend synagogue services on *Shabbat* and form meaningful communities that also become their social circles, thus bringing Jewishness into their broader lives. Practices vary among Reconstructionist congregations and groups, but the process for deciding on meaningful practices is consistent.

The Reconstructionist movement, and its congregations, need to define its path toward the Messianic age, but I'm going to make a suggestion. Presently, the largest group of Jews in the United States is Jews who are not affiliated with any movement. They lead secular lives and do not make decisions based on Jewish values. Because of the movement's liberal perspective and democratic approach, several Reconstructionist pulpit rabbis have suggested to me that the Reconstructionist approach could be attractive to secular Jews, if they had the opportunity to experience it. Thus, outreach to this large, unaffiliated Jewish population could be a very fruitful endeavor. At the same time, these rabbis noted that doing this successfully takes money and methodology, and that the movement is not providing either of these at present. We discussed the Chabad model of outreach, which is highly successful. All agreed that employing a modified form of this model could be an effective way to expand the Reconstructionist base among unaffiliated Jews.

If Reconstructionist Jews who read this book agree with this approach, then I suggest that they initiate a grassroots effort to make it a reality. This will need to include a detailed roadmap, training, and funding. It could take as long as a decade before meaningful numbers of unaffiliated Jews have joined the movement, but the results would be well worth the effort. Adding to the ranks of affiliated Jews is a noble goal. Saving future generations of these Jews from complete lack of awareness of their heritage and its practices could be a significant contribution to attainment of the Messianic age.

Chapter Eleven

WHAT WE CAN ALL LEARN FROM SEPHARDIC JUDAISM

Rabbi Ovadia Yosef's lifetime of effort has clearly defined Sephardic life in Israel, and his followers have created institutions that build on his mission to restore the crown to its original glory. Today, Rabbi Ovadia Yosef's son, Rabbi Yitzchak Yosef, is continuing in the footsteps of his father and his father's three previous successors as the Chief Sephardic Rabbi of Israel. The Sephardic path in Israel is thus well delineated.

The Sephardic path in America is somewhat harder to define because of the absence of current meaningful data about Sephardic religious observance and, equally important, about their observance of *middot*. However, the critical problem of *Sinat Chinam* that exists among Jews of different Ashkenazi movements does not appear to be a meaningful issue among Sephardic Jews, despite their wide range of religious practices. At the same time, this range leaves significant room for Sephardic communities to move toward stricter observance of religious practices and, while Chapter Five did not discuss this, there is anecdotal evidence that some Sephardic Jews could also strive for better *middot*. The fragmented leadership in the American Sephardic community makes it difficult to achieve the kind of progress that the leadership of Rabbi Ovadia Yosef and his successors in Israel spearheaded. A 1973 demographic study of the American Sephardic communities presented extensive data to demonstrate that their Jewish traditions had badly eroded over the years. It concluded with the following grim warning:

> If there is no reversal in the trends indicated by our data, no viable Sephardi communities may be left in the United States in two or three generations from now. Clearly, synagogue buildings alone cannot insure the survival, let alone growth, of Sephardi culture. Sephardim must establish good schools of their own, or insist that existing day schools teach more about the Sephardi past. They must also create meaningful cultural institutions—Sephardi theaters, newspapers, libraries. They must encourage their youth to pursue higher Jewish education and, if necessary, provide financial incentives to promising students. It is to be hoped that these efforts will strengthen religious observance, and wipe out the widespread ignorance of Judaism and Sephardi Jewish tradition. Unless this can be accomplished now, the Sephardi heritage will be lost.[1]

A 2009 study of non-Ashkenazi Jews in America,[2] demonstrated that the United States government had largely ignored Sephardic Jews when it assisted newcomers during the waves of Jewish immigration to the United States around the turn of the 20th century. Because the Ashkenazi Jewish population was so large in comparison to that of non-Ashkenazi population, the Ashkenazi Jew became the universal stereotype of the American Jew. As a result, the history and heritage of non-Ashkenazi Jews has not been recognized or recorded and their transmission therefore depends almost exclusively on oral legacies within the Sephardic Jewish communities. This situation led some Sephardic Jews to resent their Ashkenazi counterparts, although this has diminished over the years.

Fortunately, since 1973, the American Sephardic Jewish communities have grown significantly. Sephardic Jews have established numerous new Sephardic synagogues as well as many Sephardic *minyanim* in Ashkenazi synagogues. Many yeshivas, particularly in New York and Los Angeles, that were once filled almost exclusively with Ashkenazi Jews, now have a strong Sephardic presence. Yet, these non-Ashkenazi Jews lack the unified leadership that the community in Israel has. This is part of the reason why religious practices among American Sephardic communities has become so inconsistent.

One way to address these issues would be for American Sephardic Jews to establish the kind of unified leadership that Rabbi Ovadia Yosef created in Israel, whether in the form of an individual or a representative board. It is up to the Sephardic Jewish communities to define the Sephardic path and figure out their way forward. Whatever approach they choose, the goal should be increased observance of religious practices and a focus on *middot* as a way of restoring the crown of glory to American Sephardic Jewry and hastening the arrival of the Messianic age.

Part Three

THINKING DIFFERENTLY

Chapter Twelve

OVERVIEW

PART TWO PRESENTED a framework for *achdut* using a boardgame analogy as a visual image for how the different streams of Judaism within *Klal Yisrael* can do their respective parts to help bring the Messianic age. Where possible, I suggested a path that a movement or sub-stream might take and gave my rationale for the suggestion. In other cases, I identified paths that the leadership of a movement or substream might consider, recognizing that, ultimately, each one must develop its own approach. In the next paragraph, let me repeat the thesis that I stated in the Overview to Part Two:

It would be unrealistic to think that different Jewish movements can be persuaded to accept each other's theologies. What they should be able to recognize, however, is that each movement, according to its aspirational principles, has objectives that, if achieved, would encourage its adherents to engage in greater observance of *mitzvot* and *middot*. Achieving this change in perspective would lead to greater respect among the different movements, which, in turn, would break the barrier of *Sinat Chinam* that has delayed the Messianic age for almost 2,000 years.

In this part of the book, I discuss how different movements and sub-streams should think about reframing their perspectives about other movements and sub-streams. The goal is to end the *Sinat Chinam* among these groups, eliminating the biggest barrier to achieving the Messianic age. Implicit in this approach, of course, is that each movement or sub-stream will work hard to achieve the goals of its prescribed path, moving across the imaginary gameboard with increased determination.

I am asking all Jews to find the strength to think differently about their counterparts within *Klal Yisrael*, and I'm keenly aware that changing such long-standing thinking will not be easy. Now I'm going to address you directly, hoping that you will hear my plea and think seriously about its message.

At this point, it might make sense for you to go directly to the chapter that speaks to your stream of Judaism and its perspective on other streams. Then, if you are interested, feel free to read the other chapters so as to broaden your overall perspective on the attitudes of different Jews. You will find some apparent duplication among these chapters where similar principles apply, but there are subtle differences among them that make each appropriate to the movement that it is addressing.

Chapter Thirteen

CAN ORTHODOX EYES SEE THE JEWISH WORLD DIFFERENTLY?

Overview

THIS CHAPTER ADDRESSES the perspective of Orthodox Jews toward Jews of other movements within *Klal Yisrael*. First, it directly addresses Chassidic and Yeshivish Jews' general mindset regarding both non-Orthodox and Modern Orthodox Jews. Then, it addresses Modern Orthodox Jews' general mindset about non-Orthodox Jews and Chassidic and Yeshivish Jews. Finally, it addresses all Orthodox Jews' mindset toward Jews who adhere to non-Orthodox Jewish movements.

Chassidic and Yeshivish Jews

As Chassidic and Yeshivish Jews, you have embraced an all-encompassing Torah way of life that largely separates you from secular society, with the exception of the workplace in certain cases. As examples: you dress differently, strictly observe *kashrut*, daven three times a day – with a *minyan* when possible – and devote yourselves to Torah study and the yeshiva education of your children. You observe the laws of *taharas hamishpacha*. You also strictly observe special days on the Jewish calendar, including *Shabbos, Yom Tov,* and Fast Days. You refrain from cutting your hair or shaving during the *Omer* and the Three Weeks preceding *Tisha B'Av*. You obey American civil law, but you also accept all requirements of Torah law and resolve many of your disputes before a *bais din* instead of in the civil courts. You do not eat in restaurants that don't have a proper *kashrus heksher*, and you don't do activities that might compromise *tznius* or *kol isha*.

Strictly observing this way of life defines the Chassidic and Yeshivish worlds. Some Modern Orthodox Jews also observe all of these *mitzvos* and *minhagim*, and most Modern Orthodox Jews observe many of them. Even so, as Chassidic and Yeshivish Jewish communities, you are unique in your unanimous strict observance of halacha. You look to the Agudah and the Haredi Israeli Rabbinate for various types of guidance, rather than to Modern Orthodox organizations like the Orthodox Union,* the Rabbinical Council of America, or the rabbis at Yeshiva University. You've had very little exposure to the other movements in Judaism that this book describes.

Most important, you hold the fundamental belief that Jews who do not believe in *The Thirteen Principles of Faith* and who do not follow halacha are in violation, and often flagrant violation, of what the Torah requires and, therefore, are a major impediment to the arrival of *Moshiach*. Your position is understandable. After all, given the effort that you put into Jewish observance, why should others get a free pass? I have several responses to this question.

---

* Yeshivish Jews generally accept the *kashrus* approval of the Orthodox Union for food products and restaurants.

First, this attitude and the type of *Sinas Chinam* that it breeds toward other Jews is what led to the destruction of the Second Temple. It therefore seems inconceivable that *Moshisach* will come if we continue to exhibit this attitude today. Like it or not, all of us in *Klal Yisrael* are bound together in our collective mission to repair the world, and we have no idea how *Hashem* values any particular *mitzvos* or *middos*. For you, this means that the only sure approach is to continue to strictly observe the *mitzvos* and *middos* in the Torah and the Oral Law. It also means that, from deep within, you must find and exhibit love and kindness toward all Jews and encourage them to make progress along their chosen paths.

Second, it's now been several centuries since the *Haskalah*. This movement came as a shock to the Jewish world. Seemingly overnight, it challenged close to two thousand years of tradition. As secular governments gave Jews meaningful civil rights, the *rabbeim* found themselves losing control of parts of *Klal Yisrael*. There was a strong desire to nip this in the bud and return to tradition, because otherwise Chassidic and Yeshivish Judaism might not survive in the modern world. But it was not to be, and the mass migration of Jews to the United States made matters worse. America's broad religious freedoms gave Jews unprecedented protections, and with these freedoms came the ability to practice Judaism in multiple ways, of which traditional Judaism was only one option. Given these developments, it's not surprising that on *Tisha B'av*, many Orthodox Jewish communities recite a *kinah* for the loss of the Jewish way of life in Eastern Europe. But the fact remains: the Orthodox *rabbeim* no longer have civil legal control over Jews living in many parts of the world; they retain partial control in Israel, but not without heavy political friction.

At the same time, Chassidic and Yeshivish Judaism is

growing and thriving in the 21st century. Large communities in North America, Israel, and elsewhere have replaced those that the Holocaust devastated. The level of learning among these Jewish populations is unmatched, including attendance at yeshivas and *kollels*, as well as *daf yomi* participation. In contrast to the agenda of the Reform movement during the *Haskalah*, today the more liberal movements within Judaism are not focused on destroying Orthodox Judaism or persuading Orthodox Jews to join them. They are pushing hard for more recognition in Israel, but in addition to rather than instead of Orthodox Judaism.

Given this state of affairs and the inability to turn back the clock, it's time to consider carefully whether *Sinas Chinam* is the appropriate response. Wouldn't we all be better off if all Jews encouraged each other to progress along their chosen paths, and to add more *mitzvos* and *middos* than they embrace today? And wouldn't it better for a liberal Jew to keep some formal affiliation with Judaism rather than to disappear into the secular world?

Third, we've seen that, given the right conditions, Orthodox Judaism has broad appeal. I've described the magic of *Shabbos* in an Orthodox home. Just think what could happen if more people could share in this experience. This will only happen if attitudes change across *Klal Yisrael*, beginning with the attitudes of Orthodox Jews. *Sinas Chinam* breeds more *Sinas Chinam*, both within the Orthodox world, and reciprocally, from non-Orthodox Jews. Love and kindness breed reciprocal love and kindness.

I am fully aware of the risk you might feel if you think differently about non-Orthodox Jews. You don't want Orthodox Jews to make the mistake of perceiving this change in attitude as tacit acceptance of their practices as an acceptable way to fulfill their halachic obligations.

I am not asking you to take that risk. I'm only asking that you accept the principles that:

- every extra *mitzvah* and *middah* that a member of *Klal Yisrael* performs has value,
- these extra *mitzvos* and *middos*, no matter who does them, will hasten the arrival of *Moshiach*,
- *Sinas Chinam* is a serious violation of Torah law, and
- the elimination of *Sinas Chinam* will hasten the arrival of *Moshiach*.

I am not asking you to do any of the following:

- change your position on the proper practice of Judaism or compromise on any issue of public policy related to Jewish practices – e.g., *Shabbos* closing laws in Israel,
- form or join any organization that represents all of *Klal Yisrael*,
- meet or speak with clergy or leadership of any other movement,
- invite clergy from other movements to speak to members of your community, or
- speak to members of any other movement at their synagogues or in any other forum.

I am asking you to **think** differently about other Jews, and to ask members of your movement not to exhibit *Sinas Chinan* toward them. Instead, you should hope that these Jews will increase their level of *mitzvos* and *middos* along their respective paths, and, in so doing, help to bring *Moshiach* soon, in our time.

Several years ago, I heard a story about a Chassidic Rebbe who was seated next to a Conservative rabbi on a flight from

New York to Israel. They stayed up all night talking about Judaism. At one point the Chassidic Rebbe asked the Conservative rabbi whether Conservative synagogues really permit women to be called to the Torah for *aliyos*. The Conservative rabbi answered in the affirmative. In response the Chassidic Rebbe said, "when *Moshiach* comes, we will get the answer to this issue." The Chassidic Rebbe did not believe that the arrival of *Moshiach* would allow this practice, but he knew how to be warm and kind to another Jew. That's all that I'm asking of you.

It's important that this kindness be genuine. Liberal Jews, with some justification, believe that Orthodox Jews' only interest in liberal Jews is to attempt to turn them into Orthodox Jews. This belief is a powerful catalyst for the *Sinas Chinam* that liberal Jews feel toward you. They perceive Orthodox Jews as self-righteous rather than as people of humble piety. Is this how you want to be perceived? It can't be, since that runs counter to the essence of Judaism as our scripture and liturgy, including *Perkei Avo*s, describe it. It is difficult to change perceptions under any circumstances, but doing so is impossible when the perception is justified.

I'm asking for this to change. Let the other movements do the hard work of moving their adherents along their chosen paths, and be happy that they are doing so, because the alternative is the permanent loss of the majority of *Klal Yisrael*.

Mindset of Chassidic and Yeshivish Jews Toward Modern Orthodox Jews

Modern Orthodox Jews observe many of the same *mitzvos* and *minhagim* as Chassidic and Yeshivish Jews. Members of the Modern Orthodox community often daven at your *shuls* when they are away from home and need a *minyan*. You also eat at many of the same kosher restaurants and shop in the same kosher grocery stores. Most Modern Orthodox Jews daven three times a day and they overwhelmingly send their children to Orthodox schools.

Despite these similarities, there are some glaring differences between your Jewish practices and those of Modern Orthodox Jews. Here are some examples:

- All Chassidic and Yeshivish married women cover their hair at least in the presence of men other than their husbands. Many Modern Orthodox women do not, although this practice is changing with each generation.
- All Chassidic and Yeshivish men wear *kippos* all the time, including in the workplace. Some Modern Orthodox men wear *kippos* only at home, in synagogue, in kosher restaurants and around their neighborhoods, but not at work or in many public places. Modern Orthodox rabbis do wear their *kippos* all the time.
- All Chassidic and Yeshivish men wear *tzitzis* as distinct garments all the time, often visible outside their clothing. Some Modern Orthodox men do not wear *tzizis* as distinct garments at all, and instead fulfill the *mitzvah* of *tzitis* by donning a *tallis* with *tzizis* for *sharachis* and *musaf*. Modern Orthodox rabbis do wear t*zizis* all the time.
- All Chassidic and Yeshivish married couples strictly observe *taharas hamishpacha*. The level of observance of these rules is uneven, but increasing, among Modern Orthodox Jews.
- Chassidic and Yeshivish Jews strictly observe *shomer negiah*. They also date only for marriage. Many Modern Orthodox singles are not *shomer negiah* and date for reasons other than marriage. It is not uncommon for

Modern Orthodox singles to have several relationships before marriage and to defer marriage until their late 20s or beyond. This too is changing among yeshiva-educated Modern Orthodox singles.

- No Chassidic and Yeshivish Jews visit pools, beaches, or gyms where the opposite gender is present. Many Modern Orthodox Jews do not observe this rule.
- Chassidic and Yeshivish men strictly observe the prohibition of *kol isha*. Accordingly, they do not attend events like theater or films where women sing. Most Modern Orthodox men do not observe this rule.
- All Chassidic and Yeshivish Jews dress strictly according to the laws of *tznius* (see Chapter One). Modern Orthodox practices vary considerably in this area.

Underlying many of these differences is a philosophical divide between you and Modern Orthodox Jews. Modern Orthodox Jews share your beliefs in the Torah as Divinely given at Mount Sinai and in *The Thirteen Principles of Faith*. But they also accept the modern world and many of its customs. They want to be both full participants in modern society and Torah-observant Jews. This leads to many of the variations that I have just described. A good example of this is a conversation I recently had with a Modern Orthodox lawyer in New York City. I asked him whether he wears his *kippah* when he goes to court. He indicated that he does not because he wants the judge to look at him as a lawyer rather than as a Jew.

We can trace the roots of these differences to the mass immigrations of Orthodox Jews to the United States at the turn of the 20th century. They came to a country that had no appreciation of their practices and little accommodation of their need to keep *Shabbos* and observe *kashrus*. At the same time, they came from generations of near poverty in Eastern

Europe and were determined to better themselves economically, while doing their best to remain observant Jews. They came to a country that lacked a rabbinic infrastructure and Jewish institutions, largely because the Eastern European Chassidic and Yeshivish rabbinic leaders were reluctant to send to America their esteemed *rabbeim* or even many experts in such things as *shechita* and preparing meats for *kashrus*. These leaders viewed America as a halachic wasteland where proper Jewish observance was not possible. In many ways, they were right, and their reluctance made it more so. And, before they could move to fix this situation, the Holocaust arrived, decimating Eastern European Jewry.

Against this backdrop, the Modern Orthodox movement emerged and built institutions for prayer, learning, and *kashrus* in order to preserve Orthodox Judaism in America. As late as the 1960s, it was unclear whether it would succeed. It was also impossible to predict the rapid growth of Chassidic and Yeshivish Judaism in America. This development has left us with three distinctly different sub-streams of Orthodox Judaism in America: Chassidic, Yeshivish, and Modern Orthodox. Each new generation of Modern Orthodox Jews is moving slowly toward the *right* by embracing more of the practices of Chassidic and Yeshivish Jews. This process will take time and requires your patience. In the meantime, you need to embrace these fellow Orthodox Jews as individuals who are deeply invested in preserving Orthodox Judaism and bringing the ultimate redemption.

There is one further issue that we need to address: Zionism. Simply put, Modern Orthodox Jews are Zionists. Their grandparents left Eastern Europe to be free of persecution there during centuries of antisemitism. Then, they saw those Jews left behind slaughtered in the Holocaust because no country would accept them as refugees when Hitler rose to power. Because of this, Modern Orthodox Jews firmly believe that diaspora Jews need a Jewish State as a potential refuge in case of future persecution and antisemitism. This unshakable commitment to Zionism is in direct conflict with the position of Chassidic and Yeshivish Jews.

Chassidic and Yeshivish leadership opposed Zionism for two reasons. First, the early Zionists who founded and governed the new State of Israel in 1948 were secular Jews, *Maskilim*. They were products of the *Haskalah* and fiercely opposed importing the Eastern European way of life to the Holy Land. Instead, they sought farmers and soldiers capable of building and defending the new Jewish settlements. In fact, in the years preceding the Holocaust, they did their best to prevent Orthodox Jews, particularly rabbis, from settling in the Holy Land.

Second, Chassidic and Yeshivish leadership viewed the establishment a new Jewish country in the Holy Land by human political and military means as being contrary to Orthodox tradition, which says that only *Hashem*, not man, will re-establish Jewish sovereignty over the land. By tradition, this will not happen until *Klal Yisrael*, through its devotion and acts, is deserving of this redemption. A Jewish state created without Divine support would ultimately fail.*

While these arguments were once compelling, they are no longer persuasive. Many of the greatest Jewish scholars in the world live in Israel. The State has a large and growing Orthodox population with considerable political and cultural influence. Its religious institutions are extraordinary, and its infrastructure

---

* As an example, when Moshe sent a group of 12 men to spy out the land of Israel, ten of them came back with a negative report about the Jews' prospects for conquering a place where the established nations possessed great warriors and battle capabilities. *Hashem's* response to this report was to decree a 40-year exile in the wilderness for the Jewish people. When several Jews defied *Hashem's* decree and tried to conquer the land, its inhabitants routed them. *The Stone Edition, The Chumash*, trans. Rabbi Nosson Scherman (New York: ArtScroll Mesorah Publications, Ltd. 2000), 798-877. (*Bamidbar* 13:1-14:45)

supporting Orthodox religious practices is unparalleled. Viewing Israel today as the project of early secular Zionists is no longer a viable perspective. It is also noteworthy that there will soon be more Jews living in Israel than in the diaspora, and more Orthodox Jews living in Israel than outside it.

The second reason for opposing Zionism – that it jumps the gun on *Hashem's* exclusive prerogative to establish a new Jewish kingdom in the land – still has relevance in terms of not accepting the modern democratic State of Israel as the prophesized ingathering of the Jewish people at the time of *Moshiach*. But it does not justify *Sinas Chinam* toward Modern Orthodox Jews. The connection just no longer follows. Modern Orthodox Jews are religious Zionists, unlike the *Maskilim*, who were secular Zionists. Let Chassidic and Yeshivish Jews on the one hand, and Modern Orthodox Jews on the other, differ on whether to modify *Sharachis* by adding *Hallel*,* and refraining from saying *Tachanun*† on *Yom Ha'atzmaut*‡ and *Yom Yerushalayim*.§ But let's also recognize the enormous benefits to Chassidic and Yeshivish Jews from Israel's existence and the major influence that you have on life, politics, and policy in the modern State. We are all better off, in fact, much better off, because of Israel's existence. Now let's work together to bring *Moshiach*.

---

*   *Hallel* is a series of *psalms* praising *Hashem*. The sequence has an opening blessing and a concluding one. According to halacha, Jews recite it on Pesach (including at the *Pesach Seder*), *Shavuos*, *Succos*, *Chanukah*, and *Rosh Chodesh*. We recite an abridged version of *Hallel* on *Pesach* after the first two days (the first day in Israel) of the festival, as well as on *Rosh Chodesh*.

†   *Tachanun* is a daily prayer of supplication that we recite after the *Chazzan's* repetition of the silent morning prayer and at certain other times. It is not part of the liturgy on *Shabbos* morning, *Yom Tov*, the festivals, *Chanukah*, *Purim*, *Tisha B'Av*, *Rosh* Chodesh, the full Hebrew month of *Nisan*, the remainder of the Hebrew month of *Tishrei* after the festival of *Shemini Atzeret*, the morning of a *bris milah*, or when a newly married man is present at the service. It is also omitted on certain other days based on differing traditions.

‡   *Yom Ha'atzmaut* is the Hebrew name for Israel's Independence Day, which was originally declared on 5 *Iyar* 5708, May 14, 1948.

§   *Yom Yerushalayim* commemorates the reunification of Jerusalem during the 1967 (Six Day) War, on 28 *Iyar* 5727, June 7, 1967.

Modern Orthodox Jews

As Modern Orthodox Jews, you have made a lifelong commitment to the practice of Orthodox Judaism in a way that allows you to keep halacha, *Shabbat,* and *kashrut* while integrating professionally, and often socially, into the modern secular world. You grew up attending Jewish day schools, probably spanning the years from preschool through high school. Depending on where you lived, whether in a mostly Jewish community or a more mixed community, your childhood friends were almost exclusively Jewish or were a mixture of Jewish and secular children and teenagers. Even if all your friends were Jewish, probably not all of them were Orthodox. Thus, from an early age, you learned to navigate interactions with the non-Orthodox world.

These interactions included educating others about what you were not able to do on *Shabbat* as well as foods that you could not eat. Sometimes this was easy, and sometimes it wasn't. You refrained from participating in organized sports on *Shabbat,* which could be difficult for you if your friends participated. If a friend went to a fast-food restaurant that was not kosher, you might go along and have a soft drink, but you did not eat any of the food. You often had to decide whether to wear your *kippah* or to cover your head with a baseball cap when out in public. This very delicate balancing act is not easy for children and teens, and there were times that you missed out on things you wanted to do, such as attending parties on Friday evenings.

After high school, you either went straight to college or spent a year or two studying in Israel first. Some of you attended Jewish institutions such as Yeshiva University, but most of you attended secular colleges, many with significant Modern Orthodox student bodies. Or perhaps you attended secular colleges with kosher food options, but without strong Modern Orthodox infrastructures, and had to navigate your college years carefully in an environment that was not particularly supportive of your Jewish practices.

After college, you either began a career in business or went to graduate school to obtain an advanced degree in your chosen field or profession. You probably had several relationships before choosing your spouse, and probably waited to get married until at least one of you had become at least reasonably established in your career. After marriage, you probably had children fairly quickly, the number of which depended on your lifestyle choices and financial abilities, taking into account the expense of Modern Orthodox Jewish day school tuitions.

Based on your own challenges in navigating the secular world in your childhood and teenage years, you are probably now living in a heavily Modern Orthodox neighborhood where your children socialize almost exclusively with other Modern Orthodox children, as they do in school, synagogue, and summer camp. This makes things easier than they were when you were growing up, but can still be somewhat challenging; your children see you and your spouse navigating between the Jewish world and the secular world in your professional lives, on family vacations, and when attending cultural events.

You are probably successful in your profession or business where you interact regularly with the secular world. You might not wear *kippot* at work, but some of you do, especially those of you working in health professions, where it's common to see Jewish men wearing *kippot*. Perhaps you don't wear *tzizit* during the workweek, and it's possible that you don't wear them at all, except on your *tallis*. Most of you put on *tefillin* every morning, and many of you attend a morning *minyan* daily when possible. Some of you *daven* three times a day, and some of you only in the morning.

Over the years, there have been situations where you had to skip certain programs or meetings because of *Shabbat* or *Yom Tov* observance, and your non-Jewish and liberal Jewish colleagues are aware that you need to leave work on Friday afternoons in the late fall and winter, when *Shabbat* begins early. Your business requirements mean that you cannot completely avoid non-kosher restaurants, where you eat sparingly to observe *kashrut* as best as possible.

If you are a woman, you might not cover your hair in front of men who are not in your immediate family. You might wear short sleeves in warm weather and sometimes put on pants instead of a dress or skirt when it's not *Shabbat* or *Yom Tov*. Your skirts and dresses often reach to just above the knee, threading the needle between the fashions of the secular world and the stricter dress requirements of the Orthodox world. Similarly, your necklines are often lower than those of Chassidic and Yeshivish women.

Almost all Modern Orthodox Jews, other than rabbis and their families, swim in mixed-gender venues and in places where other bathers are non-Jews. Similarly, few Modern Orthodox men observe *kol isha*; you are comfortable attending events where women are singing. You are also comfortable singing with women at the *Shabbat* table.

Modern Orthodox Jews and their rabbinic leaders are ardent Zionists, but are divided on subjects such as the best way to achieve Middle East peace, and how much of a role the Israeli Orthodox Rabbinate should play with respect to issues such as marriage, divorce, and *Shabbat* closing laws.

Given your position on the spectrum of Jewish observance, you can at times resent those Jews with more liberal beliefs and practices who don't accept traditional Judaism, while recognizing that they do observe many *middot*. Yet although your practices might differ from theirs, this is not a good reason for you to display *Sinat Chinam* toward them. Rather, you should view all Jews with loving kindness and recognize that each other group needs to try to move across the imaginary gameboard that Part Two, A Framework for *Achdut*, describes, so that together we will bring *Moshiach*. So, let the other movements do the hard work of moving their adherents along their chosen paths, and be happy that they are doing so. And especially, hope that they are successful in keeping future generations within *Klal Yisroel*.

Mindset of Modern Orthodox Jews Toward Chassidic and Yeshivish Jews

You have much in common with Chassidic and Yeshivish Jews. You all observe *Shabbat, Yom Tov,* and *kashrut*. You subscribe to *The Thirteen Principles of Faith* as the basis for Jewish theology. You also sometimes attend each other's synagogues based on where you are when it's time to *daven*. But there are some noticeable differences in your practices.

At the root of these differences is the question of whether it's acceptable to modify some of the historic norms of Orthodox Jewish religious practice to accommodate living in the modern world. You believe that some relaxation of these norms is acceptable, where the Modern Orthodox rabbinate does not overtly discourage it. Chassidic and Yeshivish Jews believe that Jewish religious practices today should mirror those in Eastern Europe before the Holocaust.

You probably have mixed feelings about these differences. On the one hand, you respect the dedication that Chassidic and Yeshivish Jews bring to their practices, even at the risk of giving up career opportunities available to Modern Orthodox

Jews. On the other hand, you struggle to accept that these sacrifices are necessary now that we live in a world where, in most countries, Jews have the same rights and freedoms as non-Jews and have found acceptance in the business and professional world.

You might think that Chassidic and Yeshivish Jews have chosen to live an overly restrictive, impractical lifestyle that reduces their income and employment potential in the modern world. You probably don't feel serious resentment toward Chassidic and Yeshivish Jews, but eliminating any negative feelings would be a good way to guard against *Sinat Chinam*.

As a Modern Orthodox Jew, it might be hard for you to accept that to many Chassidic and Yeshivish Jews, you look different and are on a lower plane of piety, especially since you work so hard to fulfill the commandments of the Torah. On a typical *Shabbat,* you might pass Chassidic and Yeshivish Jews walking to or from *shul*. If you are a man, you are likely to have on a business suit and tie; a jacket, tie, and dress slacks; or a dress shirt and slacks. You are probably wearing a knit *kippah*. A Chassidic man's main garment will be a *bekishe* or a *kaputa*, he won't have a tie, and will wear a fur *shtreimel* or a *spudik* on his head. A Yeshivish man will wear a black or other dark business suit and tie, and a black fedora with a brim at least two and half inches wide. You will greet each other with a friendly "Good *Shabbos"* as you pass, but you will have an inner sense that you somehow don't measure up to their standards. And this bothers you because you are sincere in your commitment to living an Orthodox Jewish life. Your feelings in these situations probably fall short of *Sinat Chinam,* but they are not healthy. Any guilt that you might have for not fully embracing their practices is no reason for you to resent them.

Modern Orthodox Jewish women also dress differently

than Chassidic and Yeshivish women. On *Shabbat*, you wear a dress or a skirt, but your dresses and skirts might be shorter than those of Chassidic and Yeshivish women, and, while you wear a hat to *shul*, you probably do not cover your hair with a *Sheitel* or restrict yourself to long sleeves. Your neckline is also often lower than appropriate in Chassidic and Yeshivish dress.

In some communities, there is another difference. By Torah law, Orthodox Jews do not carry anything when walking outdoors on *Shabbat*. This includes pushing a baby stroller, which is considered carrying. Certain kinds of carrying are permitted, however, if the community has a proper *eruv* around its perimeter. There are differences in the way that Modern Orthodox Jews on the one hand and Chassidic and Yeshivish Jews on the other hand interpret the requirements for a proper *eruv*.

These differences can result in situations where, within a particular community, you will carry things and push strollers on *Shabbat*, while Chassidic and Yeshivish Jews will not. A good example of this is the Upper West Side of Manhattan, a community where all types of Orthodox Jews live together in harmony but only Modern Orthodox Jews accept the validity of the *eruv* for the purpose of permitting carrying on *Shabbat*. This seems not to be an issue that causes resentment between different types of Orthodox Jews.

You and Chassidic and Yeshivish Jews also differ on your views about Zionism. You are an ardent Zionist and your synagogue strongly supports the modern state of Israel. Your *siddur* includes a prayer for its success and continuation. You do not say *Tachanun* on *Yom Ha'atzmaut* or *Yom Yerushalayim*. Instead, you are likely to say *Hallel* on these days, with or without its accompanying blessings. I've previously discussed the issue of the different perspectives toward Zionism of different types of Orthodox Jews. There is no easy way to reconcile them, but they make little difference in day-to-day life and religious practices, and are not a source a *Sinat Chinam*.

There has been much less *Sinat Chinam* among different types of Orthodox Jews since Chassidic and Yeshivish Jews made peace with each other and together embraced the *Agudah* as an overall governing body. While in the United States, the Modern Orthodox community has its own such organizations, the inability of the Orthodox streams to create an umbrella governing body has not been a major source of *Sinat Chinam*.

Other issues, however, have created noticeable friction between Modern Orthodox and other Orthodox Jews. For example, several years ago, the Israeli rabbinate became concerned about the standards that some American Modern Orthodox rabbis were applying to conversions. At first, it appeared that it would not recognize the conversions of certain rabbis. Fortunately, this issue was resolved relatively quickly without invalidating the Jewish status of existing Modern Orthodox converts. In addition, the Israeli Rabbinate agreed to accept a list of American Modern Orthodox rabbis who the Rabbinical Council of America has authorized to perform conversions. All prospective Modern Orthodox Jews can reach out to the rabbis on this list to sponsor their conversions so that the Israeli rabbinate will also accept them.

There has also been frustration with the continued inability of the Chassidic and Yeshivish Rabbinates to address the status of *agunot*.* The Modern Orthodox rabbinate has addressed this issue by requiring engaged couples to sign

---

* *Agunot* (*agunah* in the singular) are women whose husbands refuse to give them a Jewish divorce (a *get*) that would allow them to remarry. Without a *get*, halacha still considers a woman to be married, even if the couple has been granted a civil divorce. A *get* is a hand-written legal document that a husband gives his wife in front of a *beit din*. A husband generally may not be compelled to grant his wife a *get*, and a wife generally may not be compelled to accept one.

a Jewish prenuptial agreement. In this document, the man commits to paying a penalty for each day that he refuses to grant a Jewish divorce to his wife if, in connection with a civil divorce, she requests one. This practice is beginning to resolve the *agunah* problem in the Modern Orthodox community.

However, the Chassidic and Yeshivish rabbinates have not accepted this approach. They agree in principle that it would be desirable to make it easier for *agunot* to obtain Jewish divorces so that they can remarry, but they do not believe that Jewish law allows them to change the 2,500-year-old language of the *ketubah*,* even if that change is in a separate document. Most Modern Orthodox Jews believe that the refusal to accept the solution of a Jewish prenup is unreasonable and that it perpetuates a legal tradition that worked in the *shtetlach* (small villages) of Eastern Europe where strong peer pressure could force Jewish men to grant Jewish divorces to their wives, but that is not effective today in Israel or the diaspora. Nevertheless, although the uncertain status of *agunot* in Israel and in America is a concern, the issue does not lead to day-to-day friction among different types of Orthodox Jews.

There are also short-term issues that can cause disagreements between Modern Orthodox Jews and other Orthodox Jews. In 2020, during the height of the COVID-19 pandemic, Modern Orthodox Jews were generally very careful about wearing masks, social distancing, and avoiding large gatherings. In contrast, there were some highly visible large *Haredi* weddings held in indoor venues without any visible precautions against the spread of the virus. The mainstream media criticized this behavior, as did some prominent members of the Modern Orthodox community. Eventually, several prominent *Haredi* rabbis insisted that their followers refrain

---

* A *ketubah* is a Jewish marriage contract. The original Aramaic language format for the *ketubah* has been used for roughly 2,500 years.

from events of this type and obtain vaccinations to protect their communities. There is no reliable data regarding how many such weddings were held, but from those that were publicized, the impression spread that such events were commonplace. Yet, even issues such as this did not create lasting schisms between different groups of Orthodox Jews, and by the summer of 2021, whatever friction had existed over this issue in 2020 was largely forgotten, further demonstrating the lack of *Sinat Chinam* between Modern Orthodox Jews and Chassidic and Yeshivish Jews.

Mindset of Orthodox Jews Toward Non-Orthodox Jews

Conservative Jews

Let's now turn to your perspective on Conservative Jews. As Chapter Two explained, there are significant theological and practice differences between Orthodox and Conservative Judaism. There is also a large gap between Conservative Jewish practices, as the movement's leadership defines them, and the practices of the vast majority of Conservative Jews. These differences make it harder for Orthodox Jews and Conservative Jews to find common ground in their practices. In fact, the Conservative movement in Israel (the *Masorti* movement) is frequently at odds with the Israeli Orthodox rabbinate over fundamental issues relating to the authority of *Masorti* rabbis, including their license to officiate at Jewish lifecycle events.

These real differences do not justify *Sinas Chinam* toward individual Conservative Jews, however. Chapter Eight demonstrates how much Conservative Jews can do to bring *Moshiach*, mostly by enhancing their practices to move closer to what the Seminary calls the *Ideal Conservative Jew*. Even modest movement along this path could make a big difference to *Klal Israel*'s overall level of observance of *mitzvos* and *middos*.

At the same time, there is little evidence that the Conservative movement today is taking the steps necessary to close this gap. I will address Conservative Jews directly in Chapter Fourteen, and they will need to do their part in helping bring *Moshiach*. Here, I'm asking you to do your part by embracing them with lovingkindness, as fellow Jews.

The differences in theology, practice, and customs between Orthodox and Conservative Jews have become so significant that it is not productive to list them in detail, but I'll highlight a few:

- Conservative Jews do not accept *The Thirteen Principles of Faith* as an absolute theological statement, particularly the Divine giving of the Torah at Mount Sinai. Instead, they look to modern multidisciplinary analysis to conclude that man wrote at least parts of the Torah.
- The Conservative movement has altered the prayer liturgy with additions, deletions, and gender-related modifications.
- The Conservative rabbinate has eased the requirements for non-Jews who wish to convert to Judaism.
- The Conservate marriage ceremony deviates from traditional Jewish wedding practices, by, for example, permitting two-ring ceremonies and modifying the *ketubah*.
- The Conservative movement ordains women as rabbis and *chazzans*.

Like Modern Orthodox Jews, Conservative Jews take Zionism seriously, although their approaches are different. The Conservative movement, through its *Masorti* arm, is pushing for broader recognition in Israel and for greater influence in

Israeli society, much to the frustration of the Orthodox Israeli rabbinate and the *Agudah*. There is no reason to think that this tension, which is closely tied to Israeli politics, will end any time soon. Nevertheless, this issue is unrelated to the average Conservative Jew's opportunity to follow the official Conservative path. If more Conservative Jews do this, we will benefit by the quicker arrival of *Moshiach*, which we strongly hope will resolve the difficult issues of today.

Reform Jews

Let's now turn to Reform Jews. As Chapter Three explained, there are significant theological and practice differences between Orthodox and Reform Judaism. The principle that halacha is a mandatory set of commandments does not exist in Reform Judaism. Instead, Reform Jews learn about Jewish traditions and practices and then pick which of them to observe based on personal criteria. This principle, which Reform literature calls "particularlism," has survived the many changes to the Reform Platform. It is a product of the Emancipation, which gave individuals free choice about how to live their lives, and it resonates with the values of the modern secular world and its increasingly progressive beliefs and politics.

In Chapter Three, we saw that the Reform Jewish Platforms have moved gradually from advocating for a complete break with tradition to calling on Reform Jews to increase their practice of traditional *mitzvos*, in addition to practicing *middos*, which are a long-standing priority of the Reform movement. As I indicated in Chapter Nine, the principles of the New Pittsburgh Platform could go a long way toward bringing *Moshiach*. Yet, adherents to Reform Judaism have been slow to implement these changes. As I stated in Chapter Three, "The average Reform Jew has little if any awareness of the movement's published principles, and Reform pulpit Rabbis are not focused on closing this gap." In Chapter Nine, I presented a possible approach for change that several Reform pulpit rabbis have suggested, while recognizing that it is up to the Reform movement to decide how to take on this issue. As I concluded there: "With the right, consistent focus and a pivot from unguided particularism to informed, nurtured particularism, the Reform movement has the opportunity to help hasten the Messianic age."

There are several other important divergences between Reform and Orthodox practices, some of which I detailed in Chapter Three. The list is long, but here is a sample of instances where the Reform movement has broken with tradition:

- Considering children with Jewish fathers and non-Jewish mothers as Jews under the Patrilineal Descent Resolution, provided that the children are raised as Jews.
- Allowing Reform rabbis to officiate at marriages between Jews and non-Jews.
- Easing conversion standards from the traditional requirements.
- Ordaining women as rabbis and *chazzans*.

Notwithstanding these differences, if Reform Jews were to embrace the principles of the New Pittsburgh Platform, they would begin to attain meaningful levels of Jewish observance and practice. Please keep in mind also that Reform Jews have made it a priority to pursue equality and social justice, which is a contribution toward bringing *Moshiach*. As with all movements within Judaism, only time will tell how the Reform leadership will define the Reform Path and whether it will undertake the necessary effort to teach its adherents to follow it. In the meantime, Orthodox Jews can do their part by eliminating *Sinas Chinam* toward Reform Jews, remembering that all of *Klal Yisrael* has a collective responsibility to bring *Moshiach*.

Reconstructionist Jews

Let's now turn to Reconstructionist Jews. There is little doubt that the Reconstructionist movement presents unique difficulties for Orthodox Jews. It rejects the basic tenets of Biblical Judaism, especially the revelation at Mount Sinai and the concept of Jews as the chosen people to bring about a better world. It also rejects the existence of God as a supernatural being, according to Rabbi Mordechai Kaplan's belief that nothing can be beyond nature, thus accepting nature as the highest monotheistic power.

Nonetheless, Reconstructionist Jews are serious about Jewish observance. Reconstructionist Jews participate in prayer and learning, and observe *Shabbos* and *kashrus* according to their congregational or group practices. The Reconstructionist movement is also an attractive choice for unaffiliated, secular Jews who otherwise would have little, if any, Jewish identity and would be lost completely to *Klal Yisrael*.

In Chapter Ten, I suggested that a productive direction for the Reconstructionist movement would be to focus heavily on outreach in order to bring unaffiliated Jews back into the fold of *Klal Yisrael*. I pointed out that this effort might take a decade to be effective, but that is not a lot of time, given how long we've already waited for the arrival of *Moshiach*.

Acknowledging the major theological differences between Orthodox Jews on the one hand and Reconstructionist Jews on the other, I nevertheless strongly assert that nothing justifies *Sinas Chinam* toward individual Reconstructionist Jews. Moreover, the more unaffiliated, secular Jews who join any movement, thus increasing the size of *Klal Yisrael*, the better the chances of their working to bring *Moshiach*.

Sephardic Jews

Because Sephardic Jews do not have a distinctive style of dress and blend in comfortably with broader society in both North America and Israel, their level of observance is not readily apparent. Chassidic and Yeshivish Jews probably view Sephardic Jews wearing *kippot* as akin to Modern Orthodox Jews. As such, the section of this chapter discussing how Chassidic and Yeshivish Jews perceive Modern Orthodox Jews and can eliminate *Sinas Chinam* toward them, applies to their approach to Sephardic Jews as well.

Chassidic and Yeshivish Jews probably presume that Sephardic Jews who do not wear *kippot* are more liberal and more like Conservative or Reform Jews. These perceptions do not justify *Sinas Chinam* toward them, any more than it would toward liberal Ashkenazic Jews.

Outwardly, Sephardic Jews do not appear distinct from Modern Orthodox Jews. As Chapter One pointed out, many Modern Orthodox Jews do not wear *kippot* in all situations. As a result, a Modern Orthodox Jew should not make assumptions about the religious practices of a Sephardic Jew based on the presence or absence of this head covering. Once Modern Orthodox Jews get to know Sephardic Jews well, they are better able to understand where they fall on the spectrum of religious practices. Even so, they are unlikely to judge them based on differences in religious practice because there are no labels for Sephardic Jews, Sephardic synagogues follow Orthodox liturgy and practices, Sephardic Jews are culturally different from Ashkenazi Jews, and even less religiously observant Sephardic Jews are almost always committed to some type of traditional *Shabbat* observance, particularly on Friday evenings. Accordingly, Modern Orthodox Jews direct little *Sinat Chinam* toward Sephardic Jews.

Sephardic Jews have different traditions based on their countries of origin, but these variations do not reflect halachic differences. As Chapter Five explained, Rabbi Ovadia Yosef, the former Sephardic Chief Rabbi of Israel, has helped to unify Sephardic practices and halacha in Israel. In Chapter Eleven, I noted the value that similar unifying rabbinic leadership could bring to American Sephardic Jewry. In the meantime, it is encouraging that there is not recognizable *Sinat Chinam* between Modern Orthodox and Sephardic Jews. As Chapter Five pointed out, there is also not a meaningful amount of *Sinat Chinam* based on level of religious observance among Sephardic Jews, although political issues have recently divided Sephardic Jews in Israel leading to *Sinat Chinam* along political lines.

Chapter Fourteen

HOW CONSERVATIVE JEWS SHOULD VIEW OTHER JEWS

Overview

THIS CHAPTER ADDRESSES the perspective of Conservative Jews toward Jews of other movements within *Klal Yisrael*. First it addresses Conservative Jews' general mindset regarding different types of Orthodox Jews. Then it addresses Conservative Jews' general mindset about Jews who adhere to streams of Judaism other than the Orthodox stream.

Orthodox Jews

Mindset of Conservative Jews Toward Modern Orthodox Jews

As a Conservative Jew, you interact with Modern Orthodox Jews in the workplace, at shopping malls, at sporting and entertainment events, and at vacation destinations. In many cases, their dress is not distinguishable from yours, particularly when Modern Orthodox men choose not to wear *kippot* and Modern Orthodox women do not observe the rules of *tzniut*, as is likely in many of these settings. Your relationship with Modern Orthodox Jews probably includes a combination of commonality and resentment.

Because they do many of the same things as you in their daily lives, generally look like you, and tend to be ardent Zionists, you and Modern Orthodox Jews have a lot in common. You might work together and commute to work together. You might eat lunch together. Your kids might attend sports, cultural, and charitable activities together. When these shared experiences are the norm, your relationships with Modern Orthodox Jews tend to be positive.

Then there is the other side of the equation. Modern Orthodox Jews don't come to work, answer their phones, or check texts or email on *Shabbat* or on Jewish holidays, while you generally do at least some work and engage in other recreational and cultural activities on these days, even if you attend synagogue services first. You might find it frustrating when your Modern Orthodox work colleagues are not available to share the workload, particularly when a project deadline approaches. You might feel that the Modern Orthodox Jew is, in effect, saying, "I'm a better Jew than you are." This can result in resentment leading to *Sinat Chinam*.

The same thing can occur in other contexts, such as when a Modern Orthodox Jewish child who is a talented athlete does not participate on a sports team on *Shabbat* or a Jewish Holiday, reducing the team's chances of winning. This can be frustrating to both you and your children, especially if the game is within walking distance of that child's home, meaning that in your view, there is no specific halachic prohibition against the child's participation in the event. Nevertheless, the Modern Orthodox child does not attend because the activity is not in the spirit of *Shabbat*. In a situation such as this, you might believe that you have enough knowledge of Jewish law to question this decision, which could lead you to feel that the Modern Orthodox family is being "self-righteous" about its level of religious observance, to the detriment of the team. This can lead to deep resentment.

An additional issue is the dichotomy between Conservative Judaism as the movement's guiding principles define it, and Conservative Judaism as most Conservative Jews practice it. The guiding principles set forth a system of laws that in many respects are close to the practices of Modern Orthodox Jews, albeit with some theological differences. Before reading this book, you were probably unaware of those principles. Thus, you have understandably believed that you were adhering to a movement that espouses the Judaism that you are practicing. You tell people "I'm Conservative," meaning that you are following the type of Judaism that a majority of American Jewry has followed for close to a century, and that is as legitimate as Orthodoxy.

Chapter Two discussed in detail the evolution of Conservative Judaism and the dichotomy between principle and practice. I described the opportunity for Conservative Jews to play their part in hastening the arrival of the Messianic age in Chapter Eight. What's important to understand is that both your practices and those of Modern Orthodox Jews are products of a mostly North American Jewish history that led each stream to these practices and perspectives. Once you accept this, you can let go of anger, blame, and resentment, and embrace each other as part of the Jewish experience that began thousands of years ago and continues today. Then, with the help of the Conservative movement's leadership, you can focus on the Conservative path for the future and your role in helping to bring *Moshiach*.

Mindset of Conservative Jews Toward Chassidic and Yeshivish Jews

As a Conservative Jew, you probably do not interact often with Chassidic and Yeshivish Jews. You don't live in the same neighborhoods, you don't dress the same way, you don't attend the same synagogues, and your children do not attend the same schools. You don't agree on many political issues in the United States or in Israel. Conservative Jews tend to look at the Chassidic and Yeshivish worlds as out-of-date throwbacks to life in Eastern Europe. You see these Jews as holding onto a medieval form of Judaism that repudiates the experiences, freedoms, and opportunities of the modern world. The media has reinforced these impressions both in films featuring the "escape" of women from the "oppressions" of the Chassidic world and by reporting on news about these communities in a one-sided and biased way.

But it goes both ways. Chassidic and Yeshivish Jews have little understanding of Conservative Judaism. This is precisely why, in Part One of this book, I explained each stream of Judaism in such detail. I wanted to give Jews of different persuasions the opportunity to understand their counterparts in different movements of Judaism. I hope that reading Part One gave you an understanding and appreciation of the beauty of Chassidic and Yeshivish Judaism.

These are happy communities who love their way of life and their families. Their version of Judaism might not include the things that are important to you such as the American cultural experience, professional sports, and a focus on secular education and career achievement. But they do not feel deprived. They are well aware that they are surrounded by a world that differs greatly from the way they live, but they have elected to live this way, sharing a deep religious and spiritual experience in large, close families and cohesive communities. The media spins these Jews, and particularly Chassidic Jews, as cult-like and brainwashed. As Part One demonstrated, nothing could be farther from the truth. It is precisely because this way of life is so alluring that so many unaffiliated Jews are attracted to outreach experiences like putting on *tefillin*, lighting *Shabbat* candles, performing the ritual of shaking a *lulav* and *etrog*, and attending *Shabbat* meals.

While you do not interact much with Chassidic and Yeshivish Jews, you might feel animosity toward them, not just because of the misperceptions that I've tried to dispel, but also because you feel that they judge you as Jews who have lost their way and who will not be worthy of redemption when the Messianic age arrives. And it goes further. They do not view your rabbis as legitimate members of the rabbinate entitled to opine on questions of Jewish law and practice. These issues have become particularly volatile in Israel where the *Masorti* movement has met determined resistance to its efforts to gain rabbinic authority on par with that of the Orthodox Rabbinate, particularly with respect to officiating at lifecycle events such as weddings and divorces.

I addressed the Chassidic and Yeshivish communities with respect to their attitudes toward Conservative Jews in Chapter Thirteen. I tried to make it clear that the *Sinat Chinam* that prevails today needs to stop in order for real change to occur and for my suggested framework to succeed. In Part Two I also emphasized that each movement within Judaism needs to work on its future path, and to appreciate the paths of other movements and the role that they will play in bringing the Messianic age. In this chapter, I am addressing you as a Conservative Jew. I am asking you please to let go of your animosity toward Chassidic and Yeshivish Jews. I recognize that it is a two-way street and that they need to respond in kind by letting go of their dislike of Conservative Jews and acknowledging that each Jewish steam's actions can improve our chances of attaining the Messianic age.

I do not expect you to agree with Chassidic and Yeshivish Jews on theological issues or on political issues in the Diaspora or in Israel. I am only asking you to let go of any *Sinat Chinam* that you presently feel toward them. Only then can Conservative, Chassidic, and Yeshivish Jews follow their respective chosen paths with a real chance of bringing the Messianic age.

Reform Jews

As a Conservative Jew, you have a lot of interaction with Reform Jews socially, in the workplace, and in your communities. Marriages between Jews of these streams are common and widely accepted. Nonetheless, most Conservative Jews have chosen Conservative Judaism over Reform Judaism. There are several reasons for this:

- Conservative Jews feel drawn to a movement that maintains traditions, such as the content of prayer services, the movement's halachic principles, and celebration of the Jewish Festivals, whether or not they choose to attend synagogue services regularly or observe specific *mitzvot*.
- Conservative Jews generally insist that their clergy observe halacha at a high level, even if most Conservative Jews do not, and they appreciate their rabbis' ability to answer questions of halachic practice based on their strong Seminary education.
- Conservative Jews enjoy belonging to synagogues that begin and end *Shabbat* and Jewish holidays according

to the prescribed halachic times, irrespective of their own levels of observance.
- Conservative Jews like that their synagogues observe *kashrut*, whether or not they choose to do so personally.
- Conservative Jews prefer to belong to a movement that recognizes the traditional Jewish calendar that includes two days for *Rosh Hashana* and the *Yom Tovim* of *Pesach*, *Shavuot*, and *Sukkot*.
- Many Conservative Jews send their children to Camp Ramah and to Conservative Jewish day schools that offer traditional educational experiences based on Conservative principles.
- Conservative Jews agree with the movement's disapproval of intermarriage between Jews and non-Jews.
- Most Conservative Jews are opposed to a determination of Jewish status based on patrilineal descent, and, while they will accept Reform Jews as marriage partners for their children, they often insist that the partner's mother is Jewish or that the prospective spouse undergo a Conservative conversion to Judaism.

Many Conservative Jews consider themselves to be more religious than Reform Jews, even when their practices are generally not particularly different from those of Reform Jews. This can create a certain tension, particularly for Reform Jews who may feel that Conservative Jews consider them to be less authentic Jews. This tension between individual Conservative and Reform Jews can contribute to *Sinat Chinam* within *Klal Yisrael*.

Jewish status issues can be particularly challenging when a Conservative Jewish parent refuses to recognize the child of a Reform couple as a Jew because the child's mother is not Jewish, notwithstanding that the child's father is Jewish and the child was raised as a Jew, consistent with the Reform definition of a Jew. There is no clear path toward eliminating these variations between Conservative and Reform practices; those facing these conflicts will need to seek the counsel of Conservative and Reform rabbis dedicated to helping their congregants move forward in a constructive way.

Recognizing that it can be hard to change behaviors, I am instead asking Conservative Jews to change their perspective toward Reform Jews, to recognize that all Jewish movements need to refine their respective paths forward, and to acknowledge that each stream has its own way to move across the imaginary gameboard. To accomplish this, those in every movement, including Conservative Jews, need to work on their perceptions and eliminate any *Sinat Chinam* that they feel today.

Reconstructionist Jews

Because the Reconstructionist movement is so small, you, as a Conservative Jew, probably don't think about Reconstructionist Jews much or encounter them often, unless you are in a community that has a reasonably large Reconstructionist synagogue. If you are knowledgeable about the Reconstructionist movement, you probably disagree with its theological positions. Giving up the concept of Jews as the chosen people and, more importantly, the concept of God as above nature is not likely to resonate with you. As such, you probably see Reconstructionist Judaism as too far a departure from traditional Jewish concepts and beliefs.

Whatever your reaction to the Reconstructionist movement's theology, it's important not to let those feelings lead to *Sinat Chinam* toward individual Reconstructionist Jews. Even if you consider that theology misguided, it's important to let the Reconstructionist movement define its own path and work to move across the imaginary game board, playing its part to help bring the Messianic age.

Sephardic Jews

As a Conservative Jew, you probably do not have an overall impression of Sephardic Jews, other than the sense that they came from different places than Ashkenazi Jews did. You might look at Sephardic Jews who observe halacha similarly to the way that you view Modern Orthodox Jews, which I discussed earlier in this chapter. The points that I made there are equally valid here. It is time to let go of anger, blame, and resentment, and embrace each other as part of the Jewish experience that began thousands of years ago and continues today. Then, with the help of the Conservative movement's leadership, you can focus on the Conservative path for the future and your role in bringing the Messianic age.

Chapter Fifteen

REFORMING REFORM JEWS' PERSPECTIVE

Overview

THIS CHAPTER ADDRESSES the perspective of Reform Jews toward Jews of other movements within *Klal Yisrael*. First, it addresses Reform Jews' general mindset regarding different types of Orthodox Jews. Then, it addresses Reform Jews' general mindset about non-Orthodox Jews who adhere to other streams of Judaism.

Mindset of Reform Jews Toward Modern Orthodox Jews

As a Reform Jew, you might interact with Modern Orthodox Jews in the workplace, at shopping malls, at sporting and entertainment events, and at vacation destinations. In many cases, their dress is not distinguishable from yours, particularly when Modern Orthodox men choose not to wear *kippot* and Modern Orthodox women do not observe the rules of *tzniut*, something that is likely in many of these settings. Your relationship with Modern Orthodox Jews probably includes a combination of commonality and resentment.

Because in their daily lives, they do many of the same things that you do, generally look like you, and tend to be ardent Zionists, you and Modern Orthodox Jews have a lot in common. You might work and commute to work together. You might eat lunch together on workdays. Your kids might attend sports, cultural, and charitable activities together. When these shared experiences are the norm, your relationships with Modern Orthodox Jews tend to be positive.

Then there is the other side of the equation. Modern Orthodox Jews don't come to work, answer their phones, or check texts or email on *Shabbat* or on Jewish Holidays, while you generally do work and engage in other recreational and cultural activities on these days. If you attend a Reform Temple regularly, you probably go on Friday night rather than on *Shabbat* morning, but do not strictly observe *Shabbat* in the traditional way. You might find it frustrating when your Modern Orthodox work colleagues are not available to share the workload on *Shabbat* or Jewish Holidays, particularly when a project deadline approaches. You might feel that the Modern Orthodox Jew is, in effect, saying, "I'm a better Jew than you are." This feeling can result in strong resentment leading to *Sinat Chinam*.

The same thing can occur in other contexts, such as when a Modern Orthodox Jewish child who is a talented athlete does not participate on a sports team on *Shabbat* or a Jewish Holiday, reducing the team's chances of winning. This can be frustrating to both you and your children, especially if the game is within walking distance of that child's home, making you wonder if there is really a halachic prohibition against the child's participation in the event. In a situation such as this, you probably don't have enough knowledge of Jewish law to question this decision publicly, but you might still feel that the Modern Orthodox family is being "self-righteous" about its level of religious observance to the detriment of the team. This can lead to deep resentment.

The Reform movement does not embrace halacha as a mandatory practice, opting instead for particularism, allowing you to choose which rituals and practices to embrace and which not to observe. Although the New Pittsburgh Platform encourages a fresh examination of Reform Jews' traditional practices, it is unlikely that you are aware of this or that it would significantly influence your choices. As a result, it is easy to view Orthodox practices as antiquated in today's modern world and to think that Orthodox Jews are taking advantage of a religious "loophole" to avoid participation in work and leisure obligations.

Notwithstanding these feelings, it is time to let go of anger, blame, and resentment and embrace Orthodox Jews as part of the Jewish experience that began thousands of years ago and continues today. Then, with the help of your Reform leadership, you can focus on the Reform path for the future and your role in bringing the Messianic age in our lifetime.

Mindset of Reform Jews Toward Chassidic and Yeshivish Jews

As a Reform Jew, you probably do not interact often with Chassidic and Yeshivish Jews. You don't live in the same neighborhoods, you don't dress the same way, you don't attend the same synagogues, and your children do not attend the same schools. You don't agree on many political issues in the United States or in Israel. Reform Jews tend to look at the Chassidic and Yeshivish worlds as out-of-date throwbacks to life in Eastern Europe. You see these Jews as holding onto a medieval form of Judaism that repudiates the experiences, freedoms, and opportunities of the modern world. The media has reinforced these impressions both in films featuring the "escape" of women from the "oppressions" of the Chassidic world and by reporting on news about these communities in a one-sided and biased way.

But it goes both ways. Chassidic and Yeshivish Jews have little understanding of Reform Judaism. This is precisely why, in Part One of this book, I explained each stream of Judaism in such detail. I wanted to give Jews of different persuasions the opportunity to understand their counterparts in different movements of Judaism. I hope that reading Part One gave you an understanding and appreciation of the beauty of Chassidic and Yeshivish Judaism.

These are happy communities who love their way of life and their families. Their version of Judaism might not include the things that are important to you such as the American cultural experience, professional sports, and a focus on secular education and career achievement. But they do not feel deprived. They are well aware that they are surrounded by a world that differs greatly from the way they live, but they have elected to live this way, sharing a deep religious and spiritual experience in large, close families and cohesive communities. The media spins these Jews, and particularly Chassidic Jews, as cult-like and brainwashed. As Part One demonstrates, nothing could be farther from the truth. It is precisely because this way of life is so alluring that so many unaffiliated Jews are attracted to outreach experiences like putting on *tefillin*, lighting *Shabbat* candles, performing the ritual of shaking a *lulav* and *etrog*, and attending *Shabbat* meals.

While you do not interact much with Chassidic and Yeshivish Jews, you might feel animosity toward them, not just because of the misperceptions that I've tried to dispel, but also because you feel that they judge you as Jews who have lost their way and who will not be worthy of redemption when the Messianic age arrives. And it goes further. They do not view your rabbis as legitimate members of the rabbinate entitled to opine on questions of Jewish law and practice. These issues have become particularly volatile in Israel where the Reform movement has met determined resistance to its efforts to gain rabbinic authority on par with that of the Orthodox rabbinate, particularly with respect to officiating at lifecycle events such as weddings and divorces.

I addressed the Chassidic and Yeshivish communities with respect to their attitudes toward Reform Jews in Chapter Thirteen. I tried to make it clear that the *Sinat Chinam* that prevails today needs to stop in order for real change to occur and for my suggested framework to succeed. In Part Two I also emphasized that each movement within Judaism needs to work on its future path, and to appreciate the paths of other movements and the role they will play in bringing the Messianic age. In this chapter, I am addressing you as a Reform Jew. I am asking you please to let go of your animosity toward Chassidic and Yeshivish Jews. I recognize that it is a two-way street and that they need to respond in kind by letting go of their dislike of Reform Jews and acknowledging that each Jewish stream's action can improve our chances of attaining the Messianic age.

I do not expect you to agree with Chassidic and Yeshivish Jews on theological issues or on political issues in the Diaspora or in Israel. I am only asking you to let go of any *Sinat Chinam* that you presently feel toward them. Only then, can Reform, Chassidic, and Yeshivish Jews follow their respective chosen paths with a real chance of bringing the Messianic age.

Conservative Jews

As a Reform Jew, you have a lot of interaction with Conservative Jews socially, in the workplace, and in your communities. Marriages between Jews of these streams are common and widely accepted. Notwithstanding this observation, most Reform Jews have chosen Reform Judaism over Conservative Judaism. There are several reasons for this:

- Reform Jews feel drawn to a movement that has historically broken with tradition, deigned its own liturgy, incorporated music into its services, and does not emphasize strict observance of *Shabbat* or the Festivals.
- Reform Jews generally prefer that their clergy do not observe halacha and instead live lives similar to those of their congregants.
- Reform Jews enjoy belonging to Temples that do not follow the prescribed halachic times for services and instead consider their congregants' convenience. Examples are prioritizing Friday night services over *Shabbat* morning ones and downplaying the importance of Festival services.
- Reform Jews do not care if their Temples observe *kashrut*, since Reform families rarely do so.
- Reform Jews prefer to belong to a movement that does not fully follow the traditional Jewish calendar and that includes only one day for *Rosh Hashana* and the Festivals of *Pesach*, *Shavuot*, and *Sukkot*.
- Reform Jews and the Reform movement accept intermarriage between Jews and non-Jews, recognizing its inevitability and seeking to support the interfaith couples in their pursuit of Jewish experiences.
- Reform Jews support the determination of Jewish status based on both patrilineal and matrilineal descent.

Many Reform Jews believe that Conservative Jews practice a form of Judaism that is the more or less same as Reform Judaism. Declining membership in Conservative Synagogues and increasing membership in Reform Temples has reinforced this belief, as the children of Conservative Jews have embraced Reform Judaism as reflecting their religious practices and upbringing, despite the differences that this chapter and Chapter Fourteen describe. Given this perception, it is upsetting to Reform Jews that many Conservative Jews consider Conservative Judaism more authentic than Reform Judaism.

There is no clear path toward eliminating the real differences in the respective positions of Reform and Conservative Jews regarding patrilineal descent and intermarriage; those facing these conflicts will need to seek the counsel of Reform and Conservative rabbis dedicated to helping their congregants move forward in a constructive way.

Recognizing that it can be hard to change behaviors, I am instead asking Reform Jews to change their perspective toward Conservative Jews, to recognize that all Jewish movements need to refine their respective paths forward and to acknowledge that each stream has its own way to move across the imaginary gameboard. To accomplish this, those in every movement, including Reform Jews, need to work on their perceptions and eliminate any *Sinat Chinam* that they feel today.

Reconstructionist Jews

As a Reform Jew, you probably do not know many Reconstructionist Jews. Your impression is likely to be that Reconstructionist Judaism is even more liberal than Reform Judaism when it comes to observing traditional Jewish practices. This is not an accurate perception. As Chapter Four explained, Reconstructionist Judaism includes many traditional elements but breaks with tradition with its rejection of the concepts that Jews are the chosen people, and of an all-knowing supernatural God who can perform miracles that defy the laws of nature. Under Reconstructionist principles, Reconstructionist Jews are also free, as congregations or smaller groups, to choose which *mitzvot* to observe and how to observe them. Thus, while theologically, Reconstructionist Judaism is well to the left of Reform Judaism, both the Reform and the Reconstructionist movements embrace particularism. In practice, however, Reconstructionist Jews embrace traditional Jewish practices and form close-knit communities far more frequently than Reform Jews do.

I don't perceive any dislike between Reform Jews and Reconstructionist Jews, although there is no reliable published data on this issue.

Sephardic Jews

As a Reform Jew, you probably do not have an overall impression of Sephardic Jews, other than the sense that they came from different places than Ashkenazi Jews did. You might look at Sephardic Jews who observe halacha similarly to the way that you view Modern Orthodox Jews, which I discussed earlier in this chapter. The points that I made there are equally valid here. It is time to let go of anger, blame, and resentment and embrace each other as part of the Jewish experience that began thousands of years ago and continues today. Then, with the help of the Reform movement's leadership, you can focus on the Reform path for the future and your role in bringing the Messianic age.

Chapter Sixteen

RECONSTRUCTIONIST JEWS ARE FEW BUT MIGHTY - WHAT DO THEY THINK?

Overview

THIS CHAPTER ADDRESSES the perspective of Reconstructionist Jews toward Jews of other movements within *Klal Yisrael*. First, it addresses Reconstructionist Jews' general mindset regarding different types of Orthodox Jews. Then, it addresses Reconstructionist Jews' general mindset about all other Jews in streams of Judaism other than the Reconstructionist stream.

Orthodox Jews

Mindset of Reconstructionist Jews Toward Modern Orthodox Jews

As a Reconstructionist Jew, you interact with Modern Orthodox Jews in the workplace, at shopping malls, at sporting and entertainment events, and at vacation destinations. In many cases, their dress is not distinguishable from yours, particularly when Modern Orthodox men choose not to wear *kippot* and Modern Orthodox women do not observe the rules of *tzniut*, as is likely in many of these settings. Your relationship with Modern Orthodox Jews probably includes a combination of commonality and resentment.

Because they do many of the same things as you in their daily lives, generally look like you, and tend to be ardent Zionists, you and Modern Orthodox Jews have a lot in common. You often work together and commute to work together. You might eat lunch together on workdays. Your kids might attend sports and cultural activities together. When these shared experiences are the norm, your relationships with Modern Orthodox Jews tend to be positive.

However, as I have noted, the Reconstructionist movement does not purport to embrace traditional halacha as mandatory, opting instead for a process by which congregations or groups choose the practices and rituals to follow, redefining them to be relevant to the modern world. As a result, traditional Judaism might feel very rigid and antiquated to you, and you might feel that your Modern Orthodox counterparts are relying on outdated practices to escape certain obligations.

For example, it can be frustrating to both you and your children when a Modern Orthodox child who is a talented athlete does not participate on a sports team on *Shabbat* or a Jewish Holiday, thus reducing the team's chances of winning. It is especially difficult when the game is within walking distance of the child's home, meaning that in your view, there is no specific halachic prohibition against the child's participation in the event. Nevertheless, the Modern Orthodox child does not attend because the activity is not in the spirit of *Shabbat*. In a situation such as this, you may believe that you have enough knowledge of Jewish law to question this decision, which often makes you feel that the Modern Orthodox family is being "self-righteous" about its level of religious observance to the detriment of the team. You might feel that the Modern Orthodox Jew is, in effect, saying, "I'm a better Jew than you are."

This feeling can result in strong resentment leading to *Sinat Chinam*, especially because you as a Reconstructionist Jew are very committed to your form of Judaism and engage in significant Reconstructionist *Shabbat* observances. It feels off-putting to have the sense that your Modern Orthodox counterparts are looking at you as a second-class Jew.

Notwithstanding these feelings, it is time to let go of anger, blame, and resentment and embrace Orthodox Jews as part of the Jewish experience that began thousands of years ago and continues today. Then, with the help of your Reconstructionist leadership, you can focus on the Reconstructionist path for the future and your role in bringing the Messianic age.

Mindset of Reconstructionist Jews Toward Chassidic and Yeshivish Jews

As a Reconstructionist Jew, you probably do not interact often with Chassidic and Yeshivish Jews. You don't live in the same neighborhoods, you don't dress the same way, and you don't agree on many political issues in the United States or in Israel. Reconstructionist Jews tend to look at the Chassidic and Yeshivish worlds as out of date throwbacks to life in Eastern Europe. You see these Jews as holding onto a medieval form of Judaism that repudiates the experiences, freedoms, and opportunities of the modern world. The media has reinforced these impressions both in films featuring the "escape" of women from the "oppressions" of the Chassidic world and by reporting on news about these communities in a one-sided and biased way.

But it goes both ways. Chassidic and Yeshivish Jews have little understanding of Reconstructionist Judaism. This is precisely why, in Part One of this book, I explained each stream of Judaism in such detail. I wanted to give Jews of different persuasions the opportunity to understand their counterparts in different movements of Judaism. I hope that Part One gave you an understanding and appreciation of the beauty of Chassidic and Yeshivish Judaism.

These are happy communities whose members love their way of life and their families. Their version of Judaism might not include the things that are important to you such as the American cultural experience, professional sports, and a focus on secular education and career achievement. But they do not feel deprived. They are well aware that they are surrounded by a world that differs greatly from the way they live, but they have elected to live this way, sharing a deep religious and spiritual experience in large, close families and cohesive communities. The media spins these Jews, and particularly Chassidic Jews, as cult-like and brainwashed. As Part One demonstrated, nothing could be farther from the truth. It is precisely because this way of life is so alluring that so many unaffiliated Jews are attracted to outreach experiences like putting on *tefillin*, lighting *Shabbat* candles, performing the ritual of shaking a *lulav* and *etrog*, and attending *Shabbat* meals.

While you do not interact much with Chassidic and Yeshivish Jews, you might feel animosity toward them, not just because of the misperceptions that I've tried to dispel, but also because you feel that they judge you as Jews who have lost their way and who will not be worthy of redemption when the Messianic age arrives. And it goes further. They do not view your rabbis as legitimate members of the rabbinate entitled to opine on questions of Jewish law and practice. These issues have become particularly volatile in Israel where the liberal Jewish movements have met determined resistance to their efforts to gain rabbinic authority similar to that of the Orthodox rabbinate, particularly with respect to officiating at lifecycle events such as weddings and divorces.

I have addressed the Chassidic and Yeshivish communities with respect to their attitudes toward Reconstructionist Jews in Chapter Thirteen. I tried to make it clear that the *Sinat Chinam* that prevails today needs to stop for real change to occur and for my suggested framework to succeed. In Part Two I also emphasized that each movement within Judaism needs to work on its future path and to appreciate the paths of other movements and the role that they will play in bringing the Messianic age. In this chapter, I am addressing you as a Reconstructionist Jew. I am asking you please to let go of your hatred of Chassidic and Yeshivish Jews. I recognize that it is a two-way street and that they need to respond in kind by letting go of their dislike of Reconstructionist Jews and acknowledging that each Jewish stream's actions can improve our chances of attaining the Messianic age.

I do not expect you to agree with Chassidic and Yeshivish Jews on theological issues or on political issues in the Diaspora or in Israel. I am only asking you to let go of any *Sinat Chinam* that you presently feel toward them. Only then, can Reconstructionist, Chassidic, and Yeshivish Jews follow their respective chosen paths with a real chance of bringing the Messianic age.

Conservative Jews

As a Reconstructionist Jew, you have a lot of interaction with Conservative Jews socially, in the workplace, and in your communities. Marriages between Jews of these streams are common and widely accepted. Nonetheless, most Reconstructionist Jews have chosen Reconstructionist Judaism over Conservative Judaism. There are several reasons for this:

- Reconstructionist Jews feel drawn to a movement that has developed its own unique theology based on the principles that Rabbi Mordechai Kaplan espoused. As such, they are not attracted to Conservative Judaism, which officially maintains much of traditional practice and liturgy, while at the same time accepting the reality that only a small percentage of Conservative Jews follow the principles and practices of the Conservative leadership. They realize that Mordechai Kaplan broke with the Conservative movement in order to help found the Reconstructionist movement.
- Reconstructionist Jews have developed tight-knit communities that share Jewish experiences in a style that Conservative Jews rarely exhibit.
- Reconstructionist Jews accept patrilineal descent in determining Jewish status, and view the Conservative movement's refusal to do so as antiquated.
- Unlike Conservative rabbis, some Reconstructionist rabbis will perform interfaith marriages.

Many Reconstructionist Jews believe that the Conservative movement has lost much of its relevance. Its members do not adhere to the movement's espoused practices, the movement has not established meaningful communities, and synagogue membership is declining in favor of the Reform and Reconstructionist movements. Yet, Conservative Jews staunchly cling to their heritage despite these alleged shortcomings, somehow believing that their brand of Judaism is more authentic than Reconstructionist Judaism because of its traditional services, its resistance to patrilineal descent, and its refusal to allow Conservative rabbis to officiate at interfaith weddings. At the same time, the typical Conservative Jew devotes far less time and effort to the practice of Judaism than does the typical Reconstructionist Jew. In light of this, it makes no sense to Reconstructionist Jews that many Conservative Jews consider Conservative Judaism more authentic than Reconstructionist Judaism. This often makes Reconstructionist Jews angry.

Another source of resentment is that because the Reconstructionist movement is small, many Conservative Jews think of it as a fringe movement rather than as a mainstream part of the American Jewish experience.

Recognizing that it can be hard to change behaviors, I am instead asking Reconstructionist Jews to change their perspective toward Conservative Jews and to recognize that all Jewish movements need to refine their respective paths forward, and to acknowledge that each stream has its own way to move across the imaginary gameboard. To accomplish this though, those in every movement, including Reconstructionist Jews, need to work on their perceptions and eliminate any *Sinat Chinam* that they feel today.

Reform Jews

As a Reconstructionist Jew, you probably know many Reform Jews. Your impression might be that Reform Jews are like Reconstructionist Jews in their rejection of the mandatory observance of the laws of traditional Judaism. You are acutely aware that the Reform movement is much larger than the Reconstructionist movement. You are also aware that Reform Jews do not generally behave like Reconstructionist Jews by engaging in group decision-making about which observances and practices to keep, modify, or reject, instead opting for individual particularism regarding this kind of decision. While you prefer Reconstructionist Judaism, including its theology that rejects both the traditional belief in a God with supernatural abilities and the concept of the Jews as the chosen people, these distinctions from Reform Judaism do not create friction between Reconstructionist and Reform Jews.

Based on my research, I don't perceive that there is discernable dislike between Reconstructionist Jews and Reform Jews, although there is no reliable published data on this issue.

Sephardic Jews

As a Reconstructionist Jew, you probably do not have an overall impression of Sephardic Jews, other than the sense that they came from different places than Ashkenazi Jews did. You might look at Sephardic Jews who observe halacha similarly to the way that you view Modern Orthodox Jews, which I discussed earlier in this chapter. The points that I made there are equally valid here. It is time to let go of anger, blame, and resentment and embrace each other as part of the Jewish experience that began thousands of years ago and continues today. Then, with the help of the Reconstructionist movement's leadership, you can focus on the Reconstructionist path for the future and your role in bringing the Messianic age.

Chapter Seventeen

THE MAGIC OF THE SEPHARDIC JEWISH PERSPECTIVE

Overview

As I explained in Chapter Five, Sephardic Jewry does not encompass denominations such as Orthodox, Conservative, etc. Sephardic Jews' religious observance spans a broad spectrum of individual practices, but without labels. Sephardic prayerbooks follow a traditional Sephardic liturgy, which in many ways resembles Ashkenazi Orthodox liturgy. Likewise, Sephardic synagogues are similar to Ashkenazi Orthodox synagogues, with services led by male clergy and congregants, separate seating for men and women, and strict *kashrut* observance at all events.

While practices of individual Sephardic Jews differ considerably, the hallmark of Sephardic Judaism is tradition. As a result, there are far fewer completely secular and unaffiliated Sephardic Jews than Ashkenazi Jews. The norm for Sephardic Jews who do not strictly observe halacha is to observe

Jewish tradition, with heavy emphasis on the laws of family purity, individual prayer, and Friday night *Shabbat* meals. This affects how Sephardic Jews view both each other and Jews from different Ashkenazi denominations.

View of Other Sephardic Jews

As a Sephardic Jew, whether in North America or in Israel, you are very accepting of other Sephardic Jews, even where your religious practices differ significantly. In North America, the cornerstone of a Sephardic community is its members' common country of origin before immigrating to North America. Within these communities, variations in the strictness of religious practices developed over time based on individual choices rather than deep philosophical principles. As a result, as long as Sephardic Jews stayed close to their families and communities, their communities and other Sephardic Jews did not judge them for their individual decisions. In contrast, for a Sephardic Jew to leave his or her community is a big deal and can, depending on the specific community and the individual's family, result in complete exclusion from the Sephardic world. Some communities also frown on marriage to a spouse from outside the community. The concept of *Sinat Chinam* based on differences in religious practices does not really exist among North American Sephardic Jews.

In contrast, strong feelings might divide different Sephardic communities in North America. The details of these divisions is beyond the scope of this book. This is far less of an issue in Israel, largely as a result of Rav Ovadia Yosef's unifying influence. In Chapter Eleven, I indicated that "American Sephardic Jews need to find a way to unify in a manner similar to Israeli Sephardic Jews to make meaningful progress and define the American Sephardic path for making progress toward bringing the Messianic Age. It is up to the Sephardic Jewish community to figure out how to achieve this result, whether by community or across multiple communities. In either case, the goal should be increased observance of religious practices and a focus on *middot*, as a way of restoring the crown of glory for American Sephardic Jewry." This should include a focus on eliminating any *Sinat Chinam* among different communities of Sephardic Jews.

Chassidic and Yeshivish Jews

As a Sephardic Jew, you are very accepting of other Jews whose levels of religious practice differ from your own. However, where you sense that Askenazi Jews are judging you negatively in instances where your religious practices differ from theirs, you feel resentful. Thus, you might have trouble fitting in with Chassidic and Yeshivish Jews in certain situations.

Chassidic Jews live mostly in communities that isolate them from the rest of society, both in North America and in Israel. They have distinctive styles of dress, depending on the specific Chassidic sect to which they belong. In all cases, this includes a black velvet *kippah*, a black hat, as well as a white shirt, and a suit with a long jacket or robe of some type. You, as a Sephardic Jew, in contrast, typically wear stylish, contemporary clothing and, if you are religiously observant, a knitted wool *kippah*, sometimes black but most often in a variety of colors and patterns. Thus, to a Chassidic Jew who does not know you, you are likely to appear like a Modern Orthodox Jew if you are wearing a *kippah*, and like a more liberal Jew if you are not wearing one. At a minimum, during these encounters, you might feel different and perhaps somewhat out of place, which is not a comfortable feeling. It doesn't take much for this to rise to the level of *Sinat Chinam*. It's extremely important to overcome any such reactions and to reframe your perceptions of Chassidic Jews. They are important partners in the mission of *Klal Yisrael* to help bring the Messianic Age speedily in our time. Focus your energies positively toward what you as a Sephardic Jew can do to move along the Sephardic Path to hasten the arrival of the Messianic Age.

As a Sephardic Jew, your exposure to Yeshivish Jews will depend on the community where you live and on your field of work. Many religiously observant Sephardic Jews attend Yeshivish or Modern Orthodox synagogues if they live in neighborhoods where there are no Sephardic synagogues. In such cases, those who attend Yeshivish synagogues have the opportunity to build close relationships with Yeshivish Jews, and this decreases the likelihood that *Sinat Chinam* will develop.

Even where you and Yeshivish Jews do not attend the same synagogue, you might meet in the workplace. Over the last few decades, Yeshivish Jews have joined the American workforce in increasing numbers. Your interaction with them facilitates greater understanding and appreciation of your respective cultures and practices. The same is true in Israel, where the Sephardic Jewish population makes up a much greater percentage of the overall Jewish population than it does in North America, further increasing opportunities for interactions between religiously observant Sephardic Jews and Yeshivish Jews.

If you are a less religiously observant Sephardic Jew, you are not likely to attend the same synagogues as Yeshivish Jews. While you might work together in the business and professional world, your differences quickly become apparent, and quite possibly you will feel that your more religiously observant Yeshivish colleagues look down on you as if you don't take Judaism seriously enough. If this happens, you are likely to be resentful. This, of course, is a two-way street, and I've addressed both Chassidic and Yeshivish Jews about this in Chapter Thirteen. It will take a mutual effort to address this issue. Here, I'm asking you as a Sephardic Jew to do your part to help bring the Messianic Age by letting go of any *Sinat Chinam* that you might feel toward Yeshivish Jews.

Modern Orthodox Jews

If you are a religiously observant Sephardic Jew, you encounter Modern Orthodox Jews in a variety of settings. You dress similarly, you might attend a Modern Orthodox synagogue, your children often go to the same Jewish day schools, you shop for food in the same kosher grocery stores, and eat in many of the same restaurants. You both might remove your *kippot* in the workplace or when attending secular events. Accordingly, there is not a strong basis for *Sinat Chinam* to develop between you.

If you are a Sephardic Jew who is not particularly religiously observant, you will have less in common with Modern Orthodox Jews. The close ties that develop through shared religious practices will not be present. Yet, Modern Orthodox Jews are not likely to regard you as they would regard a liberal Ashkenazi Jew, and you are not as likely to feel that they look down on as if you were a liberal Ashkenazi Jew. This difference results from the divergence in culture between Sephardic and Ashkenazi Jews. Even non-religiously observant Sephardic Jews have strong Jewish traditions in areas like *Shabbat* observance on Friday night and membership in synagogues that follow Orthodox practices. Thus, Modern Orthodox Jews are likely to consider that you are connected to Judaism in a significant way. This mitigates the likelihood that you or they will have negative feelings for the other and makes *Sinat Chinam* unlikely.

Conservative Jews

As a Sephardic Jew, you probably interact with Conservative Jews frequently, in the workplace, while shopping, and at entertainment venues. Your relationship with them is likely to depend on their perception of your level of religious observance. If you observe *Shabbat* and keep kosher, Conservative Jews probably view you as a Modern Orthodox Jew. This can lead to the kind of resentment toward Modern Orthodox Jews that Chapter Fourteen explained. When this happens, you are likely to resent them in return. Then, of course, everybody loses, especially *Klal Yisrael* in its quest to hasten the arrival of the Messianic Age.

If you are not particularly religiously observant, your relationship with Conservative Jews is probably better. They are not likely to have a good understanding of your Sephardic culture, but they are also not likely to harbor any resentments toward you based on religious differences. If you don't sense resentment, *Sinat Chinam* is unlikely to enter your relationship.

Reform Jews

As a Sephardic Jew, you probably also interact with Reform Jews frequently, in the workplace, while shopping, and at entertainment venues. Your relationship with them is also likely to depend on their perception of your level of religious observance. If you observe *Shabbat* and keep kosher, Reform Jews probably view you as a Modern Orthodox Jew. This can lead to the kind of resentments toward Modern Orthodox Jews that Chapter Fifteen explained. Then, you are likely to resent them in return. This reciprocal *Sinat Chinam* gets in the way of helping to bring the Messianic Age.

If you are not particularly religiously observant, your

relationship with Reform Jews is probably better. They are not likely to have a good understanding of your Sephardic culture, but they are also not likely to harbor any resentments toward you based on religious differences. If you don't sense resentment, *Sinat Chinam* is unlikely to enter your relationship.

Reconstructionist Jews

As a Sephardic Jew, you probably do not interact with Reconstructionist Jews frequently because there are so few of them. When you do, your relationship with them is likely to depend on their perception of your level of religious observance. If you observe *Shabbat* and keep kosher, Reconstructionist Jews probably view you as a Modern Orthodox Jew. This can lead to the kind of resentment toward Modern Orthodox Jews that Chapter Sixteen explained. When this happens, you are likely to resent them in return.

If you are not particularly religiously observant, your relationship with Reconstructionist Jews is probably better. They are not likely to have a good understanding of your Sephardic culture, but they are also not likely to harbor any resentments toward you based on religious differences. If you don't sense resentment, *Sinat Chinam* is unlikely to enter your relationship.

Whenever you, as a Sephardic Jew, feel resentment toward other types of Jews, I am asking you to let go of that anger, blame, and resentment, and embrace each other as part of the Jewish experience that began thousands of years ago and continues today. Then, with the help of the Sephardic movement's leadership, you can focus on the Sephardic path for the future and your role in bringing the *Messianic Age* in our lifetimes.

Part Four

TAKING ACTION

Chapter Eighteen

TO ALL JEWS: YES, WE CAN!

I'VE MADE THE case for eliminating *Sinat Chinam* among Jews and asserted that each stream within Judaism needs to define its path forward, for which, in Part Two, I suggested the metaphor of stream-by-stream movement across an imaginary gameboard. Part Three of this book speaks directly to Jews in each stream of Judaism about the need to think differently and to avoid *Sinat Chinam* toward other Jews, irrespective of their differences. But these building blocks of change based only on thoughts are not enough. Every Jew needs to take action, and all Jews, irrespective of their specific streams, beliefs, and practices, need to recognize and appreciate the steps that the others are taking. In fact, these steps need to be clear and compelling even for Jews who do not belong to any stream of Judaism, a group that I have not previously addressed in this book.

The number of unaffiliated Jews both in Israel and in the Diaspora is staggering. According to the 2016 Pew Research Center Study, 40% of Israeli Jews are secular (*Hiloni,* or *Hilonim* in the plural) as opposed to traditional or religious. Nevertheless, some members of this group observe some Jewish holidays such as *Rosh Hashana* and *Yom Kippur* and some might even keep kosher.[1]

This is not surprising since the Hebrew calendar and tradition have a critical influence on daily life in Israel, even for secular Jews. For example, on Fridays, store owners, taxi drivers, soldiers, and others wish people a *Shabbat Shalom*, even if they are all secular Jews. Similarly, because Israel is overwhelmingly a Jewish state, secular Jews are very unlikely to intermarry with non-Jews or to convert to a different faith.

Secular Israelis and religiously observant Israelis, both Chassidic and Yeshivish Jews (*Haredi* or *Haredim* in the plural) and Modern Orthodox Jews (*Dati* or *Datiim* in the plural, alternatively *Dati-Leumi* or *Datiim Leumiim* in the plural), are deeply opposed to each other's views regarding the role of religion in the decisions of the Israeli government and the level of influence that the Orthodox Israeli Rabbinate should have on domestic social policy. This division until recently has been the major factor in recent Israeli elections and had led to the inability of any political party to achieve a meaningful majority in the Israeli *Knesset* (Parliament). At present, a coalition of parties representing *Haredim*, religious *Sephardim*, and Religious Zionists holds a majority in the *Knesset*, but this has led to continuous protests by nonreligious members of Israeli society over several issues, most notably proposed judicial reform legislation and the continued exemption of most *Haredim* from serving in the military.

Accordingly, there is a significant level of *Sinat Chinam* between secular Jews and religiously observant Jews in Israel. Unlike in the Diaspora, because Sephardim make up a majority of the Jewish population in Israel, they are not insulated from this *Sinat Chinam*. In fact, the *Shas* party, which represents religious Sephardic Jews, plays an important role in determining political outcomes in Israel.

According to the 2020 Pew Research Study, 32% of American Jews are unaffiliated with any specific denomination of Judaism. This percentage is higher among American Jews ages 18-29 (41%), and ages 30-49 (36%), respectively.[2] Yet, these mostly secular unaffiliated Jews consider themselves Jewish and have the kinds of reactions to Orthodox Jews and, in some cases, other affiliated Jews, that generates *Sinat Chinam*. Given the size of the secular Jewish population in Israel and the unaffiliated Jewish population in the United States, it is not possible to address the issue of *Sinat Chinam* as a barrier to the arrival of the Messianic age without including these Jews in any suggested solution.

There is a further reason for insisting on specific action that goes beyond a call for a change of thought and mindset. While thinking differently is the ultimate goal and doing so would also change behavior toward other Jews, in practice changing behavior is a critical prerequisite to changing mindset. In fact, if we don't first take concrete steps to change our behavior, it is very unlikely that our attempts to change our mindset will be successful. The Jews at Mount Sinai recognized this principle. After receiving the Ten Commandments and other laws, they responded, "We will do and we will obey," indicating their awareness that action must precede full understanding.[3]

Before getting to my specific action proposals, it is important to mention another book relevant to the subject of *achdut*. In 1993, Rabbi Jonathan Sacks (1948-2020) wrote *One People? Tradition, Modernity and Jewish Unity*,[4] in which he asked the basic question: Does *Klal Yisrael* exist as a single entity today when Judaism is divided into multiple denominations that sanction differing sets of beliefs and practices? In analyzing the issue, he focused specifically on Orthodox Judaism and Reform Judaism as representing the two ends of the spectrum of beliefs and practices within *Klal Yisrael*. He asserted that if there were a successful resolution to the issues separating these two denominations, then a resolution could also be found that encompasses Judaism's other denominations. In his analysis, Rabbi Sacks looked at two possible approaches: Pluralism and Inclusivism.

A Pluralistic approach would recognize Orthodox Judaism and Reform Judaism as acceptable alternative approaches to beliefs and practices from the perspectives of both the Orthodox and the Reform movements. Rabbi Sacks concludes that halacha is so fundamental to the Orthodox definition of Jewish practice that it could never accept a movement within Judaism that rejects halacha in favor of individual choice regarding which aspects of halacha to follow.[5] He therefore dismisses Pluralism as a viable approach to establishing the continued existence of *Klal Yisrael*, while recognizing that Pluralism is precisely what Reform Jews would like – full recognition of Reform Judaism in Israel and the Diaspora as an acceptable approach to Judaism.[6]

Inclusivism would acknowledge the differences between Orthodox Judaism and Reform Judaism yet find a way to consider them both part of *Klal Yisrael*, descendants of the Israelites who stood at Mount Sinai and accepted the unbreakable covenant with *Hashem* for eternity. Rabbi Sacks explores this proposition at length, recognizing that the result of failed Inclusivism is the exclusion from *Klal Yisrael* of those who are beyond the theological boundaries of inclusion. Probably the best example of this result is the split that occurred between Judaism and Christianity. He acknowledges that there are those within the Orthodox world who, given a chance, would advocate for this result today with respect to Reform Jews by defining Reform Judaism as a separate and distinct religion from Judaism.

Rabbi Sacks points out that despite the differences between

Orthodox Judaism and Reform Judaism, the two denominations have coexisted within *Klal Yisroel* for close to two hundred years.* This is *de facto* proof that the covenant of Mount Sinai is strong enough to survive while continuing to include groups of Jews who do not accept the covenant's halachic terms. They might be sinners, he writes, but they are sinners within *Klal Yisrael*. He presents a litany of arguments, from an Orthodox perspective, as to why this could be acceptable. These include analogizing Reform Jews to uneducated children who cannot be held accountable for their actions and are therefore inadvertent sinners; looking at the pressures of current free societies to which Reform Jews fall victim, thus excusing them for their actions; and taking into account the opinions of a few liberal Modern Orthodox Rabbis who assert that the covenant at Mount Sinai no longer applies after the Holocaust – i.e., that *Hashem* effectively abrogated it by allowing the Holocaust to happen.

The essence of these arguments and other similar positions is that true Judaism is Orthodox Judaism and that Reform Jews because of their circumstances, or because of the Holocaust, currently get a pass from the requirement to follow halacha. Needless to say, Reform Jews do not see these arguments as an acceptable approach to Inclusiveness, and Rabbi Sacks acknowledges this.

Rabbi Sacks then makes a series of proposals to buttress the future of Inclusiveness:[7]

1. That Jews do not speak of other Jews other than with words of love and respect. In more classic language, Rabbi Sacks is asking all Jews to refrain from speaking *lashon hara*. I'll have much more to say about this subject later.

---

*   As of 1993, when Rabbi Sacks' book was published.

2. That Orthodox Jews do not use coercion to prod other Jews to return to traditional Jewish observance.
3. That universal Jewish education be made an imperative as a means to introduce all Jews to halacha.
4. That wherever possible, halacha be applied to the broadest possible constituency, within the reach of the poor, sensitive to the needs and rights of women, and opening the way to religious return.
5. That no one judge liberal and secular Jews today as heretics or rebels, but rather as unwitting sinners or products of their environment. Their favorable actions should therefore be considered as *mitzvot* even if they lack halachic intent.
6. That liberal Jews should be recognized for their positive contributions to *Klal Yisrael*, including providing a viable alternative to mass conversions to Christianity, playing a critical role as secular Zionists in establishing the modern State of Israel, and reviving the Hebrew language.
7. That value be ascribed to the steps that liberal Jewish leaders have taken to bring tradition back to their constituents, while warning these leaders to avoid more conflicting tendencies, such as their positions on such issues as conversion and patrilineal descent, in the interests of keeping all Jews within the fold of *Klal Yisrael*.
8. That exclusive-minded Orthodox leaders do not act in a way that blocks the success of Inclusivism. He recalls the great schism between Chassidic and Yeshivish Jews that threatened to divide Orthodox Jewry irretrievably, and the steps that both groups took toward resolving that schism, in the interests of the greater good.
9. That "all Jews respect the sanctity of the Jewish people, collectively and individually."

10. That all Jews remember the Holocaust, which made no distinction between Jews based on level of religious observance.

Nonetheless, Rabbi Sacks acknowledges that:

> The inclusivist understands in advance that Jews outside Orthodoxy will find his position 'patronizing' or 'imperialistic'. That is the fate of inclusivism in the modern world. The Reform or secular Jew wishes to be respected for what he is, not for what he potentially might become. Indeed, extremists on all sides prefer extremist opponents, because each reinforces the other's prejudices. The inclusivist knows that his refusal to accept pluralism or dualism will find favor with no side. ... He asks non-Orthodox Jews at least to make the effort to understand the logic of his position and why no other is available within the terms of a tradition which he believes to be true, revealed and binding. That is what I have tried to do in this book.[8]

Yet, he concludes his book on an optimistic note, drawing on the progress of Jewish history and recent accomplishments, as follows:

> The primal scene of Jewish history is of the Israelites in the wilderness, fractious, rebellious, engaged in endless divisions, yet none the less slowly journeying towards the fulfilment of the covenantal promise. No image seems to me more descriptive of contemporary Jewry. There is no

agreement on the route. But unmistakably, Jews are returning: some to faith, others to a way of life, some to a place, others to a sense of peoplehood. For eighteen hundred years of dispersion, Jews prayed for freedom, the ingathering of the exiles, the restoration of sovereignty, and the rebuilding of Jerusalem. Today they have them. If faith implies anything—faith in God, or the Jewish people, or the covenant that binds one to the other as a 'kingdom of priests and a holy nation'—it implies this: that Jews having come thus far will not now disintegrate, so advanced along the journey which Abraham began nearly four thousand years ago. The inclusivist faith is that Jews, divided by where they stand, are united by what they are traveling towards, the destination which alone gives meaning to Jewish history: the promised union of Torah, the Jewish people, the land of Israel and God.[9]

Thus, the book ends with an impassioned emotional plea to have faith in our future based on our recent past, despite our often-tragic history and the difficult road toward reaching actual or *de facto* agreement on the terms of our collective participation in *Klal Yisrael*.

Rabbi Sacks' book is important because of its exposition of the issues that divide *Klal Yisrael* and its demonstration of how challenging it would be to bridge these divisions theologically and in practice. Orthodox Jews believe in the Divine legitimacy of their beliefs and practices, and, as such, it would be unrealistic to expect the Orthodox Rabbinate to embrace the beliefs and practices of other denominations of Judaism as legitimate. This reality leads to Rabbi Sacks' conclusion that any attempt at Pluralism would be certain to fail.

At the same time, Reform Jews believe that Reform Judaism represents the correct approach to Judaism in today's world. They look at Orthodox Judaism as both antiquated and obsolete in a world where Jews participate as full members of modern society, and they dismiss the concept and historical accuracy of the revelation of the Torah and its unchangeable commandments at Mount Sinai in favor of an ongoing revelation throughout Jewish history. They also elevate the principles of kindness and *middot* written in the Torah and espoused by the Prophets over the traditional religious practices included in the Torah and elucidated by the Oral Law, although the movement encourages its members to study these practices and choose which of them to observe based on their level of personal meaningfulness.

Given this seemingly unresolvable conflict, Rabbi Sacks opts to advocate for Inclusivism, even as he recognizes that the Orthodox basis behind this approach will be unacceptable to Reform Jews and troubling to many Orthodox Jews. This leads to his plea for the continued collective recognition of *Klal Yisrael* based on the enduring covenant at Mount Sinai and the historical fact that Judaism has endured despite its different denominations. He precedes this plea with ten proposals that he believes, if adopted, will pave the way for Inclusiveness to work (although he acknowledges that several of these proposals themselves would be troubling to Reform Jews, some Orthodox Jews, or both).

Rabbi Sacks' book does not address the subject of *achdut* directly. Rather, it focuses on whether *Klal Yisrael* as we perceive it still exists, or more precisely, whether it can be defined for the future based on agreed principles of Pluralism or Inclusivism. While his concluding tone is optimistic, the book does not leave us with the clear sense that anyone will move forward with his proposals. Looking at the Jewish world close to 30 years after the book was published, three things seem clear:

1. Trying to achieve formal Inclusivism is not a productive endeavor on the path to *achdut*.
2. *Klal Yisrael*, although fragmented, has continued to exist and seems unlikely to break apart, despite the many challenges and questions that it faces.
3. It is more productive to encourage each denomination of Judaism to define its path forward, and to recognize the benefits to all of *Klal Yisrael* that this activity will bring.

This brings us to the purpose of this book, whose approach is likely to be much more successful. While is it not possible, or perhaps even desirable, to try to convince each stream of Judaism to accept other streams of Judaism as authentic in theology or practice, it is both possible and desirable for all Jews to recognize that every Jew's *mitzvot* and *middot* are worthwhile and will help us to bring the Messianic age. In fact, Rabbi Sacks hints at this approach in the last sentence of his book:

> The inclusivist faith is that *Jews… are united by what they are traveling towards*, the destination which alone gives meaning to Jewish history: the promised union of Torah, the Jewish people, the land of Israel, and God.[10] [ed.: Italics added]

I recognize the assertion that *mitzvot* require halachic intent and that doing them based on individual choice rather than on the belief that one is commanded to them, therefore undercuts their validity. There are several reasons why the Orthodox world should not take this position here however:

1. The individuals performing the acts believe that they are performing each *mitzvah* for a religious reason.
2. Some *mitzvot* are also *middot*, which are not optional for liberal Jews and which they therefore always do with religious intent.
3. *Hashem* rewards the righteous acts of non-Jews, who might also have a place in the World to Come. This principle should therefore apply to the righteous acts of secular and unaffiliated Jews, irrespective of whether strict Orthodox principles would technically characterize them as *mitzvot*.

Moreover, the framework for *achdut* that I am proposing calls for all Jews to perform acts that will help to bring the Messianic age because these acts improve the world in a way that *Hashem* desires. Thus, even if they do not all count as *mitzvot* under Orthodox scrutiny, all Jews should acknowledge them as steps toward removing the obstacles that have delayed the arrival of the Messianic age for so long.

Part Two: A Framework for *Achdut*, focused on each movement within Judaism and what it could do to refine its path to and encourage its adherents to move along this path. Part Three: Thinking Differently, addressed members of each movement within Judaism and made the case that they should view members of other movements differently and let go of the *Sinat Chinam* that exists today. Part Four, Taking Action, addresses you as Jews individually about the actions that you urgently need to take to hasten the Messianic age, without waiting for any of the streams to refine its path forward.

Chapter Nineteen

HEAR NO EVIL, SPEAK NO EVIL

RABBI SACKS CONCLUDED that advocating for Pluralism of religious beliefs and practices within *Klal Yisrael* would not be productive. According to him, it is unrealistic to think that the different movements could agree on a single approach to theology and practice or accept each other's approaches as different but acceptable. Yet, I believe that it *is* possible for *all* Jews to agree on an essential piece of Jewish practice that *all* of *Klal Yisrael* today already embraces in principle. That piece is *middot*.

While complete Pluralism is not practical, we can certainly attain a Pluralism that embraces the *middot* that the Torah enumerated and on which the Prophets, the Talmud, and the later commentators expanded, since every movement in Judaism encourages its adherents to fulfill them, and secular and affiliated Jews embrace *middot* in principle, although this is obscured by endless friction and *Sinat Chinam* over other issues. This is precisely the Pluralism that will bring the Messianic age, since it is *Sinat Chinam*, which is inconsistent with *middot*, that led to the destruction of the Second

Temple, a close to 2,000-year exile from our Homeland, and our continued wait for the Messianic age to arrive. I am asking all Jews to embrace this Pluralism immediately and to embark on a renewed focus on *middot* for the specific purpose of eliminating *Sinat Chinam* toward other Jews.

At the end of Part Three, I discussed taking specific action, because changing thought without changing behavior is nearly impossible. In addition to an overall renewed focus on *middot*, I am asking all Jews to focus specifically on the *middah* of avoiding *lashon hara* toward other Jews and instead to speak about them exclusively with words of love and kindness. In time, this change in speech will lead to change in thought and the elimination of *Sinat Chinam*. All movements within Judaism support the elimination of *lashon hara*,[1] not as an individual particularistic decision but as a fundamental part of their theology. Yet, most Jews are not aware of this or do not do the focused work necessary to learn to manage their speech.

How do we accomplish this? The Chafetz Chaim wrote the roadmap for eliminating *lashon hara*, and closely related *rechilut* (gossip), in 1873.[2] It explains the elements of *lashon hara* as engaging in negative speech and accepting the negative speech of others. It also explains the importance of avoiding speaking and listening to *rechilut*, which also triggers violations of numerous Torah commandments.

All movements within Judaism condemn *lashon hara* in any context. Eliminating it is a goal that we must embrace. We should focus on avoiding speaking or accepting *lashon hara* or *rechilut* about any other Jew. This includes Jews of different movements, unaffiliated Jews, secular Jews, and Jews who share religious preferences and affiliations.

To help you accomplish this indispensable goal in the quest to hasten the Messianic age, I'm going to present the Chafetz

Chaim's ten Principles for avoiding *lashon hara*, as well as his nine Principles regarding *rechilut*, in what I hope will be understandable and actionable language. I will then list the positive and negative Torah commandments that one violates by speaking *lashon hara* or *rechilut*.[3]

Summary of Principles Relating to Eliminating *Lashon Hara*

Principle I[4] – It is forbidden to speak negatively about another Jew, even if your words are completely true. This includes negative speech that you deliver by chance, as well as when you intend to criticize the other person. The prohibition applies whether you initiate the statement or whether you are responding to the request of a third person, including a rabbi or a parent, to engage in negative speech.[*]

The prohibitions of this *Principle* apply equally to speech, written words, and non-verbal signs, such as facial expressions. They stand even if the negative words or expressions apply to the speaker as well as to another person.

Principle II[5] – The prohibition against negative speech applies whether you are speaking to a single individual or to several listeners. The greater the number of listeners, the greater the harm.[†]

---

[*] It can be very difficult to restrain your speech in the presence of peers and authority figures, especially if you feel that your personal honor may be at stake. Yet such restraint is an essential *middah* under Jewish law. According to our Sages, a person who habitually engages in intentional negative speech with no effort to correct this behavior will be punished in this world and will have no share in the World to Come.

[†] At some point, information becomes so publicized that it becomes known broadly. Accordingly, there are some technical exceptions to the prohibition of negative speech when it is clear that the information spoken was not new news. The Chafetz Chaim urges his readers not to rely on these leniencies. In today's world, where information in the public domain so often reflects the social or political bias of the source, it is not appropriate to rely on these technical exceptions. In fact, *Sinat Chinam* among Jews of different persuasions often occurs in the public domain, in both mainstream print and social media. Relying on these technical exceptions would be counterproductive to the mission of *Klal Yisrael* to bring the Messianic age.

Principle III[6] – Negative speech is forbidden even if you are directly addressing the person that the speech is criticizing, even if you deliver it in apparent jest, and even if you are careful to couch your words as a general message, because the listener is certain to realize that they apply specifically to him.

Often, we utter negative speech when we judge another Jew "on the scales of guilt" rather than "on the scales of merit" with respect to things that person might have done. The Chafetz Chaim strongly urges us to judge others on the scales of merit wherever possible because doing so is a great *middah* and because it helps us to guard against negative speech that risks shaming someone.

Principle IV[7] – We may not mention that a Jew has failed to observe *mitzvot* that apply between man and *Hashem*, even if we know that the statement is accurate.

Observing this prohibition would go a long way toward eliminating the negative speech by Jews about Jews of other persuasions, including speech by or about unaffiliated or secular Jews.[*]

Principle V[8] – We may not speak about other people in any way that demeans their intelligence, generosity, strength, possessions, or any other possible deficiency. We must presume that speech of this nature will harm them physically or financially, or will cause them grief or fear.[†]

---

[*] This Principle addresses negative speech about performance of *mitzvot* between man and *Hashem*. Later Principles address other types of negative speech. Under strict halacha, there can be an obligation to reprove certain individuals who are known violators of *mitzvot* between man and *Hashem* when that reproof is likely to be successful. Today, such reproof is almost never likely to be successful, except perhaps between Orthodox Jews who appreciate proper reproach, and therefore no one else should attempt it.

[†] The amount of damage to the one spoken about might depend on a person's particular circumstances. Nevertheless, one should not risk causing any damage to another through speech of this type.

Principle VI[9] – We may never accept negative speech as true. We may also not listen to negative speech, even without accepting it as true, unless what we hear might enable us to prevent some type of harm to ourselves or others. In such a case, where merely hearing the negative speech might enable you to prevent harm, you may hear it, but you must not accept what you have heard as true without first carefully investigating it and establishing that there is a real harm that you can prevent.

Before even hearing the negative speech, you must ask the speaker whether what he is about to say will affect you in the future or enable you to prevent harm that otherwise might occur. Only if so, may you hear the negative speech.

You must not sit in the company of others who are engaging in negative speech. If you inadvertently find yourself in such a situation, you must firmly resolve not to believe what you hear and not indicate agreement with the negative speech, verbally or through movement, such as nodding.

Principle VII[10] – Even where negative speech occurs in public before many people, you may not accept it as true. This applies even if the subject of the negative speech was present to hear it. It is permitted, however, to suspect that the negative speech might be true and to investigate the situation for the purpose of possibly reproving the person who was the object of the negative speech.*

Principle VIII[11] – We may not speak negatively about men, women, family members, individuals of limited mental capacity, the deceased, and at-risk minors such as orphans. It is permissible to warn your spouse about potential harm,

---

* In today's world, we should give reproof gently, if at all, because of the risk that the only result of doing so will be anger and possibly retribution. For this reason, it is better not to hear the negative speech unless it implies risk of harm to yourself or another.

provided the warning does not indicate the truth of the negative speech, but just the need to be careful.

You may not listen to negative speech from anybody, including close relatives, and you have a duty to reprove them gently if they are about to speak negatively about another person.

Principle IX[12] – You may not speak lavish words of praise[*] about a third party because the listener might react by trying to find a fault in the otherwise praiseworthy person. This risk of stimulating a negative reaction is especially true when you are praising someone in front of those who don't like him or her, and who are certain to respond with negative comments. You should also avoid public praise because there will certainly be a detractor among the broad spectrum of listeners. You may also not explicitly refuse to speak about a person in a tone that conveys that you are withholding information about him.

We consider this Principle to be the "dust" of *lashon hara* because it is not about negative speech, but rather the stimulation of negative speech by others.

Principle X[13] – There is an exception from the prohibition against negative speech for reporting on the damage – by robbery, wrongdoing, or negative speech – that one Jew caused another Jew. In such instances one might be permitted to relate what happened in order to help the Jew to whom wrong was done. For this exception to *lashon hara* to apply, several conditions must be met:[†]

1. It must be clear that the wrongdoer did not make restitution to the one whom he harmed.

---

[*] The key is to avoid lavish words of praise in favor of gentle ones.

[†] The Chafetz Chaim lists seven conditions. I have presented them as ten, by dividing some of them into two.

2. It must be clear that the wrongdoer did not ask forgiveness from the one whom he harmed.
3. You must have personally seen the wrongdoing, or it must be clear to you that the wrongdoing took place as assumed.
4. You must carefully analyze the situation to determine that the act of wrongdoing was illegal.
5. You must first reprove the wrongdoer in the hope that the wrongdoer will repair the wrong without the need for disclosure to others to accomplish this result. If you determine that reproval will not be effective, then when you reveal the wrongdoing, you must do so in the presence of at least three individuals, as evidence of your conviction that what you are saying is correct.
6. You must not exaggerate the degree of wrongdoing.
7. You must not intend to benefit personally from your speech.
8. You must not speak out of hatred for the wrongdoer or any other person.
9. There must be no way to help repair the wrongdoing other than by revealing it to others.
10. You must ensure that the damage to the wrongdoer will be limited to the damages that the person harmed would receive in a halachic court of law.

It should be clear to the reader how difficult it would be to meet all of these conditions.* But the rule of thumb here is straightforward – in all situations, we should be careful to avoid negative speech when trying to repair damage that someone else's negative speech has caused.

---

* There are further conditions that apply in a case where it was the negative speech of the wrongdoer that caused the wrong. Rather than expand on these further conditions, it's better to suggest that, in all situations, the reader should avoid using negative speech to repair damage stemming from the negative speech of another.

The exception of *Principle X* only applies to instances of individual wrongdoing or harm that are generally unrelated to differing religious convictions among Jews; one can imagine, perhaps the rare instance that would trigger a Jew who feels sufficient *Sinat Chinam* toward a fellow Jew to harm him. However, the exception does not justify negative speech toward other Jews because of the belief that their actions are damaging to Judaism or to a political goal.

Summary of Principles Related to Eliminating *Rechilut*

Principle I[14] – You may not tell another Jew, verbally or in writing, what a third Jew said about him, even if it is completely true, even if you do not intend to cause the listener to hate the third Jew, and even if you are speaking to many people. If the listener knows the story but not the source, you may not reveal the source to him. You are also not allowed to remind the listener of a story that he already knows, directly or by innuendo, thus stirring up an old quarrel.

The prohibition includes not completing a story at the urging of the listener who already knew part of the story. It applies even when you will risk ridicule or harm for your silence.

Principle II[15] – You may not repeat a story about someone even if the story can be taken two ways, only one of which would demean the listener, because human nature often leads listeners to find negative inferences from what they hear.

Principle III[16] – You may not tell a Jew what a third Jew said about a fourth Jew, even if what you say is true. In this case the listener is not the subject of the gossip. Nevertheless, you may not repeat it even if you ask the listener not to reveal the matter to others.

Principle IV[17] – Even if someone has already heard about comments about himself, you may not repeat them to him in a way that gives him a fresh negative perspective about them and about the source of the comments. Even if someone else has already delivered such a fresh negative perspective, you may not repeat it again and risk intensifying the listener's hatred for the original source of the comments.[*]

Principle V[18] – You may not accept as true gossip about what a third person said about you or did to you. You may not even listen to it without accepting it as true unless what you hear can help you to guard against future harm to yourself. In this case, before accepting what you hear, you must first carefully investigate its truth and establish that there is a real harm that you can prevent.

If someone wants to tell you gossip about yourself, you must ask him whether what he is about to say will affect you in the future or enable you to prevent harm to your safety. Only if it will, may you hear the gossip.

Principle VI[19] – Even when someone gossips in public about what a third person said or did to you, you may not accept it as true. This applies even if that third party was present to hear it. If, however, you suspect that the gossip might be true, you may investigate the situation if doing so will prevent future harm to your safety or to confirm a loss to your property.

Principle VII[20] – You may not relate gossip about what a third person said about or did to the listener irrespective of the status of the third party. It applies for men, women, relatives, and strangers, and with respect to listeners who are

---

[*] If one gossips about his friend, he must ask forgiveness from his friend and console him. He must then repent to *Hashem* for his behavior.

men, women, adults, minors, and individuals of limited mental capacity.

Principle VIII[21] – You may not tell a listener that, when asked, a third party refused to discuss the listener. You may not praise an individual in front of his friend because doing so might make the friend jealous. You may not ask a friend for a favor on the grounds that he did a similar favor for a third party.

We consider these prohibitions to be the "dust" of *rechilut*, because they do not directly involve gossip about what a third party said about or did to the listener but are likely to cause similar damage.

Principle IX[22] – There is an exception to the prohibition against relating gossip about what a third party said about the listener that applies in situations where you are doing so to prevent possible harm or address existing harm to the listener. In such instances you might be permitted to relate gossip to the Jew to whom harm could otherwise result. For this exception to *rechilut* to apply, several conditions must be met:

1. You must reflect very carefully on whether the listener is really in imminent danger of or has already sustained possible harm.
2. You must not exaggerate the level of harm or any other aspect of the situation.
3. You must not be speaking out of hatred for the third party.
4. You must truly believe that the listener will take heed based on what he hears from you.
5. You must not be able to prevent the threatened harm or address the existing harm in any other way, such as

convincing the third party not to act to the detriment of the listener or to make restitution to the listener.
6. You must be certain that your speech will not result in harm to the third party without really benefiting the listener.
7. You must be certain that the listener will act responsibly and not place himself in greater harm if he reacts in anger toward the third party in response to what you tell him.
8. If you feel that it will be productive, you must first reprove the third party, in the hope that the third party will change his position without the need for your disclosure.
9. You must determine that the harm, once it has occurred is one that a halachic court of law can address. But, if the listener would have no such recourse because of the passage of time or otherwise, then you must remain silent.
10. You must be confident that the listener will resolve the matter in a halachic court of law where possible, rather than acting on his own.
11. You must ensure that the damage to the wrongdoer will be limited to the amount of the damages that a halachic court of law would impose.
12. In a case when you are accusing a third party of having cheated the listener, there must be two speakers with knowledge of the cheating.

It should be clear to the reader how difficult it would be to meet all of these conditions. The exception of *Principle IX* only applies to instances of individual wrongdoing or harm generally unrelated to differing religious convictions among Jews; one can imagine, perhaps the rare instance that would trigger a Jew to harm a fellow Jew because he feels *Sinat Chinam* toward him. However, the exception does not apply to justify relating gossip about the view of one Jew toward another based on the first Jew's belief that the other Jew's practices are damaging to Judaism or to a political goal.

These are the details of how to avoid *lashon hara* and *rechilut*. At first blush, internalizing all these Principles may seem daunting. With a little practice though, you will be able to incorporate them into your thinking and understand how to use them in common situations where they apply. Even after you master this, however, it will be difficult to train yourself not to engage in speaking or listening to *lashon hara* or *rechilut*. In today's world, the compulsion toward *lashon hara* is overwhelming, as is the impulse to share gossip, often to the point where it feels like required behavior in normal social interactions.

The Torah and later sources make it clear that negative speech of these types is fundamentally damaging to a just society. In the introduction to his book, the Chafetz Chaim lists the *mitzvot*, most of which are *middot*, from the Torah, that speaking and hearing *lashon hara* and *rechilut* violate.[23] It is far more extensive than you would assume.

Negative Commandments that You Violate by Engaging in *Lashon Hara* and *Rechilut*

1. "You shall not be a gossipmonger among your people."[24] This is a negative commandment not to engage in *rechilut*. It serves as a strong guard against spreading *Sinat Chinam* among *Klal Yisrael*. It also prohibits listening to *rechilut*, as that would facilitate the speaker's spreading gossip.
2. "Do not accept a false report."[25] We understand that

this also refers to spreading a false report,[26] so it prohibits speaking or listening to false *lashon hara* as well as false *rechilut*. Any false negative speech violates this negative *mitzvah*. It is very easy to violate this negative *mitzvah* unknowingly because all too often neither the speaker nor the listener knows whether the information or rumor in question is true.

3. "Beware of a *tzaraas* affliction, be very careful."[27] This refers to the leprosy* that Miriam contracted when she spoke *lashon hara* about her brother, Moses. It is phrased as a negative mitzvah not to speak *lashon hara* because of the affliction that *lashon hara* inflicts on both Jews – the speaker and the one who hears this negative speech. There is no doubt that *lashon hara* stemming from *Sinat Chinam* has inflicted great harm to countless Jews over the generations and has delayed the arrival of the Messianic age.

4. "[Y]ou shall not place a stumbling block before the blind."† Speaking or hearing *lashon hara* or *rechilut* endangers the person spoken about, and he is blind to the danger because the speaker did not direct the negative speech at him. He cannot defend himself and does not know how many other people might have heard it. If he heard the *lashon hara* or *rechilut*, he might well be blindsided by what he is hearing and unaware of how many other people may also hear it.

5. "Take care lest you forget *HASHEM*, your God, by not observing His commandments, His ordinances, and His decrees, which I command you today."[28] This

---

* *Tzaraas* is often translated as leprosy, but it is better understood as damage done to the speaker of *lashon hara* that may be emotional, spiritual, or physical.

† Ibid., p. 661. (*Vayikra* 19:14) The Chafetz Chaim identifies certain situations where only the speaker, but not the listener, transgresses this prohibition, but he cautions against relying on these exceptions.

commandment includes remembering not to speak or receive *lashon hara* or *rechilut*. If we want *Hashem* to bring the Messianic age, we need to avoid doing the things that will spread *Sinat Chinat* among Jews.

6. "You shall not desecrate My holy Name, rather I should be sanctified among the Children of Israel."[29] For a person, who is created in *Hashem's* image, to speak or hear *lashon hara* is a desecration of *Hashem's* name because it shows the speaker's visible lack of respect for *Hashem* and undermines the goal of the Jewish people to repair, rather than damage, the world by their acts.

7. "You shall not hate your brother in your heart."[30] This is the Biblical prohibition against *Sinat Chinam*. This hatred, which *lashon hara* or *rechilut* reflects, damages everyone involved. The importance of this *mitzvah* validates this book's basic proposition that learning to avoid negative speech is directly linked to eliminating *Sinat Chinam* and bringing the Messianic age.

8. "You shall not take revenge and you shall not bear a grudge against the members of your people."[31] These are two separate *mitzvot*, both of which are products of *Sinat Chinam*. You violate them when you use *lashon hara* or *rechilut* to demean or damage another person. Bearing a grudge alone, without negative speech, is also *Sinat Chinam*.

9. "A single witness shall not stand up against any man for any iniquity or for any error, regarding sin that he may commit."[32] This prohibition relates to the requirement that two witnesses must testify against a defendant in order for a halachic court to hold him liable for a wrong in a civil matter or to convict him for a criminal offense. Thus, where only a single witness offers testimony and the court therefore does not have enough

evidence upon which to render a decision, the testimony has no purpose and is therefore considered *lashon hara* and perhaps *rechilut*.*

10. "Do not be a follower of the majority for evil."³³ People who are inherently evil will speak *lashon hara*. Those who join a group of them, even briefly, put themselves in a position to hear *lashon hara* and *rechilut*.

11. "[T]he Children of Israel… [shall] not be like Korach and his assembly."³⁴ Korach led a rebellion against Moshe when the Jews were in the wilderness. His followers encouraged Korach's quarrel with Moses. Using negative speech, either *lashon hara* or *rechilut*, to nurture a quarrel violates this *mitzvah*.

12. "Each of you shall not aggrieve his fellow."³⁵ This relates to damaging another person verbally by, say, demeaning him for past deeds, for a family trait, for not being well educated, or for doing poor work. We may not use speech of this type either to the person's face or to others. One who speaks *lashon hara* or *rechilut* is likely to also violate this *mitzvah*. All too often, *Sinat Chinam* leads to this type of negative speech.

13. "[Y]ou shall reprove your fellow and do not bear a sin because of him."³⁶ The Torah obliges us to reprove a fellow Jew whose wrongdoing has caused him to stray from the proper path, but we must be careful to do this in a gentle way, so as not to shame or demean him. If it does, as evidenced by his face turning pale, we have violated this *mitzvah*, and our negative speech becomes *lashon hara* or *rechilut*, rather than proper reproof. This damaging result is even worse if it takes place in public.

14. "You shall not cause pain to any widow or orphan."³⁷

---

* Secular courts of law generally require only one witness in order to convict a defendant or to hold him liable. Halachic courts continue to apply the two-witness rule.

One who speaks *lashon hara* or *rechilut* directly to a widow or orphan is violating this *mitzvah*, as is speaking negatively about them to a third party who, in response, then acts in a way that pains the widow or the orphan.

15. "You shall not [flatter]... the [men of] the land."[38] If a person hears flattery about someone he doesn't like, those words could provoke his anger toward the third party. This gives positive speech the effect of negative speech and constitutes *lashon hara* or *rechilut*. In the context of the *Sinat Chinam* of a Jew in one stream of Judaism toward a Jew in a different stream, saying flattering things about the second Jew to the first one is *lashon hara* or *rechilut*.

16. "You shall not curse the deaf."[39] This can apply in two ways. First, if you curse another Jew, but not to his face, that Jew is deaf to your words and the damage they may cause. Second, if you curse the Jew to his face and he hears your words, the damage is worse than if he were deaf. Either way, it is *lashon hara*. Sadly, this happens all too often because of *Sinat Chinam* based on religious differences.

Positive Commandments that You Violate by Engaging in *Lashon Hara* and *Rechilut*

1. "Remember what HASHEM, your God, did to Miriam on the way, when you were leaving Egypt."[40] Here, the Torah is giving us a positive *mitzvah* stemming from the same event – Miriam speaking *lashon hara* about Moses – that we saw in the negative *mitzvah* "3" above. The fact that one instance of *lashon hara* transgresses both positive and negative *mitzvot* emphasizes

the seriousness of *lashon hara* and the care that we must take to avoid it. This reinforces my premise that eliminating *Sinat Chinam* – and its inevitable product, *lashon hara* – is essential to bringing the Messianic age.

2. "[Y]ou shall love your fellow as yourself."[41] *Lashon hara* and *rechilut* are incompatible with love. Rather, they reflect *Sinat Chinam* because they express negative feelings through damaging negative speech.

3. "[W]ith righteousness shall you judge your fellow."[42] We have the choice of whether to view another Jew's behavior positively or negatively. Judging another Jew negatively and speaking *lashon hara* or *rechilut* based on this negative judgment violates this positive *mitzvah*. All too often one Jew will judge another Jew negatively because of their differences in religious beliefs or practices.

4. "If your brother becomes impoverished and his means falter in your proximity, you shall strengthen him… so he can live with you."[43] "And let your brother live with you."[44] In both cases, the "brother" means a fellow Jew. These sentences describe the positive *mitzvah* of supporting fellow Jews in need. When our *lashon hara* or *rechilut* damages another Jew, resulting in his loss of income, we have done the opposite of what this positive *mitzvah* requires; we have impoverished another Jew rather than helping him to escape poverty. This can happen when a Jew with certain religious beliefs or practices acts with *Sinat Chimam* toward another Jew whose beliefs or practices differ, denying him a financial opportunity, an employment opportunity, or a promotion by speaking *lashon hara* or *rechilut* about him.

5. "[Y]ou shall reprove your fellow." This refers to listening to someone's *lashon hara* or *rechilut* rather than

reproving him before he manages to speak negatively. The obligation of reproof only applies where there is a possibility that the words of reproof will be accepted. Imagine a situation in which someone's reproof of a Jew with *Sinat Chinam* against another Jew in his heart, inspired him not to speak his intended *lashon hara* or *rechilut*. This act of reproof could prevent so much damage.

6. "[T]o him you shall cleave."[45] This refers to selecting the right people with whom to associate. If you choose to gather with people who feel *Sinat Chinam* toward other Jews and who express *lashon hara* and *rechilut* about them, you will be inclined to participate in the spreading of *lashon hara* and *rechilut*, delaying the Messianic age.

7. "My sanctuary you shall revere."[46] There is a positive *mitzvah* to revere and fear *Hashem* when praying or studying in a synagogue. If you engage in *lashon hara* or *rechilut* in the synagogue, you are actively violating many of *Hashem's mitzvot* in God's presence. Think about it. How can we work for the arrival of the Messianic age when our prayers and studies are polluted with *Sinat Chinam* that we are spreading to others through *lashon hara* and *rechilut* in *Hashem's* very sanctuary?

8. "In the presence of an old person you shall rise and you shall honor the presence of a sage."[47] Here, we have the positive *mitzvah* to honor people who are elderly or scholarly. If we speak *lashon hara* or *rechilut* directly to an elderly or a wise person, we are demeaning that person, which is the opposite of honoring him, and we have let our *Sinat Chinam* cause us to violate this *mitzvah*.

9. "You shall sanctify him."[48] This refers to the special honor that we give to *kohanim* –priests, the descendants of

Aaron, the first high priest. If you speak *lashon hara* or *rechilut* about a *kohen*, you are demeaning or shaming him, which directly conflicts with this *mitzvah*. In today's world, when a speaker does not necessarily know whether the individual he is discussing is a *kohen*, it is all the more important to refrain from using negative speech.

10. "Honor your father and your mother."[49] "Accursed is the one who degrades his father and his mother."[50] Our sages have interpreted the first of these *mitzvot*, which is included in the Ten Commandments, to apply to older siblings and one's parents-in-law as well. One who speaks *lashon hara* or *rechilut* about these individuals violates this *mitzvah*. One who speaks *lashon hara* or *rechilut* about his parents violates both *mitzvot*. And it is far worse if the listener is one of the people whom the speaker must honor and the listener accepts the *lashon hara* or *rechilut*. In this case, instead of honoring the listener, the speaker has enticed him into listening to forbidden negative speech.

11. "HASHEM, your God, shall you fear."[51] Willingness to speak or hear *lashon hara* or *rechilut* is not consistent with fearing *Hashem*, as this positive *mitzvah* requires. One who does this instead of fearing *Hashem* is forgetting the reason for the destruction of the Second Temple and is letting his *Sinat Chinam* cause him to speak *lashon hara* or *rechilut*. Engaging in negative speech is inconsistent with behavior that will help to bring the Messianic age.

12. "You shall teach them [the words of the Torah] thoroughly to your children."[52] This positive *mitzvah* requires us to learn Torah so that we can pass it on to the next generation. Many activities – such as earning a living and dealing with family and personal matters – limit the amount of time that we can dedicate to

this *mitzvah*. But we also fulfill it when we mindfully conduct our lives in accordance with the *middot* of the Torah and set an example for others – particularly our children. When we speak or accept *lashon hara* or *rechilut*, we are doing the opposite by giving in to *Sinat Chinam*, and thus disparaging the Torah and its teachings.

13. "Distance yourself from a false word."[53] This is the positive *mitzvah* to speak truthfully to others. When we speak *lashon hara* or *rechilut* that contains false words, we are violating this positive *mitzvah* and also enticing the listener to accept false words. This is a particularly evil expression of *Sinat Chinam* because the speaker is willing to lie to damage another Jew.

14. "[A]nd you shall go in His ways."[54] This positive *mitzvah* reflects the fact that man was created in *Hashem's* image.[55] Exhibiting *Sinat Chinam* and speaking *lashon hara* and *rechilut* are strikingly inconsistent with the way that *Hashem* thinks or speaks.

Before beginning the final chapter of this book, let me briefly summarize where we are. We've established that all movements in Judaism have a strong interest in bringing the Messianic age, although each defines it differently. The main impediment to this outcome is the continued *Sinat Chinam* among Jews, and particularly among Jews of different streams of Judaism. I've proposed that each movement within *Klal Yisrael*

1. should envision an imaginary gameboard across which all Jews should strive to move in an effort to bring the Messianic age, and
2. should take steps to define its own path across that gameboard.

We've also established that all movements within Judaism support observance of the *middot* of the Torah and particularly the prohibition against speaking *lashon hara*, which is closely related to the companion prohibition of speaking *rechilut*. As a result, I've asked all Jews to work on avoiding *lashon hara* and *rechilut* as a way to eliminate the verbal expression of *Sinat Chinam* toward other Jews. Over time, this will lead to the elimination of *Sinat Chinam* among Jews.

To assist in this effort, I've explained the elements of *lashon hara* and *rechilut* as the Chafetz Chaim defined them, as well as the *mitzvot* that one violates when speaking or hearing *lashon hara* or *rechilut*.

Chapter Twenty

CHOOSE LIFE!

WHAT DO WE mean by *achdut*? The literal translation of *achdut* is "unity." Yet, by acknowledging that pursuing absolute *Pluralism* is not a fruitful objective, I am recognizing that complete unity across all streams of *Klal Yisrael* is not possible. Instead, I propose a unity of purpose to bring the Messianic age as each stream defines it. This will be possible when we treat each other respectfully, let each stream define its path forward, and recognize progress along these paths as a positive benefit to *Klal Yisrael*. At the same time, if all Jews work to mitigate both *lashon hara* and *rechilut*, we will successfully attack *Sinat Chinam*, the main obstacle to the arrival of the Messianic age. In simple language, I am prescribing a formula by which to achieve universal respect of Jews for each other, in place of the destructive *Sinat Chinam* that has existed among us for so long.

Our ancestors saw redemption with their own eyes, first from Egypt, and later from the exile that followed the destruction of the First Temple in Jerusalem. The redemption from Egypt was the fulfillment of *Hashem*'s promise to Abraham. Because the destruction of the First Temple resulted from *Klal Yisrael's* observance of idol worship (*avodah zarah*), the Second Temple was established after *Klal Yisrael* abandoned this practice. The Second Temple was destroyed because of *Sinat Chinam*, and intense *Sinat Chinam* within *Klal Yisrael* has lasted to this day because we as a people have not done the hard work necessary to eliminate it. As a result, the Messianic age has not arrived.

Let's give this a little context. In the book of Leviticus, the Torah sets forth most of the laws regarding the Temple rituals, the Priests' and Levites' performance of them, and the related laws of ritual purity. Leviticus, chapter 19, also contains most of the *middot* in the Torah, including the prohibition against speaking *lashon hara* and *rechilut*. *Lashon hara* and *rechilut* are the fruits and the seeds of *Sinat Chinam*. They are the fruits because those who feel *Sinat Chinam* toward other Jews express their feelings by speaking *lashon hara* and *rechilut*. They are the seeds because those who hear *lashon hara* and *rechilut* fall prey to *Sinat Chinam* as a result of the negative words that they have accepted. For close to two thousand years, this vicious cycle has persisted.

The 26th chapter of Leviticus contains the curses that will befall *Klal Yisrael* if it does not observe the Torah's commandments. It reads in part: *"I will turn My attention against you, you will be struck down before your enemies, those who hate you will subjugate you – you will flee with no one pursuing you."*[1] The message from Leviticus is clear: If *Klal Yisrael* does not keep the commandments of the Torah, it will suffer terribly at the hands of their enemies. This is precisely what has happened to us since the destruction of the Second Temple. The specific commandment that we keep failing to keep is in plain sight twice in Leviticus chapter 19, first as a negative commandment: *"You shall not hate your brother in your heart,"*[2] and again as a positive one: *"[Y]ou* *shall love your fellow as yourself."*³ Nothing could be clearer. The Torah is imploring us to avoid *Sinat Chinam*. Yet, we have not been successful at doing this. The result? We continue to suffer from *Hashem's* bitter curse. Instead of doing our part to bring the Messianic age, we keep moving in the opposite direction. [ed.: Italics in quoted text.]

No movement in Judaism has rejected the Torah's prohibition of *Sinat Chinam* and the related prohibition of *lashon hara*. *Klal Yisrael* is already unified in accepting these principles. But we have failed miserably to observe them. The results of this failure have been devastating for the Jewish People:

- The Romans' destruction of the Second Temple, exiling us from The Holy Land and condemning us to live as foreigners in other peoples' countries where we were subject to persecution.
- The Crusades, which ravaged Jewish communities throughout Europe.
- The Spanish Inquisition, which ended centuries of Jewish life in Spain and scattered Sephardic Jews throughout Europe, North Africa, and the Middle East.
- The Pogroms in Eastern Europe, which often made Jewish life there intolerable.
- World War I, which destroyed much of Jewish life in Europe by subjecting Jews as foreigners to continued persecution and abuse.
- The Russian Revolution, which ended Jewish life for the largest Eastern European community thus ending Jewish continuity for millions of Jews.
- The Holocaust, which killed six million Jews and effectively ended centuries of Eastern European Jewish life.
- The global resurgence of antisemitism in the 21st Century.

- The rising threats today from terrorists on Israel's borders as well as within the country.
- The continuing Iranian nuclear threat.

What more evidence do we need to make us take serious note of our failure and embark on a concerted effort to change? I'm not saying that *Hashem* caused each of these events as punishment for our *Sinat Chinam*. Rather, I'm pointing out that so long as we do not take the steps that will hasten the Messianic age, we are vulnerable to the evil forces in the world and their self-interests, which pose a threat to our safety and existence. Note that each of these events involved world powers and their aspirations. There is no realistic way for a people who constitute such a small percentage of the world's population to have protected itself from the consequences of these events without *Hashem's* help. If we want this protection, we need to earn it. We must end our own evil behavior in the form of *Sinat Chinam* and *lashon hara.*

Recently, under the auspices of China, Iran and Saudi Arabia have restored their relationship after years of mutual hatred. There is, perhaps, no greater threat to the future of Israel. If Israel is not safe, neither are Jews in the diaspora who are now experiencing real antisemitism for the first time in decades.

Beginning with the *Haskalah*, the level of *Sinat Chinam* within *Klal Yisrael* intensified. The leadership of Orthodox Jewry saw itself in an existential battle to preserve Orthodox Judaism in the face of significant defections to Reform Judaism. The leadership of Reform Judaism saw itself as the proponent of a new Judaism, separated from the Holy Land and traditional practices, and assimilated into the secular culture of European society. These Reform leaders believed that Jews who didn't act like Jews would not suffer the same persecution as in the past, and that it would be best if all Jews adopted this approach.

The existence of these perspectives from the beginning of the *Haskalah* until the Holocaust is understandable, but they no longer seem relevant. Today, Orthodox Jewry is vibrant and growing. The institutions of learning that it has established throughout the Western World and in Israel rival and, in many cases, surpass those of Eastern Europe before the Holocaust. At the same time, Reform Jewry has abandoned its belief that assimilated Jews are safe from antisemitism and that a State of Israel is not important to the Jewish future. Perhaps most important, neither Orthodox Jews nor Reform Jews see persuading Jews who adhere to other movements in Judaism to switch their allegiance as their main focus.*

I strongly believe that the issues and fears that drove the spread of *Sinat Chinam* from the dawn of the *Haskalah* until the Holocaust no longer exist. This presents us with a magic moment in which to unite our collective efforts and finally put an end to *Sinat Chinam* and herald the arrival of the Messianic age.

For Orthodox, some Conservative, and many Sephardic Jews, this would fulfill the prophecy of the arrival of *Moshiach*, the descendant of King David whom *Hashem* will anoint to lead the *Klal Yisrael* into the Messianic age. The unanswered questions in Scripture that await the arrival of *Moshiach* would finally be resolved. For liberal Jews, this would mean the attainment of a just society, ultimately encompassing all peoples of the world, not just Jews, who would treat each other with respect and universally practice the *middot* that every movement within Judaism embraces.

The contrast in these perspectives is especially interesting.

---

* It is true that the Israeli Orthodox rabbinate has thwarted the efforts of the Reform and Conservative movements to expand their institutions, presence, and authority in Israel, a political battle that shows no signs of ending. But this is different from any of the movements making concerted efforts to attract members away from other movements. The political battles should not stand in the way of the initiatives that I am proposing.

The traditional Jewish concept of *Moshiach* is based on prophesy, belief, and the principles that only *Hashem* will determine the exact date on which *Moshiach* will arrive and who will be anointed to this role. *Klal Yisrael* can work to hasten *Moshiach's* arrival, but only *Hashem* can bring *Moshiach*. In contrast, the liberal Jewish concept of the Messianic age, which Reconstructionist theology most clearly reflects, represents the attainment of a state of human civilization in which *middot* are universally observed and the principles of *tzedakah* and *chesed* guide the world. In theory, there is no reason, why we cannot achieve this concept of the Messianic age without Divine intervention if we set the right example for all world civilizations. Either way, there is no doubt that elimination of *Sinat Chinam* and its closely related fruits and seeds, *lashon hara* and *rechilut*, are essential to reaching the Messianic age.

What about secular and unaffiliated Jews? Some of them follow the principles that liberal, affiliated Jews espouse. But many of them do not embrace the concept of a Messianic age. They do, however, endorse the liberal values of equality, justice, fairness, and respect. Their goal is the attainment of a fair and just society, as well as protection of the environment and preservation of our planet. While *Sinat Chinam*, *lashon hara*, and *rechilut* are not terms that secular and unaffiliated Jews usually use, the benefits that will flow from eliminating these behaviors are not only consistent with liberal values, they are also essential to achieving the state of civilization to which these Jews aspire. Thus, I am appealing to secular and unaffiliated Jews to join the rest of *Klal Yisrael* in the effort to eliminate *Sinat Chinam*, *lashon hara*, and *rechilut*.

This appeal is applicable equally in the diaspora and in Israel. Before the Gaza war, *Sinat Chinam*, *lashon hara*, and *rechilut* had taken hold of Israel at perhaps the highest levels in history. Now, we see a new hope as Israeli society has come together to support the war. But, this unity is fragile, and, despite the current optimism, it can't last without addressing the underlying issues of *Sinat Chinam, lashon hara, and rechilut*. There has never been a better time to do this, especially since we now have a taste of what success can feel like.

I have made my case for change, a change led by all movements within Judaism as well as all Jews. I am not proposing that we all agree on Jewish theology or practice. I am proposing that each stream of Judaism clarify its own path forward and engage its adherents in a way that will drive real progress. We need to end the disparity between religious principles and religious practice within each movement. Most importantly, we need to work collectively and vigorously to end *Sinat Chinam* among Jews, beginning with a relentless focus on eliminating *lashon hara* and *rechilut*. Each one of us has the power to move us forward toward this objective. Let us work together energetically, beginning today, to bring the Messianic age in our time.

ENDNOTES

Introduction

1. *The Complete Artscroll Siddur, Nusach Sefard*, trans. Rabbi Nosson Scherman (New York: ArtScroll Mesorah Publications, Ltd. 1985, Ninth Impression 2002), 153.

2. Joseph Telushkin, *Rebbe, The Life and Teachings of Menachem M. Schneerson, the Most Influential Rabbi in Modern History* (New York: Harper Wave, 2016), 159.

3. See, Rabbi Herschel Schachter, Minhagei Sefirah, Daily Shiur Series, Yeshiva University, Wilf Campus, May 16, 2016, discussing the view of Rabbi Yoseph Eliyahu Henkin (1881-1973). http://www.yutorah.org/lectures/lecture.cfm/857286/rabbi-hershel-schachter/minhagei-sefirah/

4. See The Biblical Book of Esther of which there are many editions. See for example Rabbi Meir Zlotowitz and Rabbi Meir Nosson Scherman, *The Five Megillos* (Brooklyn, New York: Mesorah Publications, Ltd, Synagogue Edition, Second Impression 1995), 13-52.

Chapter One

1. For a thorough comparison of Orthodoxy in the Diaspora with Religious Judaism in Israel see: Eliezer Don-Yehiya. "Orthodox Jewry in Israel and in North America." *Israel Studies* 10, no. 1, (2005): 157–187. *JSTOR*, www.jstor.org/stable/30245757

2. *The Complete Artscroll Siddur, Nusach Sefard*, trans. Rabbi Nosson Scherman (New York: ArtScroll Mesorah Publications, Ltd. 1985, Ninth Impression 2002), 196-199.

3. Ibid., footnote pp. 196-198.

4. Ibid, footnote p.198, item 13.

5. See, for an example, ibid, pp. 13-17.

6. Ibid, pp. 198-199.

7. To learn more about Orthodox Jewish practices, see: Rabbi Hayim Halevi Donin, *To Be a Jew: A Guide to Jewish Observance in Contemporary Life* (New York: Basic Books 1972).

8. Genesis or *Bereishis* in Hebrew.

9. *The Stone Edition, The Chumash*, trans. trans. Rabbi Nosson Scherman (New York: ArtScroll Mesorah Publications, Ltd. 1993, Eleventh Edition 2000), pp. 2-11.

10   For the background and history of *daf yomi*, see Shimon Finkelman, *5 Great Leaders* (Brooklyn, New York: Mesorah Publications Ltd. 2005), 195-219.

11   Rabbi Yaakov Yosef Reinman, *Rabbi Levi Yitzchak of Berdichev, Stories and Thoughts Arranged According to the Weekly Parsha*, (New York: ArtScroll Mesorah Publications Ltd. 2011), 165-166. At the time, the Vilna Gaon's opposition to Chassidism was quite understandable. A string of false *Messiahs* over the years, including Shabtai Tzvi just 55 years before the Vilna Gaon's time, had disrupted the Jewish world, so the rabbis tended to respond negatively to any hint of non-traditional Jewish practices. And there was sufficient variation in Chassidic practices to concern the Vilna Gaon and his contemporaries that these new, mystical cults would threaten authentic Torah-based Judaism. The pressure that the Vilna Gaon and others exerted on the Chassidic leadership of the time helped to steer the Chassidic movement away from such threats. At the same time, the Chassidic movement injected new life into Orthodox Judaism, which had become more the province of yeshiva scholars than of the average Jew. See Betzalel Landau, *The Vilna Gaon*, (New Jersey: Mesorah Publications, Ltd. Second Edition, Third Impression 2022), 181-199, for a complete discussion of this subject.

12   See, Rabbi Moses M. Yoshor, *The Chafetz Chaim, The Life and Works of Rabbi Yisrael Meir Kagan of Radin* (New Jersey: Mesorah Publications, Ltd. 1997, Third Edition 2013), 427-434. Although *Agudas Yisrael* was formed in 1913, the outbreak of World War I delayed efforts to operationalize its initiatives.

13   Rabbi Yisroel Friedman of Chortkov, 1854 - 1934, the leader of the largest Chassidic movement in pre-war Eastern Europe with perhaps as many as 50,000 followers, of whom only about 300 survived the Holocaust.

14   See, Rabbi Yisroel Friedman, *The Rebbes of Chortkov* (New York: Mesorah Publications, Ltd. 2003), 270-285.

15   Excerpted from, Rebecca Beck, "The Hasidic Way of Dating and Marriage," *Orthodox Sunflower*, February 12, 2015.
https://orthodoxsunflower.com/the-hasidic-way-of-dating-and-marriage-in-honor-of-valentine

16   Pew Research Center, May 11, 2021, "Jewish Americans in 2020," Washington, DC. For convenience this study is referred to as the "2020 Pew Study", p. 79.

17   Readers who wish to learn more about Chabad Chassidim should read: Joseph Telushkin, *Rebbe, The Life and Teachings of Menachem M. Schneerson, the Most Influential Rabbi in Modern History* (New York: Harper Wave 2016).

18   See footnote 13.

19   See, *The Stone Edition, The Chumash*, trans. Rabbi Nosson Scherman (New York: ArtScroll Mesorah Publications, Ltd. 2000), 817 (*Bamidbar* 15:37).

20   Yeshivat Chovevei Torah Rabbinical School website, https://www.yctorah.org/about/, March 17, 2022.

21   Yeshivat Maharat website, https://www.yeshivatmaharat.org/, May 21, 2020.

22   The Hebrew Institute of Riverdale, The Bayit, website, https://www.thebayit.org/, March 17, 2022.

23   See for example https://shirahadasha.org

Chapter Two

1. Neil Gilman, *Conservative* Judaism *in the New Century* (New Jersey: Behrman House, Inc. 1993), 22-23.

2. See Chapter Three: Reform Judaism.

3. Ibid., pp. 29-30.

4. Gilman op. cit., p. 94.

5. Ibid., pp. 94-95.

6. Pew Research Center, October 1, 2013, "A Portrait of Jewish Americans," Washington, DC. For convenience, I refer to this study as the "2013 Pew Study."

7. Pew Research Center, May 11, 2021, "Jewish Americans in 2020," Washington, DC. For convenience, I refer to this study as the "2020 Pew Study."

8. 2020 Pew Study, p. 9.

9. Gilman op. cit., p. 130.

10. *Emet Ve-Emunah, Statement of Principles of Conservative Judaism* (New York: 1988, The Jewish Theological Seminary of America, The Rabbinical Assembly and The United Synagogue of America. Second Printing 1990). (Page numbers cited are from of a PDF of a scanned text of the Second Printing, 1990.)

11. Ibid., pp. 17-19.

12. Ibid., pp. 19.

13. Ibid., pp. 20-23.

14. Ibid., pp. 23-24.

15. Ibid., pp. 24-27.

16. Ibid., pp. 28.

17. Ibid., pp. 29-31.

18. Ibid., pp. 31-33.

19. Ibid., pp. 33-34.

20. Ibid., pp. 34-36.

21. Ibid., pp. 36-38.

22. Ibid., pp 38-39. In the years following the issuance of *Emet Ve-Emunah*, the Conservative movement approved the ordination of women as rabbis and cantors.

23. Ibid., pp. 39-40.

24. Ibid., pp. 40-43.

25 Ibid., pp. 43-45.

26 Ibid., pp. 45-46.

27 Ismar Schorsch, "The Sacred Cluster: The Core Values of Conservative Judaism", *Conservative Judaism* 47, no.2 (Spring 1995), pp. 3-12.

Chapter Three

1 "*Reform Judaism: History & Overview*" The Jewish Virtual Library, a Project of AICE, Chevy Chase, MD 1998 – 2022, American-Israeli Cooperative Enterprise). Jewish Virtual Library website, https://www.jewishvirtuallibrary.org/history-and-overview-of-reform-judaism

2 "Declaration of Principles, The Pittsburgh Platform" (Pittsburgh: 1885, Central Conference of American Rabbis), Central Conference of American Rabbis website. https://www.ccarnet.org/rabbinic-voice/platforms/article-declaration-principles

3 "*Reform Judaism: History & Overview*," The Jewish Virtual Library op. cit.

4 "The Guiding Principles of Reform Judaism, The Columbus Platform," (Columbus, Ohio: 1937, Central Conference of American Rabbis), Central Conference of American Rabbis website. https://www.ccarnet.org/rabbinic-voice/platforms/article-guiding-principles-reform-judaism

5 "Reform Judaism: A Centenary Perspective" (San Francisco: 1976, Central Conference of American Rabbis), Central Conference of American Rabbis website. https://www.ccarnet.org/rabbinic-voice/platforms/article-reform-judaism-centenary-perspective

6 "A Statement of Principles for Reform Judaism" (Pittsburgh: 1999, Central Conference of American Rabbis), Central Conference of American Rabbis website. https://www.ccarnet.org/rabbinic-voice/platforms/article-statement-principles-reform-judaism

7 "*Reform Judaism: History & Overview*" The Jewish Virtual Library, op. cit.

8 "*Judaism: Patrilineal Descent*" The Jewish Virtual Library, a Project of AICE, (Chevy Chase, MD 1998 – 2022, American-Israeli Cooperative Enterprise). Jewish Virtual Library website. https://www.jewishvirtuallibrary.org/patrilineal-descent

9 In June 1997, just two years before issuing the New Pittsburgh Platform, the Reform Movement, in commemoration of the centenary of the first World Zionist Congress, published a statement of principles specifically related to Judaism and Zionism: "Reform Judaism & Zionism: A Centenary Platform." This statement of principles is referred to as "The Miami Platform," according to "Reform Judaism: A Centenary Platform" (Miami: 1997, Central Conference of American Rabbis), Central Conference of American Rabbis website. https://www.ccarnet.org/rabbinic-voice/platforms/article-reform-judaism-zionism-centenary-platform

10 Pew Research Center, May 11, 2021, "Jewish Americans in 2020," Washington, DC. For convenience, I refer to this study as the "2020 Pew Study."

11 Pew Research Center, October 1, 2013, "A Portrait of Jewish Americans," Washington, DC. For convenience, I refer to this study as the "2013 Pew Study."

12 2020 Pew Study, op. cit., p. 63.

13 2020 Pew Study, op. cit., p. 66.

14 2013 Pew Study, op. cit., p. 64.

15 The percentages in both Pew Studies would, of course, vary significantly among different American Reform Jewish communities.

Chapter Four

1   Neil Gilman, *Conservative Judaism in the New Century* (West Orange, New Jersey: Behrman House, Inc. 1993), p. 75.

2   Ibid., p. 76.

3   Ibid. p. 79.

4   Ibid., p. 82.

5   "*Reconstructionist Rabbinical College,*" The Jewish Virtual Library, a Project of AICE, (Chevy Chase, MD 1998-2022, American-Israeli Cooperative Enterprise). Jewish Virtual Library website. https://www.jewishvirtuallibrary.org/reconstructionist-rabbinical-college

6   Rebecca T. Albert and Jacob J. Straub, *Exploring Judaism, a Reconstructionist Approach* (Elkins Park, PA: The Reconstructionist Press, Expanded and Updated 2000), 39.

7   Alpert and Staub, op. cit., pp. 48-50.

8   Ibid., p. 101-102.

9   Ibid., p. 51.

10 Ibid., pp. 97-98.

Chapter Five

1   Suheil Bushrui, ed., *The World's Favorite Love Poems* (Oxford, England: Oneworld Publications 2008), 93, 162-163.

2   Yehudah HaLevi, *The Kuzari: In Defense of the Despised Faith*, trans. Rabbi N. Daniel Korobin (Spring Valley, NY: Feldheim Publishers 2013).

3   *The Complete Tishah B'Av Service,* Nusach Sefard, trans. and commentary Rabbi Avrohom Chaim Feuer and Rabbi Avie Gold (New York: Artscroll Mesorah Publications, Ltd. 1992, Second Edition, Seventh Impression 2016), fn. pp. 334-335.

4   For a more extensive discussion on the *Rambam*, see Joseph Telushkin, *Jewish Literacy* (New York: William Morrow and Company 1991), 175-177.

5   For a complete discussion of the history of Sephardic Jews, see Ron D. Hart, *Sephardic Jews: History, Religion and People* (Santa Fe, NM: Gaon Books 2016).

6   For a discussion about the life of Rabbi Yosef Karo, see Telushkin, op. cit., pp. 208-209.

7   For an extensive treatment of the life of Rabbi Ovadia Yosef, see Rabbi Yehuda Heimiowitz, *Maran HaRav Ovadia, The Revered Gaon and Posek Who Restored the Crown of Sephardic Jewry* (New York: Mesorah Publications, Ltd. 2014).

8   For an example of Sephardic cuisine, see Poopa Dweck, *Aromas of Aleppo* (New York: Harper-Collins 2007).

Chapter Seven

1   *The Stone Edition, The Chumash*, trans. Rabbi Nosson Scherman (New York: ArtScroll Mesorah Publications, Ltd. 2000), 661. (*Vayikra* 19:13)

2   Ibid., p. 657. (*Vayikra* 19:1-2)

3   *Talmud Bavli, The Schottenstein Day Yomi Edition, Tractate Yevamos*, ed. Rabbi Yisroel Simcha Schorr and Rabbi Chaim Malinowitz (Brooklyn, NY: Mesorah Publications, Ltd., 2005), 20a.

4   Scherman op. cit., p. 656-657, fn. 2. (*Vayikra* 19:2)

5   Ibid., pp. 659, 661, 665. (*Vayikra* 19:11-18,35)

6   Ibid., p. 1195. (*Yeshayahu* 1:10-17)

Chapter Eight

1   *Emet Ve-Emunah, Statement of Principles of Conservative Judaism* (New York: 1988, The Jewish Theological Seminary of America, The Rabbinical Assembly and The United Synagogue of America. Text scanned to PDF from the Second Printing 1990).

2   Ismar Schorsch, "The Sacred Cluster: The Core Values of Conservative Judaism," *Conservative Judaism* 47, no.3 (Spring 1995), 3-12.

3   *Emet Ve-Emunah, Statement of Principles of Conservative Judaism op. cit.*, pp. 56-57.

Chapter Nine

1   "A Statement of Principles for Reform Judaism" (Pittsburgh: 1999, Central Conference of American Rabbis), Central Conference of American Rabbis website. https://www.ccarnet.org/rabbinic-voice/platforms/article-statement-principles-reform-judaism

Chapter Eleven

1   Marc Angel, "The Sephardim of the United States: An Exploratory Study", *The American Jewish Yearbook* (New York: The American Jewish Committee and The Jewish Publication Society 1973), 77-138.

2   Aviva Ben-Ur, *Sephardic Jews in America: A Diasporic History* (New York: New York University Press 2009).

Chapter Eighteen

1   Pew Research Center 2016, "Israel's Religiously Divided Society," Washington, DC, p. 6.

2   Pew Research Center 2021, "Jewish Americans in 2020," Washington, DC, p. 10.

3   *The Stone Edition, The Chumash*, trans. Rabbi Nosson Scherman (New York: ArtScroll Mesorah Publications, Ltd. 2000), p. 441. (*Shemot* 24:7)

4   Rabbi Jonathan Sacks, *One People? Tradition, Modernity, and Jewish Unity* (London: The Littman Library of Jewish Civilization 1993). Rabbi Sacks was the Chief Rabbi of the United Hebrew Congregations of the Commonwealth from 1991 to 2013. He was also appointed as a member of the House of Lords on June 15, 2009.

5   Ibid., p. 151.

6   Ibid., p. 152.

7   Ibid., pp. 217-227.

8   Ibid., p. 224.

9   Ibid., p. 224.

10 Ibid.

Chapter Nineteen

1   See for example, Margaret Moers Wenig, "Sacred Speech — Sacred Communities," *The Reconstructionist*, (Fall 2002).

2   Rabbi Yisrael Meir Kagan, Chafetz Chaim, trans. Rabbi Shraga Silverstein (New Haven, CT: Rabbi Shraga Silverstein 2014 and 2021). See also Joseph Telushkin, *Words That Hurt, Words that Heal, How the Words You Choose Shape Your Destiny* (New York: William Morrow, revised edition 2019) for a contemporary, anecdotal treatment of the respective effects of negative and positive speech.

3   Ibid., pp. 10-17.

4   Ibid., pp. 26-27.

5   Kagan op. cit., pp. 28-32.

6   Kagan op. cit. p. 33-35.

7   Ibid., pp. 36-42.

8   Kagan op. cit., pp. 43-48.

9   Ibid., pp. 49-53.

10 Ibid., pp. 54-57.

11 Kagan op. cit., pp. 58-62.

12 Ibid., pp. 63-64.

13 Ibid., pp. 65-72.

14 Kagan op. cit., p. 73-75.

15 Ibid., pp. 76-77.

16 Ibid. pp. 78-79.

17 Ibid. pp. 80.

18 Kagan op. cit., pp. 81-83.

19 Ibid., pp. 84-87.

20 Ibid., pp. 88-89.

21 Ibid., p. 90.

22 Ibid., pp. 91-98.

23 Ibid., pp. 13-23. The *mitzvot* quoted in this section appear in the English translation of the Chaftez Chaim's book. I have based the English quotations on the translation in: *The Stone Edition, The Chumash*, trans. Rabbi Nosson Scherman (New York: ArtScroll Mesorah Publications, Ltd. 2000).

24 Ibid., p. 661. (*Vayikra* 19:16)

25 Ibid., p. 443. (*Shemot* 23:1)

26 Kagan op. cit., p. 13.

27 Scherman op. cit., p. 1061. (*Devarim* 24:8)

28 Ibid., p. 98. (*Devarim* 8:11)

29 Ibid., pp. 681-683. (*Vayikra* 22:23)

30 Ibid., p. 661. (*Vayikra* 19:17)

31 Ibid., p. 661. (*Vayikra* 19:18)

32 Ibid., p. 1037. (*Devarim* 19:15)

33 Scherman op. cit., p. 443. (*Shemot* 23:2)

34 Ibid., p. 829. (*Bamidbar* 17:5)

35 Ibid., p. 699. (*Vayikra* 25:17)

36 Ibid., p. 661. (*Vayikra* 19:17)

37 Ibid., p. 431. (*Shemot* 22:21)

38 Ibid., p. 933. (*Bamidbar* 25:33) The text here reads: "You shall not bring guilt upon the land." The translator in Kagan op. cit., p. 16 translates the text as: "And you shall not flatter [the men of] the land." In this case, the preferred English translation of the Torah's Hebrew text uses the verb "to flatter" rather than "to bring guilt."

39 Ibid., p. 661. (*Vayikra* 19:14)

40 Ibid., p. 1061. (*Devarim* 24:9)

41 Ibid., p. 661. (*Vayikra* 19:18)

42 Ibid., p. 661. (*Vayikra* 19:15)

43 Ibid., p. 703. (*Vayikra* 25:35)

44 Ibid., p. 703. (*Vayikra* 25:36)

45 Ibid., p. 903. (*Devarim* 10:20)

46 Ibid., p. 665. (*Vayikra* 19:30)

47 Ibid., p. 665. (*Vayikra* 19:32)

48 Ibid., p. 685. (*Vayikra* 21:8)

49 Ibid., p. 410 (*Shemot* 20:12); and Ibid. Page 970. (*Devarim* 5:16)

50 Ibid., p. 1075. (*Devarim* 27:16)

51 Ibid., p. 975. (*Devarim* 6:13)

52 Ibid. p. 975. (*Devarim* 6:7) See also Rabbi Yisrael Meir Kagan, *The Concise Book of Mitzvoth*, trans. Charles Wengrov (Jerusalem/New York: Feldheim Publishers 1990), 27. The quotation comes from the first full paragraph of the *Shema*, a prayer that appears in the prayerbook and that all denominations of Judaism accept as fundamental. See for example, *The Complete Artscroll Siddur, Nusach Sefard*, trans. Rabbi Nosson Scherman (New York: ArtScroll Mesorah Publications, Ltd. 1985, Ninth Impression 2002), 94-99.

53 Ibid., p. 435. (*Shemot* 23:7)

54 Ibid., p. 1077. (*Devarim* 28:9)

55 Ibid., p. 9. (*Bereishit* 1:26)

Chapter Twenty

1 *The Stone Edition, The Chumash*, trans. Rabbi Nosson Scherman (New York: ArtScroll Mesorah Publications, Ltd. 2000), 711. (*Vayikra* 26:17)

2 Ibid., p. 661. (*Vayikra* 19:17)

3 Ibid., p.661. (*Vayikra* 19:18)

BIBLIOGRAPHY

"A Statement of Principles for Reform Judaism" (Pittsburgh: 1999, Central Conference of American Rabbis), Central Conference of American Rabbis website. https://www.ccarnet.org/rabbinic-voice/platforms/article-statement-principles-reform-judaism

Albert, Rebecca T. and Straub, Jacob J., *Exploring Judaism, a Reconstructionist Approach* (Elkins Park, PA: The Reconstructionist Press, Expanded and Updated 2000).

Angel, Marc, "The Sephardim of the United States: An Exploratory Study", *The American Jewish Yearbook* (New York: The American Jewish Committee and The Jewish Publication Society 1973), 77-138.

Ben-Ur, Aviva, *Sephardic Jews in America: A Diasporic History* (New York: New York University Press 2009).

Bushrui, Suheil, ed., *The World's Favorite Love Poems* (Oxford, England: Oneworld Publications 2008).

"Declaration of Principles, The Pittsburgh Platform" (Pittsburgh: 1885, Central Conference of American Rabbis), Central Conference of American Rabbis website. https://www.ccarnet.org/rabbinic-voice/platforms/article-declaration-principles

Emet Ve-Emunah, Statement of Principles of Conservative Judaism (New York: 1988, The Jewish Theological Seminary of America, The Rabbinical Assembly and The United Synagogue of America. Second Printing 1990).

Finkelman, Shimon, *5 Great Leaders* (Brooklyn, New York: Mesorah Publications Ltd. 2005).

Friedman, Yisroel, *The Rebbes of Chortkov* (New York: Mesorah Publications, Ltd. 2003).

Gilman, Neil, *Conservative* Judaism *in the New Century* (New Jersey: Behrman House, Inc.1993).

HaLevi, Yehudah, *The Kuzari: In Defense of the Despised Faith*, trans. Rabbi N. Daniel Korobin (Spring Valley, NY: Feldheim Publishers 2013).

Hart, Ron D., *Sephardic Jews: History, Religion and People* (Santa Fe, NM: Gaon Books 2016).

Heimowitz, Yehuda, *Maran HaRav Ovadia, The Revered Gaon and Posek Who Restored the Crown of Sephardic Jewry* (New York: Mesorah Publications, Ltd. 2014).

Kagan, Yisrael Meir, *Chafetz Chaim*, trans. Rabbi Shraga Silverstein (New Haven, CT: Rabbi Shraga Silverstein 2014 and 2021).

Kaplan, Dana Evan, *A Life of Meaning, Embracing Reform Judaism's Sacred Path*, (New York: CCAR Press 2018).

Kaplan, Mordechai M., *Judaism as a Civilization, Toward a Reconstruction of American-Jewish Life*, (New York: The Reconstructionist Press, Second Printing 1972).

Landau, Betzalel, *The Vilna Gaon*, (New Jersey: Mesorah Publications, Ltd. Second Edition, Third Impression 2022).

Pew Research Center, October 1, 2013, "A Portrait of Jewish Americans," Washington, DC.

Pew Research Center 2016, "Israel's Religiously Divided Society," Washington, DC.

Pew Research Center, May 11, 2021, "Jewish Americans in 2020," Washington, DC.

"Reform Judaism: A Centenary Perspective" (San Francisco: 1976, Central Conference of American Rabbis), Central Conference of American Rabbis website. https://www.ccarnet.org/rabbinic-voice/platforms/article-reform-judaism-centenary-perspective

"*Reform Judaism: History & Overview*" The Jewish Virtual Library, a Project of AICE, Chevy Chase, MD 1998 – 2022, American-Israeli Cooperative Enterprise). Jewish Virtual Library website, https://www.jewishvirtuallibrary.org/history-and-overview-of-reform-judaism

Sacks, Jonathan, *One People? Tradition, Modernity, and Jewish Unity* (London: The Littman Library of Jewish Civilization 1993).

Schorsch, Ismar, "The Sacred Cluster: The Core Values of Conservative Judaism", *Conservative Judaism* 47, no.2 (Spring 1995).

The Complete Artscroll Siddur, Nusach Sefard, trans. Rabbi Nosson Scherman (New York: ArtScroll Mesorah Publications, Ltd. 1985, Ninth Impression 2002).

The Complete Tishah B'Av Service, Nusach Sefard, trans. and commentary Rabbi Avrohom Chaim Feuer and Rabbi Avie Gold (New York: Artscroll Mesorah Publications, Ltd. 1992, Second Edition, Seventh Impression 2016).

"The Guiding Principles of Reform Judaism, The Columbus Platform," (Columbus, Ohio: 1937, Central Conference of American Rabbis), Central Conference of American Rabbis website. https://www.ccarnet.org/rabbinic-voice/platforms/article-guiding-principles-reform-judaism

The Stone Edition, The Chumash, trans. Rabbi Nosson Scherman (New York: ArtScroll Mesorah Publications, Ltd. 1993, Eleventh Edition 2000).

Telushkin, Joseph, *Jewish Literacy* (New York: William Morrow and Company 1991).

Telushkin, Joseph, *Rebbe, The Life and Teachings of Menachem M. Schneerson, the Most Influential Rabbi in Modern History* (New York: Harper Wave 2016).

Telushkin, Joseph, *Words That Hurt, Words That Heal* (New York: William Morrow, revised edition 2019)

Yoshor, Moses, *The Chafetz Chaim, The Life and Works of Rabbi Yisrael Meir Kagan of Radin* (New Jersey: Mesorah Publications, Ltd. 1997, Third Edition 2013).

Zev, Eleff, *Modern Orthodox Judaism, A Documentary History*, (Philadelphia: The Jewish Publication Society, 2016).

GLOSSARY OF ITALICIZED AND FREQUENTLY USED TERMS

Aron Kodesh: The Ark, or closet, in the front of the synagogue where the Torah scrolls are kept.

Avodah Zara: Idol worship, generally associated with polytheistic, pagan religions.

Badchan: Chassidic storyteller.

Bekishe: A special robe worn by Chassidic men. Many of these robes are black, but some Chassidic sects have unique styles of bekishes in solid or patterned colors. Some Chassidim wear their bekishes every day. Other Chassidim wear their bekeshes only for special occasions such as Shabbat, Yom Tov and Weddings.

Beit Din, Beis Din: Jewish court of law.

Bar Mitzvah: The status attained by a Jewish boy at his 13th Hebrew birthday. This is usually celebrated in the synagogue on a Shabbat morning, followed by a celebratory luncheon or party.

Bat Mitzvah, Bas Mitzvah: The status attained by a Jewish girl at her 12th or 13th Hebrew birthday, depending on the stream of Judaism. In non-Orthodox synagogues, this occasion may be celebrated by the girl's participation in a Shabbat morning service. For all streams of Judaism, it is marked by a celebratory luncheon or party.

Birkat Hamazon, Birchas Hamazon: The blessing recited at the conclusion of any meal at which bread is eaten.

Ben adam l'chavero: Literally between a man and his fellow man. This refers to mitzvot governing how Jews are required to treat each other.

Challah: Traditional braided bread served as part of any Shabbat or Jewish holiday meal.

Chatan, Chasson: A Jewish bridegroom.

Glossary of Italicized and Frequently Used Terms | 321

Chazzan: The cantor who leads synagogue prayer services.

Daven: To pray.

Deveikus: The ability to get spiritually close to Hashem. The term is generally associated with the intensity of prayer of Chassidic Rebbes.

Gartel: A woven cloth belt worn during prayer by male Chassidim to separate the upper body from the less pure lower body

Halacha: Jewish law.

Haredi, Charedi: Literally one who trembles before Hashem. The term is used to describe Chassidic and Yeshivish Jews, particularly in Israel.

Hallel: A series of psalms praising Hashem. The sequence has an opening blessing and a concluding one. According to halacha, Jews recite it on Pesach (including at the Pesach Seder), Shavuot, Sukkot, Chanukah, and Rosh Chodesh. An abridged version of Hallel is recited on Pesach after the first two days (the first day in Israel) of the festival, as well as on Rosh Chodesh.

Havdalah: The prayer signifying the conclusion of Shabbat. It is recited with a multi-wick candle, wine and spices.

Heksher: Certification by a recognized authority that a food product or an eating establishment is kosher.

Kallah: A Jewish bride.

Kapota: A special long double-breasted coat worn by Chassidic men. Most of these robes are black or blue. Some Chassidim wear a kapota every day. Other Chassidim wear a kapota only for special occasions such as Shabbat, Yom Tov and weddings.

Kashrut, Kashrus: The body of rules for determining whether food is kosher.

Kiddush: The prayer recited over wine on Shabbat and other special occasions.

Kinah: Any poem of lamentation recited on Tisha B'Av.

Kippah (skullcap in English, yarmulke in Yiddish): the head covering worn by Orthodox Jews and, at times, such as in synagogue, by other Jews.

Kiruv: Jewish outreach.

Klal Yisrael: The Jewish people.

Kol Isha: Literally the voice of a woman. The rule prohibiting men from listening to the singing of women other than immediate family members. This rule is observed strictly by Chassidic and Yeshivish Jews and less strictly by Modern Orthodox Jews.

Korbanot, Korbanos: Ritual offerings of animals and grains in the ancient Temples.

Korim: The practice of bowing from the knees fully to the floor during the Musaf prayers in synagogue on Rosh Hashana and Yom Kippur.

Lashon hara: Prohibited negative speech about others.

Leibedik: A lively, enthusiastic, heartfelt way of praying, dancing and singing.

Litvish: Following the traditions of the non-Chassidic Lithuanian Jews from Eastern Europe.

Lulav and etrog, lulav and esrog:- A palm branch, myrtle twigs, weeping willow twigs, and a citron fruit bound together and waved and paraded around the synagogue on Sukkot.

Masorti: The name for the Conservative movement in Israel.

Mechilah: Complete forgiveness by a Jew for harm done by him or her to another Jew. Traditionally, Orthodox Jews ask for mechilah from others from the days preceding Rosh Hashana through the day before Yom Kippur.

Megillah: Literally any of the five Megillot included in the Tanach. More commonly, the term megillah is used to refer specifically to the Book of Esther that is read on Purim.

Minhagim: Traditional practices kept by Klal Yisrael, a particular stream of Judaism, a community, a family or an individual.

Mikveh: A Jewish ritual bath immersed in at night by married women several days after menstruation, before marriage and on certain other occasions. Men bathe in a mikveh during the daytime, most frequently before a Yom Tov, but traditions vary widely on use of the mikveh by Jewish men.

Minyan: Ten Jewish men, which is the minimum number of Jewish men required for a public prayer service that includes certain prayers and sometimes the reading of the Torah. Non-Orthodox streams also include Jewish women in determining whether a minyan is present.

Misheberach: The traditional prayer for healing generally recited in synagogue when the Torah is read.

Mishneh Torah: The first Code of Jewish law often referred to as the Yad Chazakah. It was written by the Rambam (1138-1204).

Misnagdim: Traditional Orthodox Jews who were not Chassidim. The term Misnagdim preceded the term Yeshivish Jews that is used today.

Mitzvah, mitzvot, mitzvos: A Commandment under Jewish law, which may have its source in the Torah or a rabbinical decree.

Moshiach: The Hebrew term for the Messiah descended from King David.

HaMotzi, The Motzi: The traditional blessing recited over bread after ritually washing the hands.

Musaf: An additional prayer service supplementing the regular morning prayers on special days such as Shabbat.

Pesach: The common name given to the Biblical holiday of Chag HaMatzot that commemorates the exodus from Egypt.

Posek, poskim: An expert whose rulings on matters of Jewish law are respected as authoritative.

Psak halacha: A ruling on Jewish law given by a posek.

Niggunim: Melodies, often accompanied by lyrics, sung by Jews on festive occasions.

Rabbeim, Rabbanim: Plural for rabbi.

Refuah sheleima: Complete healing or recovery from a physical, mental or spiritual affliction.

Rosh Hashana: The Jewish New Year observed every year in the late summer or fall.

Simcha: A happy occasion such as a wedding, engagement, birth of a child, bar mitzvah or bat mitzvah.

Sanhedrin: The supreme Jewish legal tribunal in the ancient Land of Israel.

Seudah shlishit, shalosh shudess: The third Shabbat meal generally eaten late on Shabbat afternoon.

Shabbat, Shabbos: Saturday, the seventh day of the week under the Hebrew calendar, which is observed as a day of rest from regular weekday activities in commemoration of Hashem resting on that day after the six days of creation as described in the Torah.

Shacharit, Shacharis: The daily morning prayer service.

Shavuot, Shavuos: The festival commemorating the giving of the Torah to the Children of Israel at Mount Sinai. Also called the Feast of Weeks because it is observed beginning seven weeks following the second night of Pesach.

Sheitel: A wig worn by Chassidic, Yeshivish and some Modern Orthodox women to cover their hair in the presence of men who are not part of their immediate families.

Shiduchim: The prescribed dating-for-marriage process in the Orthodox world.

Shadchan: A matchmaker who introduces marriageable-age men and women to each other as possible marriage candidates.

Shechita: The process for the proper ritual slaughter of animals so that their meat can be kosher.

Shemeni Atzeret, Shemeni Atzeres: The festival held the day after Sukkot.

Shemitah: The requirement to let the land of Israel lay fallow every seven years.

Shomer negiah: The requirement that Jewish men and women who are not married to each other not touch, including when they are dating.

Shtender: A podium on which to rest books when standing during prayer or learning from Jewish texts.

Shtetl, shtetlach: A small Orthodox Jewish community in Eastern Europe before the Holocaust.

Shulchan Aruch: The authoritative code of Jewish law authored by Rabbi Joseph Karo in Safed in 1563 and published in Venice, Italy in 1565.

Sinat Chinam, Sinas Chinam: Baseless hatred among Jews.

Snoods: Fabric hair coverings worn by Orthodox women as an informal alternative to a sheitel.

Sukkot, Succos: The festival of Tabernacles observed each year five days after Yom Kippur.

Shul: Yiddish for synagogue.

Spudiks: Tall fur hats worn by many Chassidim on Shabbat and for special occasions such as weddings.

Streimels: Short, wide fur hats worn by many Chassidim on Shabbat and for special occasions such as weddings.

Tachanun:- a daily prayer of supplication recited after the Chazzan's repetition of the silent morning prayer and at certain other times. It is not recited on Shabbos morning, Yom Tov, Chanukah, Purim, Tisha B'Av, Rosh Chodesh, the full Hebrew month of Nisan, the remainder of the Hebrew month of Tishrei after the festival of Shemini Atzeret, and at a service when a brit milah takes place following the service or when a newly married man is present at the service. It is also omitted on certain other days based on differing traditions.

Tanach: The complete text in book form of the Torah, the Prophets, the Megillot, the Psalms and certain other writings.

Tallit, tallis, tallitot: A prayer shawl traditionally worn by Jewish men for daily morning prayer services and on certain other occasions. Special fringes called tzitzit are attached to the four corners of a tallit. Non-Orthodox Jewish women sometimes also wear tallitot.

Tefillin: Passages from the Torah that are written on parchment and placed in leather boxes that are worn by wrapping straps attached to the boxes around the left arm (or right arm for a left-handed person) and around the top of the head. Jewish men wear tefillin during weekday morning prayers in fulfillment of the Torah mitzvah to place "these words" "on your arm and between your eyes." Some non-Orthodox Jewish women also wear tefillin.

Tzedakah: Literally righteous deed but used most often to refer to charitable giving.

Thaharat HaMishpacha, Taharas HaMishpacha: The laws of family purity related to menstruation and immersion in a mikveh.

Tehillim: Passages from the Book of Psalms.

Tikun olam: The Jewish obligation to repair the world spiritually through performance of mitzvot and middot.

Torah: The Five Books of Moses: Genesis (Bereshit), Exodus (Shemot), Leviticus (Vayikra), Numbers (Bamidbar) and Deuteronomy (Devarim). When these books are written in sequence on a parchment scroll, the scroll is referred to as a Torah scroll. When they are printed in a book, the book is referred to as The Chumash. The term Torah is also commonly used to describe the full body of Jewish law including The Tanach, The Talmud, commentaries and codes of Jewish law.

Torah U'Mada: Literally Torah and science. This, until recently, represented the Modern Orthodox approach to teaching both Torah and secular subjects in Jewish schools. It was exemplified by Yeshiva University, which used Torah U'Mada as part of its brand.

Tzniut, Tznius: Modesty in dress, demeanor and speech.

Yad: A silver pointer used by one reading from a Torah scroll in synagogue.

Yad Chazakah: See Mishneh Torah.

Yom Ha'atzmaut:- The Hebrew name for Israel Independence Day, which was originally declared on 5 Iyar 5708, May 14, 1948.

Yom Yerushalayim: The day commemorating the reunification of Jerusalem during the 1967 (Six Day) War, on 28 Iyar 5727, June 7, 1967.

Yom Kippur: The Jewish Day of Atonement. A full day of prayer and fasting observed each year nine days after the first day of Rosh Hashana.

Yetzer hara: The evil inclination that distracts Jews from the path of righteousness and inspires them to do evil things, including speaking lashon hara.

Yetzer hatov: The good inclination that inspires Jews to observe the mitzvot and the middot.

Zmirot, Zmiros: Traditional songs generally associated with the three Shabbat meals.

ACKNOWLEDGMENTS

I WOULD LIKE TO thank Rabbi Allen Schwartz for his help in carefully reviewing the manuscript, giving me page-by-page comments, discussing them with me, helping me refine my thesis and making suggestions for the best approach to the book's publication. Second, I would like to thank Rabbi Michael Stanger for his help in thoroughly reviewing the manuscript, suggesting changes to content and tone, being enormously supportive throughout the editing process, and introducing me to several of his colleagues so that I could interview them. Third, I would like to thank Rabbi Herschel Schacter for his endorsement of the book and for taking time from his busy schedule to meet with me to discuss it in detail. His endorsement appears at the front of the book and on the book's website: www.apathtojewishsurvival.net. Fourth, I would like to thank Rabbi Mordechai Willig for reviewing the manuscript, meeting with me to discuss it and expressing sincere enthusiasm for the fact that I'd written it and the benefit that it may bring to *Klal Yisrael*. His endorsement appears on the book's website. Fifth, I would like to thank Rabbi Nechemia Steinberger for his elucidating *Divrei Torah* that convinced me that the book's objectives should be more than helping to bring the Messianic Age, and should focus equally on the risks to *Klal Yisrael* both in Israel and the Diaspora stemming from lack of unity within *Klal Yisrael*. I want to thank him for meeting with me and reviewing the pertinent sources on this subject in *Tanach* as elucidated by distinguished commentators over time. Sixth, I would like to thank Rabbi Rashi Shapiro, my teacher and study partner for his poignant comments as I was working on the book, which helped refine my thinking as he does every day in our studies together. Seventh, I would like to thank Rabbi Jonathan Morgenstern for inspiring this book by his consistent advocacy for *achdut*, and for reviewing parts of the manuscript. Last, I want to acknowledge the help that I received from numerous rabbis, most of whom asked to remain anonymous, who allowed me to interview them about specific aspects of their respective streams of Judaism. Without their help, the level of detail contained in the text would not have been possible. Thanks to all of you for your help and for believing in the timeliness and concept of this book.

I would also like to thank the exceptional team of professionals that helped me bring this work to fruition: Fern Reiss, my publishing consultant, Ruth Kahan, my editor and Shanie Cooper, my cover and interior designer.

Finally, I would like to thank *Hashem* for giving us the guidance and the urgency in the *Tanach* for achieving *achdut* within *Klal Yisrael*, and who, in His patience, has given us the time to address this existential issue. May we find the strength and the wisdom to do so before it is too late.

www.ingramcontent.com/pod-product-compliance
Lightning Source LLC
Chambersburg PA
CBHW060942230426
43665CB00015B/2032